REFERENCE GUIDES TO RHETORIC AND COMPOSITION

Series Editor, Charles Bazerman

REFERENCE GUIDES TO RHETORIC AND COMPOSITION
Series Editor, Charles Bazerman

The Series provides compact, comprehensive and convenient surveys of what has been learned through research and practice as composition has emerged as an academic discipline over the last half century. Each volume is devoted to a single topic that has been of interest in rhetoric and composition in recent years, to synthesize and make available the sum and parts of what has been learned on that topic. These reference guides are designed to help deepen classroom practice by making available the collective wisdom of the field and will provide the basis for new research. The Series is intended to be of use to teachers at all levels of education, researchers and scholars of writing, graduate students learning about the field, and all who have interest in or responsibility for writing programs and the teaching of writing.

Parlor Press and The WAC Clearinghouse are collaborating so that these books will be widely available through low-cost print editions and free digital distribution. The publishers and the Series editor are teachers and researchers of writing, committed to the principle that knowledge should freely circulate. We see the opportunities that new technologies have for further democratizing knowledge. And we see that to share the power of writing is to share the means for all to articulate their needs, interest, and learning into the great experiment of literacy.

EXISTING BOOKS IN THE SERIES
Invention in Rhetoric and Composition (2004, Lauer)
Reference Guide to Writing across the Curriculum (2005, Bazerman, Little, Bethel, Chavkin, Fouquette, and Garufis)
Revision: History, Theory, and Practice (2006, Horning and Becker)
Writing Program Administration (2007, McLeod)
Community Literacy and the Rhetoric of Local Publics (2008, Long)
Argument in Composition (2009, Ramage, Callaway, Clary-Lemon, and Waggoner)
Basic Writing (2010, Otte and Mlynarczyk)
Genre: An Introduction to History, Theory, Research, and Pedagogy (2010, Bawarshi and Reiff)

Genre

An Introduction to History, Theory, Research, and Pedagogy

Anis S. Bawarshi and Mary Jo Reiff

Parlor Press
West Lafayette, Indiana
www.parlorpress.com

The WAC Clearinghouse
http://wac.colostate.edu/

Parlor Press LLC, West Lafayette, Indiana 47906

Printed in the United States of America

S A N: 2 5 4 - 8 8 7 9

Library of Congress Cataloging-in-Publication Data

Bawarshi, Anis S.
 Genre : an introduction to history, theory, research, and pedagogy / Anis S. Bawarshi and Mary Jo Reiff.
    p. cm. -- (Reference guides to rhetoric and composition)
 Includes bibliographical references and index.
 ISBN 978-1-60235-171-4 (hardcover : alk. paper) -- ISBN 978-1-60235-170-7 (pbk. : alk. paper) -- ISBN 978-1-60235-172-1 (adobe ebook) -- ISBN 978-1-60235-173-8 (epub ebook)
  1. Literary form--Handbooks, manuals, etc. 2. Literary form--Study and teaching--Handbooks, manuals, etc. I. Reiff, Mary Jo. II. Title.
 PN45.5.B36 2010
 808'.0066--dc22
                               2010008725

Series logo designed by Karl Stolley. Copyediting by Rebecca Longster.
This book is printed on acid-free paper.

Parlor Press, LLC is an independent publisher of scholarly and trade titles in print and multimedia formats. This book is available in paperback, cloth, and Adobe eBook formats from Parlor Press on the World Wide Web at http://www.parlorpress.com. For submission information or to find out about Parlor Press publications, write to Parlor Press, 816 Robinson St., West Lafayette, Indiana, 47906, or e-mail editor@parlorpress.com.

The WAC Clearinghouse supports teachers of writing across the disciplines. Hosted by Colorado State University's Composition Program, it brings together four journals, three book series, and resources for teachers who use writing in their courses. This book will also be available free on the Internet at The WAC Clearinghouse (http://wac.colostate.edu/).

In memory of Larry Tinklepaugh (1938-2005)

To Aden and Daliah

Contents

Series Editor's Preface

Charles Bazerman

The longer you work with genre, the more it reveals and the more it connects with—perhaps because genre is at a central nexus of human-sense-making, where typification meets utterance in pursuit of human action. To communicate effectively we need to know what kind of situation we are in, what kinds of things are being said, and what kinds of things we want to accomplish. The evolving variety of human circumstances, the creative potentials of language, and the cleverness of human action challenge us to know where we are and where we are going in interactions, especially since we must be intelligible to other people equally struggling to make sense of communicative situations from their separate perspectives. Shared social attributions of genre help us and those we communicate with to be on the same page, or close enough for our practical purposes.

Many aspects of communication, social arrangements, and human meaning-making are packaged in genre recognition. Genres are associated with sequences of thought, styles of self-presentation, author-audiences stances and relations, specific contents and organizations, epistemologies and ontologies, emotions and pleasures, speech acts and social accomplishments. Social roles, classes, institutional power are bound together with rights and responsibilities for producing, receiving, and being ruled by genres. Genres shape regularized communicative practices that bind together organizations, institutions, and activity systems. Genres by identifying contexts and plans for action also focus our cognitive attention and draw together the dynamics of our mind in pursuit of specific communicative relations, thereby exercising and developing particular ways of thinking. I would not be surprised if brain researchers were to find that typification and genre leave their mark on brain organization as the child matures into an articulate and literate adult.

By following genres we can see both the complex regularities of communicative life and the individuality of each situated utterance. Awareness of robust types and purposeful individual variation responsive to local circumstances provides an antidote to over-simplifying models of writing instruction. Genre helps us see the purposefulness and flexibility of form, rather than form being just a matter of correctness and fulfillment of a few school-based tasks, created purely for instruction and assessment. A proper understanding of genre also reveals the underlying communicative action and social situation which give reason to the form and motive to acts of reading and writing. An understanding of genre brings us into touch with the manifold uses of writing in different parts of society, the economy, governance and culture. Awareness of genre and skill in adapting to the varieties of action possible, using a wide range of linguistic tools, prepares us and our students for wide ranging participation and purposeful innovation.

Given the richness of the concept of genre, it is no wonder that many approaches to understanding and teaching genre have developed, in many regions of the world. This volume provides an informed and thoughtful introduction to all of these approaches and provides means for understanding their relation as well as pursuing deeper study of each. I am deeply appreciative for the work of the authors and am confident you will find their work useful as you explore the meaning of genre for yourselves as writers, as teachers of writing, and as students of the wonder of human communicative accomplishment.

Acknowledgments

As we developed this book, we benefited greatly from the vibrant intellectual community of scholars in Rhetorical Genre Studies, many of whom are featured in this book. We especially thank Chuck Bazerman, the editor of this series and a renowned genre scholar, for his generous feedback and invaluable, expert advice. His careful reading and insightful responses have made this a much better book, helping us to tighten the manuscript and pushing us to consider and to integrate additional perspectives on genre, including international perspectives.

A special thanks to our friend, colleague, and mentor, Amy Devitt, whose seminar in genre theory at the University of Kansas in 1994 initiated and inspired our interest in genre and whose rich body of scholarship on genre and collaborative endeavors with us (conference presentations, articles, and a textbook on genre) have informed and enriched our understanding of genre.

In addition, we have had the good fortune of working with truly exceptional graduate students who have contributed to and deepened our investigations and understanding of genre over the years, with a special thanks to the students in the Spring 2008 genre theory seminar (English 564) at the University of Washington. We are also indebted to our research teams at the University of Tennessee and the University of Washington, without whose collaboration we could not have carried out a large, cross-institutional empirical study of genre learning: Bill Doyle, Cathryn Cabral, Sergio Casillas, Rachel Goldberg, Jennifer Halpin, Megan Kelly, Melanie Kill, Shannon Mondor, and Angela Rounsaville.

We would also like to thank Rebecca Longster for her skilled copyediting and careful and thorough reading of our manuscript and David Blakesley for his guidance through this project and for his superb editing and production of the book. A special thanks also to Melanie Kill, who generously contributed a comprehensive glossary and annotated bibliography.

Additionally, we are grateful for the institutional support we have received from our department heads, Chuck Maland and Gary Handwerk, as well as our colleagues at the University of Tennessee and University of Washington. Our project was funded in part by the Office of Research Exhibit, Performance, and Publication Expenses (EPPE) Fund, the College of Arts and Sciences, and the John C. Hodges Better English Fund at the University of Tennessee-Knoxville, for which we are thankful.

We are especially grateful to our families for their patience and encouragement as we completed this project. For Mary Jo, a special thanks to Dan; and for Anis, a special thanks to Amy, and to Daliah and Aden.

Finally, and perhaps most importantly, we thank each other. We completed this project while both of us were serving as Writing Program Administrators and directing large programs. But despite the challenges of finding the time and energy to pursue this project, the collaborative process kept us going, creating a shared commitment and intellectual energy that would have been much more difficult to muster on our own. This shared intellectual vision—along with a lot of laughter and good humor—inspired and motivated us to persevere.

Genre

1 Introduction and Overview

Over the past thirty years, researchers working across a range of disciplines and contexts have revolutionized the way we think of genre, challenging the idea that genres are simple categorizations of text types and offering instead an understanding of genre that connects kinds of texts to kinds of social actions. As a result, genres have become increasingly defined as ways of recognizing, responding to, acting meaningfully and consequentially within, and helping to reproduce recurrent situations. This idea of genres as typified rhetorical ways of interacting within recurring situations (Miller, "Genre as Social Action") has had a profound impact on the study and teaching of writing. Researchers and teachers working across borders (North America, Australia, Brazil, France and Switzerland), across disciplines (applied linguistics, TESOL, rhetoric, composition studies, technical communication, critical discourse analysis, sociology, education, literary theory), and across grade levels and contexts (primary, secondary, post-secondary as well as professional and public writing) have explored the analytical and pedagogical implications of genre in ways that reveal genres as significant variables in literacy acquisition. In order to consider what a genre approach to the study and teaching of writing means and how it can best be implemented, this book examines the various traditions that have shaped our understanding of genre, and how these traditions have informed work in genre research and pedagogy.

Despite the wealth of genre scholarship over the last thirty years, the term *genre* itself remains fraught with confusion, competing with popular theories of genre as text type and as an artificial system of classification. Part of the confusion has to do with whether genres merely sort and classify the experiences, events, and actions they represent (and are therefore conceived of as labels or containers for meaning), or whether genres reflect, help shape, and even generate what they represent in culturally defined ways (and therefore play a critical role in meaning-making). Interestingly, these competing views of genre are reflected in the etymology of the word *genre*, which is borrowed from French. On the one hand, *genre* can be traced, through its related word *gender*, to the Latin word *genus*, which refers to "kind" or "a class of things." On the other hand, *genre*, again through its related word *gender*, can be traced to the Latin cognate *gener*, meaning to generate. The range of ways genre has been defined and used throughout its history reflects its etymology. At various times and in various areas of study, genre has been defined and used mainly as a classificatory tool, a way of sorting and organizing kinds of texts and other cultural objects. But more recently and, again, across various areas of study, genre has come to be defined less as a means of organizing kinds of texts and more as a powerful, ideologically active, and historically changing shaper of texts, meanings, and social actions. From this perspective, genres are understood as forms of cultural knowledge that conceptually frame and mediate how we understand and typically act within various situations. This view recognizes genres as both organizing *and* generating kinds of texts and social actions, in complex, dynamic relation to one another.

Such a dynamic view of genre calls for studying and teaching genres beyond only their formal features. Instead, it calls for recognizing how formal features, rather than being arbitrary, are connected to social purposes and to ways of being and knowing in relationship to these purposes. It calls for understanding how and why a genre's formal features come to exist the way they do, and how and why they make possible certain social actions/relations and not others. In short, it calls for understanding genre knowledge as including not only knowledge of formal features but also knowledge of what and whose purposes genres serve; how to negotiate one's intentions in relation to genres' social expectations and motives; when and why and where to use genres; what reader/writer relationships genres maintain; and how genres relate to other genres in the coordination of social life.

How to implement this deeper understanding of genre and activate this kind of genre knowledge has varied across genre approaches, informed as these have been by different traditions and intellectual resources as well as by different pedagogical imperatives and conditions. Part 1 of the book will examine these approaches in more detail as they emerge, over time, in different areas of study, from literary theory to systemic functional linguistics (what is often called the "Sydney school" of genre theory) to historical/corpus linguistics to English for

Specific Purposes to Rhetorical Genre Studies (what is often termed the "North American" approach to genre theory) to the French and Swiss pedagogical traditions to the Brazilian synthesis. It matters, as we will describe, that the Sydney school genre approach emerged in response to a national curriculum aimed at K-12 students; that the English for Specific Purposes approach emerged in response to the needs of graduate student, non-native speakers of English; that the Brazilian synthesis has been energized by the Brazilian Ministry of Education's National Curricular Parameters and the International Symposium on Genre Studies (SIGET), held since 2003; that the Rhetorical Genre Studies approach has been informed by rhetorical theory and sociology and has targeted college-level, native speakers of English. But what connects these various approaches is a commitment to the idea that genres reflect and coordinate social ways of knowing and acting in the world, and hence provide valuable means of researching how texts function in various contexts (the focus of Part 2 of the book) and how to teach students to act meaningfully in various contexts (the focus of Part 3).

The interest in genre study and teaching has been broad in scope and has been enriched by multidisciplinary and international perspectives. In their introduction to *Genre in a Changing World*, a recently published collection of twenty-four papers selected from the Fourth International Symposium on Genre Studies (SIGET IV), Charles Bazerman, Adair Bonini, and Débora Figueiredo describe genre studies' global reach, with authors in the collection representing Argentina, Australia, Brazil, Canada, Chile, Finland, France, Portugal, the United Kingdom, and the United States. As Bazerman, Bonini, and Figueiredo explain, the concept of genre has been particularly useful in helping literacy educators respond to the demands of a global world and information-based economies (ix-x). Genre, they argue, by helping to "elaborate writing as a focused, purposive, highly-differentiated task," helps us understand and prepare students for the increasingly specialized communicative needs of disciplines, professions, and everyday life (x). At the same time, genre can help provide "access to the benefits of advanced levels of education" to an increasing number of people around the world (x), as we will see in the case of Australia and Brazil. As Bazerman, Bonini, and Figueiredo eloquently conclude:

> A world tied together by communication and knowledge, enacting increasingly complex cooperations

on many levels, puts an increasing demand on the genres that share our meanings and knowledge, that coordinate our actions, and that hold our institutions together. A world being transformed by new technologies and media as well as new social and economic arrangements creates the need for rapid and deep transformation of genres. In a world where pressing problems require increasing levels of coordination and mutual understanding, forging effective genres is a matter of global well-being. In a world where increasingly high degrees of literate participation are needed by citizens of all nations, advancing the communicative competence of all, making available the genres of power and cooperation, is a matter of social capacity and social justice. (xiv)

In the U.S., and within Rhetoric and Composition studies, the concept of genre has begun to inform the study and teaching of writing in important and exciting ways. In the past few years, a number of edited collections and books that examine and apply genre theory have been published, targeting a mainstream composition audience; various composition journals have published scholarship in genre theory; the number of conference sessions devoted to genre at major conferences is on the rise, each drawing increasingly larger audiences; and several composition textbooks have recently appeared with genre as their guiding concept (we will discuss some of these in Chapters 10 and 11). Indeed, it would not be an exaggeration to say that we are witnessing something of a "genre turn" in Rhetoric and Composition studies, one that is informing various aspects of the field's commitments: from the teaching of writing at various levels and in various contexts to the study of writing as a form of ideological action and social participation to research on writing, metacognition, and transferability. In his 2005 *College Composition and Communication* essay, "Composition at the Turn of the Century," Richard Fulkerson calls for an overview of genre scholarship within composition and rhetoric that can delineate the various genre traditions and applications.

Two recent books targeting secondary school audiences attest to the growing influence of genre on writing instruction in the U.S. Deborah Dean's *Genre Theory: Teaching, Writing, and Being* introduces genre studies to high school writing teachers, arguing that a genre approach in the secondary classroom can teach students a view of writing as situated and can connect reading and writing, product and process. Cathy Fleischer and Sarah Andrew-Vaughan's *Writing Outside Your Comfort Zone: Helping Students Navigate Unfamiliar Genres,* building on the work of Heather Lattimer (*Thinking Through Genre*) and Tony Romano (*Blending Genre, Altering Style*), develops a genre-based curriculum in which students select, analyze, and produce unfamiliar genres in response to various literacy tasks. This pedagogy, they argue, helps students develop the analytical, transferable skills to write in a range of genres and for a variety of purposes. Such a genre-informed curriculum is reflected in a 2008 policy research brief titled "Writing Now" produced by the National Council of Teachers of English. The research brief identifies genre as a key component in writing instruction, and proposes that "writing instruction . . . would benefit from deep study of genre considerations" ("Writing Now" 17).

The "Writing Now" brief is careful to acknowledge and to dispel myths of genre as formulaic writing, a concern echoed by Barbara Little Liu in "More than the Latest P.C. Buzzword for Modes: What Genre Theory Means to Composition." Liu points out that while the word *genre* plays a key role in the influential Council of Writing Program Administrators' "WPA Outcomes Statement for First-Year Composition" ("Write in several genres," "Develop knowledge of genre conventions ranging from structure and paragraphing to tone and mechanics," "Understand how genres shape reading and writing"), the concept of genre remains under-defined and not well understood (73). As such, Liu cautions that the "WPA Outcomes Statement for First-Year Composition" reintroduces genre into the mainstream discourse of Rhetoric and Composition without informing the concept of genre with new insights from recent work in genre theory, thus risking the possibility that a "genre-based approach reverts to a product-centered approach, and the writing process becomes a series of increasingly accurate attempts to replicate an ideal text rather than an engaged understanding of how writing and writers work within a complex world" (73-74). To address this concern, Liu calls for "an introduction to genre theory for nonspecialist composition instructors" (224).

This volume aims to provide a reference guide to genre for writing instructors and writing program administrators working in various institutional contexts, such as first-year composition programs, TESOL programs, graduate-level writing programs for international students, and writing in the disciplines/writing across the curriculum programs. The volume is also aimed at scholars, beginning and advanced, in Rhetoric and Composition and in related areas such as rhetorical criticism, applied linguistics, discourse analysis, cultural studies, education, and sociology, who are interested in theorizing, researching, and applying genre to the study and teaching of writing.

OVERVIEW OF THE BOOK

In the chapters that follow, we will provide an overview of genre theory, research, and pedagogy, tracing the different traditions that inform them in order to account for the variations and overlaps in genre application. We will present an historical overview of genre; describe and explain key issues and scholarship that have led to the reconceptualization of genre over the last 30 years and what such a reconceptualization has meant for the study and teaching of writing; examine current research and lines of development in the study of genre; provide examples of various methodologies for conducting genre research; and explore the possibilities and implications for using genre to teach writing at various levels and within different disciplines. In short, we will examine genre historically, theoretically, and pedagogically, in ways which we hope will be useful for new and experienced teachers and researchers who are interested in locating and exploring the scholarly and pedagogical possibilities of genre.

Part 1 (Chapters 2 through 6) of the book examines the various traditions that have informed current understandings and applications of genre. Chapter 2 traces genre study within literary traditions in order to describe how these have contributed to widespread attitudes about genres as either exclusively aesthetic objects or as impositions on the artistic spirit, and how recent literary and cultural studies approaches expand the scope of genre study in ways that align with linguistic and socio-rhetorical traditions.

Chapters 3 and 4 examine genre study within linguistic traditions, which were the first to identify genre's pedagogical implications. Chapter 3 focuses on genre within systemic functional linguistics as well as historical and corpus linguistics, describing how genre researchers in Australia brought genre to bear on systemic functional linguistics and applied it to literacy education in primary and secondary schools. We will examine how such an approach challenged process-based writing instruction, and we will describe some of the critiques of such an approach. Chapter 3 also describes how genre is becoming a significant variable in historical and corpus linguistics.

Chapter 4 continues to explore genre study within linguistic traditions by focusing on the rich tradition of work done in genre analysis and teaching within English for Specific Purposes. We describe John Swales's influential work in developing a genre analytical method that accounts for discourse community and communicative purpose, and we trace developments in the field over the last twenty years as they bridge linguistic and rhetorical traditions and address the specialized literacy needs of graduate-level non-native speakers of English.

Chapter 5 examines genre study within rhetorical and sociological traditions, describing how these traditions helped shift the emphasis of genre study from the communicative actions to the social actions genres perform. We distinguish between communicative and sociological genre approaches and then trace how Carolyn Miller's groundbreaking work in "Genre as Social Action" was informed by research in rhetorical criticism and social phenomenology, which created new possibilities for the study and teaching of genre. The chapter concludes with an overview of the French and Swiss pedagogic traditions and how that tradition, along with linguistic and socio-rhetorical traditions, has been synthesized within Brazilian genre studies.

Chapter 6 describes how scholars in Rhetorical Genre Studies have extended the idea of genre as social and rhetorical action over the past twenty-five years. We identify and explain key developments in genre study, including concepts such as genre sets and systems, uptake, meta-genres, distributed cognition, genre chronotope, and activity systems. As we will describe throughout Part 1, the various traditions and intellectual resources that have been brought to bear on genre study help to clarify the analytical and pedagogical uses to which genres have been applied.

Part 2 of the book (Chapters 7 through 9) examines a wide range of empirical genre research conducted in multiple contexts (academic, workplace, and public), in various countries, for various purposes, utilizing a range of methods. The chapters cover a range of research studies in order to showcase trends in research interests, kinds of study designs and methods used, findings, and areas of future research. Chapter 7 traces genre research within academic contexts, focusing on studies of genre acquisition and development that have shaped debates over the efficacy of explicit genre teaching. The chapter examines studies of genre and early childhood writing development, secondary and college-level studies of genre teaching and learning, studies of genre and advanced literacy, studies of cultural influences on genre acquisition, as well as historical and international studies.

Chapter 8 focuses on genre research in workplace and professional contexts. The chapter includes historical studies of scientific articles, economics textbooks, legal genres, and business communication, as well as international studies from Brazil. As well, the chapter includes a range of studies that examine how genres mediate social activities, power relations, and identities within professional contexts, such as banks, social work agencies, and insurance companies.

Chapter 9 describes future directions in genre research, examining genre research in public and electronic contexts as well as in new media. This chapter as well draws on international and historical studies (for example, letters and land deeds) as well as new genres such as blogs and websites and instant messaging.

Part 3 of the book (Chapters 10 and 11) explores pedagogical approaches to genre. Drawing on the various genre traditions and research studies described in Parts 1 and 2, Chapter 10 examines the range of ways genre scholars have used genre to support writing instruction. Along the way, and drawing on international and U.S. perspectives, we describe the debates over the explicit teaching of genre and situate them within the traditions and pedagogical conditions (secondary, undergraduate, graduate; native, non-native speakers of English) that inform them.

Chapter 11 examines Rhetorical Genre Studies-based pedagogical approaches, with a focus on how to develop students' genre knowledge within first-year composition courses that transfers across writing situations; how to teach a critical awareness of genre; how to teach students to move from critique to production of alternative genres; and, finally, how to situate genres within the contexts of their use, whether public, professional, or disciplinary contexts.

The overarching goal of all these chapters is to provide readers with an overview of what genre approaches have to offer for the study and teaching of writing. As a result, we hope readers will be better able to account for various genres approaches and be better positioned to make use of genre as a research and teaching tool.

Part 1: Historical Review and Theories of Genre

2 Genre in Literary Traditions

In this and the next four chapters of Part 1, we will examine the various ways genre has been defined and used (historically and currently) in literary theory, Systemic Functional Linguistics (what is often called the "Sydney school" of genre study), historical/corpus linguistics, English for Specific Purposes, and Rhetorical Genre Studies (what is often termed "North American" genre study), with the goal of tracing how this dynamic, inter-related history has informed current understandings and syntheses (see for example the discussion of the Brazilian tradition in Chapter 5) of genre and its implications for writing instruction and writing program development. Certainly, an entire book, let alone a few chapters, will not be able to capture the complexity of this history in all the areas in which genre theory has played a significant role. Brian Paltridge, for example, has described the important work on genre done in folklore studies and linguistic anthropology, while Rick Altman and Steve Neale have examined genre in film studies. In the following chapters, we will instead describe the range of ways genre has been understood, synthesized, and used, over time, in those areas of study that have had the most impact on the study and teaching of writing: literary, linguistic, and rhetorical/sociological genre traditions. An understanding of these traditions will help situate various genre approaches and reveal their analytical and pedagogical possibilities, which Parts 2 and 3 will take up in more detail.

The traditions we examine illustrate a range of pedagogical and analytical trajectories, from textual trajectories that examine genres' formal features for purposes of classification, description, and/or teaching to contextual trajectories that examine how genres reflect, shape and enable participants to engage in particular social and linguistic events, including how genres mediate social and linguistic events in ways that reproduce social activities and relations, how genres relate to larger social structures in ways that allow for cross-cultural analysis, and how genres can be used as forms of resistance and change. This range—

from taxonomic and descriptive approaches to explanatory approaches to pragmatic approaches to critical approaches that link genres to ideology and power—can be seen at work in literary approaches to genre study, which this chapter takes up.

Of the traditions we examine in Part 1, literary approaches to genre have been the least directly concerned with writing instruction and writing program development. Yet the analytical perspectives they offer, including those about genre and creativity (see Devitt, *Writing Genres* 163–90), and the ways that they have informed widespread beliefs about genre make literary genre traditions significant to scholarship in linguistic and rhetorical studies of genre. In what follows, we will first examine how literary approaches to genre have traditionally maintained culturally-widespread, bipolar attitudes toward genre as either an exclusively aesthetic object or as a constraint on the artistic spirit, and then we will consider more recent literary genre scholarship that challenges bipolar attitudes and offers a larger landscape for genre action that can include linguistic and socio-rhetorical studies of genres. We will describe what we perceive as five major trajectories of literary genre study: Neoclassical approaches to genre; Structuralist (or literary-historical) approaches to genre; Romantic and post-Romantic concerns about genre; Reader Response approaches to genre; and Cultural Studies approaches to genre. These trajectories will help highlight the range of ways literary theories have defined and made use of genre and their implications for the study and teaching of writing.

NEOCLASSICAL APPROACHES TO GENRE

In *The Fantastic* and "The Origin of Genres," Tzvetan Todorov distinguishes between what he calls "theoretical" and "historical" approaches to genre, a distinction we can see at work in the first two literary traditions we will examine: the Neoclassical and Structuralist. Theoretical approaches define genres based on abstract, analytical categories that critics use to classify texts (*Fantastic* 13-14). These categories are "theoretical" because, rather than beginning with actual practices and texts, they begin with apriori categories, which are then applied to texts for purposes of classification. An example of such a theoretical approach, which Todorov critiques, is Northrop Frye's well-known work in *Anatomy of Criticism*, which classifies literary texts according to archetypal themes and images. Historical approaches, on the other hand, recognize genres as resulting "from an observation of literary reality," meaning that genres are defined based on an inductive method, whereby critics identify genre categories based on perceived structural patterns in texts, as these texts exist historically within particular literary contexts (*Fantastic* 13-14). (Todorov's approach to genre study can be described as historical in this way.) While Todorov does not deny the usefulness of theoretical or "abstract analysis" for the designation of what he prefers to call "types" of genres, he wants to reserve the word "genre" to designate "only those classes of texts that have been historically perceived as such" ("Origin" 198).

What we are calling Neoclassical approaches to genre utilize a theoretical, trans-historical set of categories (or taxonomies) in order to classify literary texts. Such taxonomic approaches start with apriori, macro-categories which are then used to define and clarify kinds of literary texts according to internal thematic and formal relations. As Todorov's critique suggests, Neoclassical approaches to genre tend to rely on these taxonomies to classify and describe relations between literary texts, rather than examine how genres emerge from and are codified by users within actual contexts of use.

Gérard Genette has described how Neoclassical literary taxonomies have their basis in the famous literary triad of lyric, epic, and dramatic, which is mistakenly attributed to Aristotle but is actually more the product of Romantic and post-Romantic poetics (Genette 6-12).[1] According to Genette, "the whole history of the theory of genre [within the literary tradition] is imprinted with these fascinating patterns that inform and deform the often irregular reality of the literary field" (45). This triad has traditionally been used to define the literary landscape: the novel, novella, epic (epical); the tragedy, comedy, bourgeois drama (dramatic); ode, hymn, epigram (lyrical) (49). As a taxonomy, the classical triad has also been used to describe genre change. For example, citing Ernest Bovet's theory of how the triad evolved naturally to reflect biological and social evolution, Genette writes: "To Bovet, as to Hugo and the German Romantics, the three 'chief genres' are not merely forms . . . but rather 'three basic ways of imagining life and the universe,' which correspond to three stages of evolution, as much ontogenetic as phylogenetic . . ." (56). So within a given historical era, different periods will mark stages of generic evolution reflecting, say, an "epic world," a "lyric consciousness," and a "dramatic milieu" (Genette 62). At other times, the triad has been associated with spatial presence and temporal perspective. Lyric, for instance, is at times defined as subjective, dramatic as objective, and epic as subjective-objective (Genette 38), so that in each formation we have a different notion of presence—each, that is, articulates a different spatial dimension in which a particular literary action takes place.[2]

As illustrated by the lyric, dramatic, and epic triad, what distinguishes Neoclassical genre approaches is their pursuit of systematic and inclusive rules based on universal validity for classifying and describing kinds of literary texts (Frow 52). As such, we can describe Northrop Frye's well-known work on genre as Neoclassical insofar as it seeks a transhistorical system of archetypes in order to describe literary texts and their relations. For example, in *Anatomy of Criticism,* Frye identifies four archetypal mythos: comedy, romance, tragedy, and irony/satire. These narratives are associated with the cycle of the seasons, such that Winter is associated with irony/satire, Spring with comedy, Summer with romance, and Autumn with tragedy. Each of these narratives unfolds within archetypal plots (for example, the movement from one type of society to another within comedy), and each of these plots unfolds within archetypal phases (for example, the movement from complete innocence to tragic flaw to unrelieved shock and horror within tragedy). And the phases themselves are associated with archetypal characters and traits (for example, the quest plot of romance includes archetypal characters such as youthful hero, aged magician, sibylline, monster, nymphs, as well as archetypal imagery such as water, fertility, wooded landscapes, valleys, brooks, friendly companions, and so on). As Frye explains of Neoclassical approaches, "the purpose of criticism by genre is not so much to classify as to clarify such traditions and affinities, thereby bringing out a larger number of literary relationships that would not be noticed as long as there were no context established for them" (247-48).

While Neoclassical taxonomies seek to organize relations between literary texts, the main critique of such approaches has been the way they universalize the ideological character of genres rather than seeing genres as emerging from and responding to socio-historically situated exigencies. In terms of their impact on writing instruction, such attitudes toward genre have helped to authorize the creation of decontextualized taxonomies which have resulted in the use of modes of writing such as the still widely-taught "description," "narration," "persuasion," and "exposition." These artificial modes isolate form from content and presume that all writing (and associated cognitive processes) can be classified and explained by way of universally applicable categories. At the same time, such an abstract view of genre constrains writing teachers and students from treating genres as dynamic, situated actions, in ways articulated in more recent literary, linguistic, and rhetorical genre studies.

STRUCTURALIST APPROACHES TO GENRE

While Frye's archetype-based taxonomy invites criticism such as Todorov's for being theoretical rather than historical, Frye's work also provides a way of describing how literary texts do not function as free standing entities, but exist in systematic, intertextual relation to one another within a literary universe. In *Anatomy of Criticism*, Frye proposes an approach to literary criticism rooted not in ideological perspectives, personal taste, and value judgments, but in a systematic study of literary texts, one that sought a "coordinating principle" through which to identify and describe literary texts as parts of a larger whole (16). In tracing the archetypal patterns (rituals, myths) that permeate and help distinguish literary texts, Frye delineated a complex, intertextual literary universe in which literary texts participate and are defined. All literary texts draw on a finite set of available archetypes, configuring these archetypes according to the genres in which the literary text functions. In this way, Frye's work can also be seen as operating in part within another of the literary approaches to genre: the structuralist approach.

Structuralist (or literary-historical) approaches understand genres as organizing and, to some extent, shaping literary texts and activities within a literary reality. In *Metaphors of Genre: The Role of Analogies in Genre Theory*, David Fishelov explores the connections between literary reality and genre theory, explaining that the metaphor "genres are social institutions" is commonly used by literary scholars to describe how literary genres coordinate textual relations, organization, and change. Fishelov, for example, explains that as "a professor is expected to comply with certain patterns of action, and to interact with other role-players (e.g. students) according to the structure and functions of an educational institution . . . , a character in a comedy is expected to perform certain acts and to interact with other characters according to the structural principles of the literary 'institution' of comedy" (86).

So genres are literary institutions that make certain literary activities possible and meaningful, both in terms of the subjects who participate within them and in terms of the writers and readers who produce and interpret them. Structuralist approaches, thus, examine how genres structure literary texts and contexts within what Todorov calls "literary reality" (*Fantastic* 13-14).

Whereas Neoclassical approaches to genre use transhistorical categories (such as epic, lyric, and dramatic) to classify and clarify literary texts and their relations at an abstract level, Structuralist approaches are more concerned with how socio-historically localized genres shape specific literary actions, identifications, and representations.[3] In this way, according to Fredric Jameson, "genres are essentially literary institutions, or social contracts between a writer and a specific public, whose function is to specify the proper use of a particular cultural artifact" (106). Likewise, Jonathan Culler explains, the activity of writing a poem or a novel "is made possible by the very existence of the genre, which the writer can write against, certainly, whose conventions he may attempt to subvert, but which is none the less the context within which his activity takes place, as surely as the failure to keep a promise is made possible by the institution of promising (116). This genre context is as conceptual as it is discursive, regulating not only certain formal and textual conventions, but also certain ways of organizing and experiencing literary reality. For example, Heinz Schlaffer, describing Walter Benjamin's understanding of how the "wholeness and distinctiveness of the world of art is created," writes: "Benjamin's decisive contribution to genre theory lies in his thought that genres are condensed world-images. . . . Organized by means of ideas, genres are pregnant outlines which contrast with the endlessness and indefiniteness of the real world (qtd. in Beebee 259). Literary genres bound the "endlessness and indefiniteness of the real world" in ways that create particular literary-historical meanings and values.

One specific way that genres structure literary meanings and values is by establishing particular space-time configurations within which texts discursively function. Käte Hamburger, for example, argues that genres structure a particular temporal orientation, so that at the grammatical level, for instance, the "past tense in fiction does not suggest the past tense as we know it but rather a situation in the present; when we read 'John walked into the room,' we do not assume, as we would if we encountered the same preterite in another type of writing, that the action being described occurred prior to one in our world" (qtd. in Dubrow 103).

At the same time, genres also structure our perceptions of literary actions, representations, and identifications. For example, Heather Dubrow asks readers to consider the following hypothetical paragraph:

> The clock on the mantelpiece said ten thirty, but someone had suggested recently that the clock was wrong. As the figure of the dead woman lay on the bed in the front room, a no less silent figure glided rapidly from the house. The only sounds to be heard were the ticking of that clock and the loud wailing of an infant. (1)

How we make sense of this piece of discourse and the event it represents, Dubrow suggests, points to the significance of genre in structuring literary events. For instance, knowing that the paragraph appears in a novel with the title *Murder at Marplethorpe,* readers can begin to make certain decisions about the action taking place when they recognize that the novel they are reading belongs to the genre of detective fiction. The inaccuracy of the clock and the fact that the woman lies dead in the front room become meaningful clues in that context. Likewise, the figure gliding away is more likely to be identified as a suspect, in which case the gliding figure and the dead woman assume a certain genre-mediated cause/effect relationship to one another as possible murder victim/suspect. However, if, as Dubrow suggests, the title of the novel was not *Murder at Marplethorpe* but rather *The Personal History of David Marplethorpe,* then the way we encounter the same discourse changes. Reading the novel as a Bildungsroman (life novel), we will place a different significance on the dead body or the fact that the clock is inaccurate. Likely, we would not be trying to identify a suspect. The crying baby, as Dubrow suggests, will also take on more relevance, perhaps being the very David Marplethorpe whose life's story we are about to read. In short, the actors in the discourse embody particular actions, identifications, and representations in relation to one another within the structure of the genre.

In localizing the ideological character of genre and recognizing genre's role in structuring aesthetic worlds, Structuralist approaches acknowledge the power of genre to shape textual interpretation and production. Yet, as we will discuss later in this chapter and then in our discussion of linguistic and rhetorical genre traditions, by focusing on genres as literary artifacts that structure literary realities, Structuralist genre approaches overlook how all genres, not just literary ones, help organize and generate social practices and realities in ways that prove important for the teaching of writing.

ROMANTIC AND POST-ROMANTIC APPROACHES TO GENRE

While Structuralist approaches understand genres as structuring textual actions and relations within a literary universe, certain Romantic and post-Romantic approaches have rejected genre's constitutive power, arguing instead that literary texts achieve their status, in fact, by exceeding genre conventions, which are perceived as prescriptive taxonomies and constraints on textual energy (Frow 26). Such a denial of genre, which asserts that "to be a modern writer and write generically is a contradiction in terms" (Rosmarin 7), can be traced to German Romanticism and the work of Freidrich Schlegel in the late eighteenth century. Schlegel insisted on the singularity of literary texts, with Romantic poetry serving as the ideal example: "only Romantic poetry is infinite as only it is free. . . . the genre of Romantic poetry is the only one that is more than a genre: it is, in a way, the very art of poetry[;] in a certain sense, all poetry is or should be Romantic" (qtd. in Threadgold 112). Following Schlegel a century later, Benedetto Croce argues that classifying any aesthetic work according to genre is a denial of its true nature, which is based in intuition, not logic. Genres, Croce claims, are logical concepts, and as such cannot be applied to literary works, which resist classification and are indeterminate (38). Perhaps the most famous dismissal of genre comes from Maurice Blanchot, who, in *Le Livre à venir*, writes:

> The book alone is important, as it is, far from genre, outside rubrics . . . under which it refuses to be arranged and to which it denies the power to fix its place and to determine its form. A book no longer belongs to a genre; every book arises from literature alone, as if the latter possessed in advance, in its generality, the secrets and the formulas that alone allow book reality to be given to that which is written. (qtd. in Perloff 3)

In Blanchot's formulation, literature becomes a transcendental domain that exists outside of or beyond genre's ability to classify, clarify, or structure texts.

Jacques Derrida, for one, has seized upon the apparent contradiction in Blanchot's formulation of the text's autonomy and its relationship to Literature. In the "Law of Genre," Derrida acknowledges that "as soon as the word 'genre' is sounded, as soon as it is heard, as soon as one attempts to conceive it, a limit is drawn. And when a limit is established, norms and interdictions are not far behind" (221). Yet he responds to Blanchot with this often-cited hypothesis: "Every text participates in one or several genres, there is no genreless text; there is always a genre and genres, yet such participation never amounts to belonging. And not because of an abundant overflowing or a free, anarchic and unclassifiable productivity, but because of the *trait* of participation itself . . ." (230). In so doing, Derrida preserves what Blanchot recognizes as a text's indeterminacy while presenting that indeterminacy as emerging from a complex relationship between literary texts and genres. Texts do not *belong* to a genre, as in a taxonomic relation; texts *participate in* a genre, or more accurately, several genres at once. "Participation" for Derrida is a key word, as it suggests something more like a performance than a replication or reproduction. Every textual performance repeats, mixes, stretches, and potentially reconstitutes the genre(s) it participates in. As such, for Derrida, genres are not apriori categories that classify or clarify or even structure texts, but rather are continuously reconstituted through textual performances (Threadgold 115). Indeed, for Derrida, one of the marks of literary texts is their ability to "re-mark" (self-consciously, self-reflectively) on their performances: "This re-mark—ever possible for every text, for every corpus of traces—is absolutely necessary for and constitutive of what we call art, poetry or literature" (229). In short, genres are the preconditions for textual performances.

For all that it offers in response to Romantic and Post-Romantic denials of genre and contributes to a dynamic understanding of the relationship between texts and genres, Derrida's argument still ultimately perceives genre as an imposition on literature (Beebee 8), a necessary imposition, perhaps, but an imposition nonetheless which literary texts must grapple with, mix, and perform themselves against. For this reason, as John Frow argues, Derrida's argument "participates in . . . a familiar post-Romantic resistance to genre understood as a prescrip-

tive taxonomy and as a constraint on textual energy" (26). What matters in the end is the singularity of the literary text, which exceeds the
genre(s) it performs. Such resistance to genre has had implications for
writing instruction, in the form of debates over constraint and choice,
convention and creativity. These dichotomies have created a false set
of choices for student writers and their instructors, where students'
"authentic" voices and visions are perceived to be in tension with the
"constraining" forces of genre conventions. As Amy Devitt has argued,
however, and as we will discuss in Part 3, genres offer teachers and
students a way of seeing constraint and choice, convention and creativity as interconnected (see Devitt, "Integrating Rhetorical and Literary
Theories of Genre" as well as Chapter 6 of *Writing Genres*).

READER RESPONSE APPROACHES TO GENRE

Reader Response approaches to genre follow Derrida in presenting a
complex relationship between texts and genres. Yet whereas Derrida
recognizes a literary text as a performance of genre, reader response
approaches recognize genre as a performance of a reader, particularly
the literary critic, upon a text. In *The Power of Genre*, Adena Rosmarin
identifies genre's power in just this way: "The genre is the critic's heuristic tool, his chosen or defined way of persuading his audience to see
the literary text in all its previously inexplicable and 'literary' fullness
and then to relate this text to those that are similar or, more precisely,
to those that may be similarly explained" (25). Within such an approach, genre becomes an argument a critic makes about a text. Such
an argument does not necessarily alter the text, being more of a localized and even temporary explanation of a text that may itself be
subject to multiple genre explanations or performances. As Rosmarin
explains, "The critic who explicitly uses genre as an explanatory tool
neither claims nor needs to claim that literary texts should or will be
written in its terms, but that, at the present moment and for his implied audience, criticism can best justify the value of a particular literary text by using these terms" (50-51). The same text can be subject
to different genre explanations without compromising its integrity,
so that, along with Rosmarin, a critic could say, "let us explore what
'Andrea del Sarto' [a poem by Robert Browning] is like when we read
it as a dramatic monologue . . ." (46). Such an approach acknowledges

genre's constitutive power, albeit as an interpretive tool, involved in literary consumption, not literary production.

E.D. Hirsch has likewise argued for a view of genres as interpretive frameworks, claiming that a reader's "preliminary generic conceptions" are "constitutive of everything that he subsequently understands" and remains so until that conception is challenged or changed (Hirsch 74). Genres thus function as conventionalized predictions or guesses readers make about texts. Summarizing such an approach to genre, John Frow writes: "genre is not a *property* of a text but is a function of reading. Genre is a category we *impute* to texts, and under different circumstances this imputation may change" (102). Such an approach begins to offer a more dynamic view of genre that leads into Cultural Studies approaches, which we describe next, and it has offered a way of teaching reading in terms of what reading theorist Frank Smith has called "specifications," which enable a reader to identify, make predictions about, and negotiate a text. Yet by psychologizing genre as the performance of a reader and perceiving it as an interpretive tool, Reader Response approaches to genre have overlooked the social scope of genre and its role in the production as well as interpretation of texts.

CULTURAL STUDIES APPROACHES TO GENRE

While traditional literary approaches have contributed to culturally-widespread, bipolar attitudes toward genre as either an exclusively aesthetic object or as a constraint on the artistic spirit, the final tradition we will examine (Cultural Studies approaches to genre) challenges such bipolar attitudes and offers a larger landscape for genre action. Cultural Studies genre approaches seek to examine the dynamic relationship between genres, literary texts, and socio-culture—In particular, the way genres organize, generate, normalize, and help reproduce literary as well as non-literary social actions in dynamic, ongoing, culturally defined and defining ways.

In reaction to Reader Response approaches to genre, for instance, a Cultural Studies approach would be interested in how and which genres become available as legitimate options for readers or critics to use. Hirsch and Rosmarin, for example, do not account for the socially regulated ways that readers and critics impute genres to texts, suggesting instead that genres are interpretive frameworks readers simply select. In fact, however, there is a great deal socially at stake in what texts are identified with what genres. Cultural Studies approaches are thus concerned with how genre conventions hail certain texts and readers in "shared and shareable ways, and are built into more or less durable infrastructures" (Frow 102), so that the choice of genre a reader or critic "selects" as an interpretive framework is guided by his or her knowledge of certain social practices. Focusing on genre in the film industry, Rick Altman suggests that "we may fruitfully recognize the extent to which genres appear to be initiated, stabilized and protected by a series of institutions essential to the very existence of genres" (85). These institutions include literary institutions, but also other social institutions such as schools, publishing companies, marketing agencies, and so on, which constitute what John Frow has called "reading regimes" that regulate habits of reading. According to Frow, "it is through our learning of the structure of reading regimes that we acquire the background knowledges, and the knowledge of rules of use and relevance, that allow us to respond appropriately to different generic contexts" (140). The knowledge of "rules of use and relevance" that shape how readers identify, select, value, and experience literary texts is acquired through social practices (including genres), thus linking literary genres to social institutions in more than simply the analogous ways suggested by structuralist approaches.

An important aspect of Cultural Studies approaches to genre is the way they define and use genres to examine dynamic relations between literary texts and historically situated social practices and structures. As Todorov puts it, "Like any other institution, genres bring to light the constitutive features of the society to which they belong;" as such, "a society chooses and codifies the [speech] acts that correspond most closely to its ideology; that is why the existence of certain genres in one society, and their absence in another, are revelatory of that ideology . . ." (200). For example, in *Epic and Empire: Politics and Generic Form from Virgil to Milton,* David Quint describes how epic as a genre "encodes and transmits" an "ideology of empire" by shaping human history into narrative (8). As Quint explains, "To the victor belongs epic, with its linear teleology; to the loser belongs romance, with its random or circular wandering. Put another way, the victors experience history as a coherent, end-directed story told by their own power; the losers experience a contingency that they are powerless to shape their own ends" (9). As such, epic carries an "idea of narrative itself" through western history, one that equates power with narrative in a way that eventually becomes 'universalized' and codified as the epic becomes part of a larger literary history" (13-15). Far from being simply a Neo-classical category used to classify kinds of literary texts, then, epic reflects and participates in maintaining a view of narrative that has proven to be historically durable. Not only are literary genres linked in dynamic ways to ideology, so too, Peter Hitchcock claims, is the urge to classify genres, which is itself a historical and socio-cultural impulse connected to colonialism and nationalism. "The classificatory ambition in literature," Hitchcock argues, "is indissoluble from a particular history of self and society" (308). For example, the urge to codify the novel as genre in the 1960s and 70s was a conservative gesture in the face of popularizations of and the rise in subgenres of the novel, especially connected to a rise in decolonization and postcolonial states asserting their autonomy and difference (Hitchcock 309-10). Hitchcock calls for a "mode of analysis that *takes genre seriously* enough to fathom the conditions under which particular genres may appear and expire . . . while allowing for a law of genre that is not in itself ahistorical" (311; emphasis added). Genre formations and transformations are linked to social formations and transformations in ideological, powerful ways; to take "genre seriously enough," according to Cultural Studies approaches, means both examining how genres reflect and participate in legitimizing social practices *and* recognizing how generic distinctions maintain hierarchies of power, value, and culture.

In a way hinted at already, Cultural Studies approaches to genre tend to complicate traditional boundaries between literary and non-literary genres in ways that acknowledge how all genres reflect and shape texts and social actions. As John Frow offers, "Genre theory is, or should be, about the ways in which different structures of meaning and truth are produced in and by the various kinds of writing, talking, painting, filming, and acting by which the universe of discourse is structured" (10). Mikhail Bakhtin has been an especially important figure in describing the complex relations between genres: literary and everyday genres, written and spoken. We will revisit Bakhtin's work on speech genres in Chapter 6, when we examine rhetorical approaches to genre. Here, we will focus on what we will describe as two axes of genre relations in Bakhtin's work, horizontal and vertical. Horizontal relations describe the dialogic nature of genres, as one genre becomes a response to another within a sphere of communication. For example, a call for papers leads to proposals which lead to letters of acceptance or rejection, and so on. Vertical relations involve what Bakhtin calls primary and secondary genres ("Problem" 61-62). For Bakhtin, primary genres take form in "unmediated speech communion," meaning that they maintain an "immediate relation to actual reality and to the real utterances of others" (62). Examples of primary genres include rejoinders in everyday dialogue and private letters (62). Secondary genres (which for Bakhtin include "novels, dramas, all kinds of scientific research, major genres of commentary") are more complex: "During the process of their formation, [secondary genres] absorb and digest various primary (simple) genres. . . . These primary genres are altered and assume a special character when they enter into complex ones" (62). When we answer the phone with "hello" during an actual phone conversation, for instance, we are using a primary genre, but if that rejoinder and the phone conversation that ensues were recorded and included as part of a cross examination in a trial, then the primary genre becomes recontextualized and altered as part of the secondary genre of cross examination.

The vertical relation in which secondary genres absorb and alter primary genres (as well as other secondary genres) offers insight into how literary and everyday genres interact to form and transform social practices and actions. For one thing, it suggests that literary genres, which are secondary genres, are not pure but are rather made up of other genres, including everyday, vernacular genres such as phone conversations, tax forms, contracts, prayers, and so on. For Bakhtin, the novel offers the clearest example of such a herteroglosia of genres. The novel recontextualizes multiple genres into its symbolic world. According to Bakhtin, "Each of these genres possesses its own verbal and semantic forms for assimilating various aspects of reality. The novel, indeed, utilizes these genres precisely because of their capacity, as well worked-out forms, to assimilate reality in words" (*Dialogic* 320-21). In so doing, the novel can be understood as re-assimilating realities within realities, so that the realities represented by the various genres the novel incorporates become recontextualized within its own reality. The novel *uses* the various genre realities to construct its own reality. This process of genre transformation works in two directions. On the one hand, once a literary genre absorbs other genres, say legal genres, it transforms them, so that these genres are no longer defined by what Thomas Beebee calls their cultural "use values" as legal documents that have cultural consequences, such as getting someone put in jail.

On the other hand, though, a literary genre can supply an alternative vision of how everyday legal or public genres can be used, thereby transforming their cultural use values. That is, literary genres such as the novel have the potential to "de-form" or destabilize the realities represented by the genres they recontextualize. As Beebee explains, "In terms of my theory of genre as use-value, the purpose of the novel would be to provide a discursive space for different genres to critique one another" (154). In this way, literary genres can reveal cultural ideologies by denaturalizing and reconfiguring relations between everyday genres and their use values.[4]

For Beebee, "primarily, genre is the precondition for the creation and the reading of texts" (250), because genre provides the ideological context in which a text and its users function, relate to other genres and texts, and attain cultural value: "Genre gives us not understanding in the abstract and passive sense but use in the pragmatic and active sense" (14). It is within this social and rhetorical economy that a genre attains its use-value, making genre one of the bearers, articulators, and reproducers of culture—in short, ideological. In turn, genres are what make texts ideological, endowing them with a social use-value. As ideological-discursive formations, then, genres delimit all discourse into what Beebee calls the "possibilities of its usage" (278). Philippe Gardy describes this transformation as a "movement of actualization" in which "brute information" or the "brute 'facts' of discourse" (denotation) becomes actualized as "ideological information" (connotation) (qtd. in Beebee 278). So genre is an "actualizer" of discourse, transforming general discourse into a socially recognized and meaningful text by endowing it with what Foucault calls a mode of being or existence. It is genre, thus, that gives a text a social reality in relation to other texts. Beebee concludes, "The relation of the text to the 'real' is in fact established by our willingness to place it generically, which amounts to our willingness to ideologically appropriate its brute information" (278). Genres frame systems of relations (intra-generically and inter-generically) within which texts become identifiable, meaningful, and useful in relation to one another.

Bakhtin and Beebee offer a situated view of literary genres, one that is situated not only within a literary universe as Structuralist approaches understand it, but also situated in relation to other genres within a culture's system of genres. Todorov has defined a system of genres as "the choice a society makes among all the possible codifications of discourse" (*Genres* 10). Such codifications include literary as well as legal, public, political, disciplinary, and other everyday genres, and together the complex relations of these genres organize and help generate a society's social structures, practices, events, and discourses in dynamic inter-related ways. As a result, Todorov asserts, "in place of literature alone we now have numerous types of discourse that deserve our attention on an equivalent basis" (*Genres* 12). It is this understanding of the multiplicity of genres, their functions, and situations that, as Amy Devitt has argued, can integrate literary and rhetorical approaches. While literature courses may emphasize the role of the reader and composition courses the role of the writer, there is the potential for a shared understanding of "genres as involving readers, writers, text, and contexts; that sees all writers and readers as both unique and as necessarily casting themselves into common, social roles; that sees genres as requiring both conformity with and variation from expectations; and that sees genres as always unstable, always multiple, always emerging" ("Integrating" 715). In the next four chapters, we will describe how scholarship in Systemic Functional Linguistics, historical/corpus linguistics, English for Specific Purposes, rhetorical theory and sociology, and Rhetorical Genre Studies has paid attention to these other various types of discourse, in ways that have come to inform the study and teaching of writing.

3 Genre in Linguistic Traditions: Systemic Functional and Corpus Linguistics

While current approaches to genre in Rhetoric and Composition studies draw in part from work in literary theory, they draw more so from linguistic, rhetorical, and sociological traditions. In this and the following chapter, we will examine genre studies within linguistic traditions, namely Systemic Functional Linguistics, Corpus Linguistics, and English for Specific Purposes. Then in Chapters 5 and 6, we will focus on genre studies within rhetorical and sociological traditions, since Rhetorical Genre Studies (RGS) has been most closely linked with and has most directly informed the study and teaching of genre in Rhetoric and Composition studies.

GENRE AND SYSTEMIC FUNCTIONAL LINGUISTICS

Systemic Functional approaches to genre have contributed richly to how genre is understood and applied in textual analysis and language teaching over the last twenty-five years. Influenced in large part by the work of Michael Halliday (Halliday; Halliday and Hasan) at the University of Sydney, and applied to genre particularly in the work of J. R. Martin, Frances Christie, Bill Cope and Mary Kalantzis, Gunther Kress, Brian Paltridge, Joan Rothery, Eija Ventola, and others, Systemic Functional Linguistics (SFL) operates from the premise that language structure is integrally related to social function and context. Language is organized the way it is within a culture because such an organization serves a social purpose within that culture. "Functional" thus refers to the work that language does within particular contexts. "Systemic" refers to the structure or organization of language so that it can be used to get things done within those contexts. "Systemic" then refers to the "systems of choices" available to language users for the *realization* of meaning (Christie, "Genre Theory" 759; emphasis added). The concept of "realization" is especially important within SFL, for it describes the dynamic way that language *realizes* social purposes and contexts as specific linguistic interactions, at the same time as social purposes and contexts *realize* language as specific social actions and meanings.

A great deal of the work in SFL can be traced to Halliday's *Language as Social Semiotic*, in which Halliday describes how "the network of meanings" that constitute any culture, what he calls the "social semiotic," is to a large extent encoded in and maintained by its discourse-semantic system, which represents a culture's "meaning potential" (100, 13). This is why, as Halliday argues, language is a form of socialization, playing a role in how individuals become socialized and perform meaningful actions within what he calls "contexts of situation."

Halliday explains that contexts of situation are not isolated and unique, but often reoccur as "situation types," a set of typified semiotic and semantic relations that make up "a scenario . . . of persons and actions and events from which the things which are said derive their meaning" (28-30). Examples of situation types include "players instructing novice in a game," "mother reading bedtime story to a child," "customers ordering goods over the phone" (29). Because contexts of situation reoccur as situation types, those who participate in these situation types develop typified ways of linguistically interacting within them. As these situation types become conventionalized over time, they begin to "specify the semantic configurations that the speaker will typically fashion" (110).

Halliday refers to this "clustering of semantic features according to situation types" as *register* (68). By linking a situation type with particular semantic and lexico-grammatic patterns, register describes what actually takes place (the "field"), how participants relate to one another (the "tenor"), and what role language is playing (the "mode"). For example, the "field" of discourse represents the system of activity within a particular setting, including the participants, practices, and circumstances involved. The "tenor" of discourse represents the social relations between the participants—their interactions—within the discourse. And the "mode" of discourse represents the channel or wavelength of communication (face-to-face, via e-mail, telephone, and so on) used by the participants to perform their actions and relations

(Halliday 33). When linguists identify a "scientific register," then, they not only describe a style of language but also the practices, interactional patterns, and means of communication associated with scientific contexts.

What happens at the level of context of situation in terms of field, tenor, and mode corresponds to what happens at the linguistic level in terms of what Halliday refers to as the three language "metafunctions": ideational, interpersonal, and textual. "Ideational" refers to the linguistic representation of action (who is doing what, to whom, when, and where). As such, the ideational metafunction corresponds with *field*. "Interpersonal" describes interactions between participants (such as asking questions, making statements, or giving commands) at the linguistic level. The interpersonal corresponds with *tenor*. "Textual" describes the flow of information within and between texts, including how texts are organized, what is made explicit and what is assumed as background knowledge, how the known and the new are related, and how coherence and cohesion are achieved. The textual metafunction thus corresponds to *mode*. At the level of register, then, context of situation and language realize one another as follows (informed by Martin, "Analysing" 34-40):

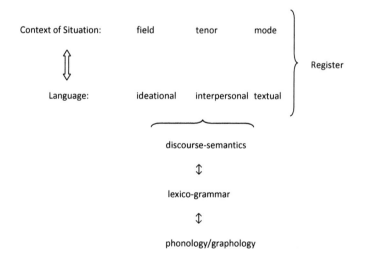

In connecting situation types and semantic/lexico-grammatic patterns, Halliday's work has served as a foundation for Systemic Functional (what is commonly known as "Sydney School") approaches to

genre and their focus on helping students "learn to exercise the appropriate linguistic choices relevant to the needs, functions or meanings
at any time" (Christie, "Genres as Choice" 24).[5] Led by the work of
J.R. Martin and supported by scholarship in the field of education linguistics in Australia, Systemic Functional approaches to genre arose in
part in response to concerns over the efficacy of student-centered, process-based literacy teaching, with its emphasis on "learning through
doing." Such an approach, its critics argued, ignores the contexts in
which texts are acquired and function, in ways that naturalize and
privatize what is actually a social process of literacy acquisition. As
such, process approaches deprive students of access to the systemic,
patterned textual choices that function within different contexts of situation. Far from empowering students via a student-centered approach
that encourages student expression and discovery, process approaches
instead reproduce social inequality by denying traditionally marginalized students access to academic and cultural texts. As Bill Cope
and Mary Kalantzis explain, process-based approaches are actually
"culture bound;" with their focus on student agency and ownership,
the power of voice and expression, student control and motivation,
such approaches reflect and privilege the "cultural aspirations of middle-class children from child-centered households" (6). By the same
token, "its pedagogy of immersion 'naturally' favours students whose
voice is closest to the literate culture of power in industrial society"
(6). In short, by keeping textual structures and their social functions
hidden, process approaches exclude even further those students whose
cultural and linguistic backgrounds leave them on the margins of the
dominant culture. An explicit focus on genre in literacy teaching, its
proponents argue, helps counter such imbalance by revealing the relationship between text structures and social purposes in ways that enable all students to produce texts more effectively and critically.

Beginning in the early 1980s with research that examined children's writing in Australian elementary and secondary school classrooms, and extended in the early 1990s through research related to the
New South Wales Department of Education's Disadvantaged Schools
Program, SFL approaches to genre have been influenced most widely
by the work of J.R. Martin, who has helped define genres as "staged,
goal-oriented social processes through which social subjects in a given
culture live their lives" ("Analysing" 43). As further explained in Martin, Christie, and Rothery, genres function as *social processes* "because

members of a culture interact with each other to achieve them; as *goal-oriented* because they have evolved to get things done; and as *staged* because it usually takes more than one step for participants to achieve their goals" (59).

Martin builds on Halliday's work by locating genre in relation to register so that genre and register relate to and realize one another in important ways. According to Martin, while register functions on the level of *context of situation*, genre functions on the level of *context of culture*. The relationship can be diagrammed as follows:

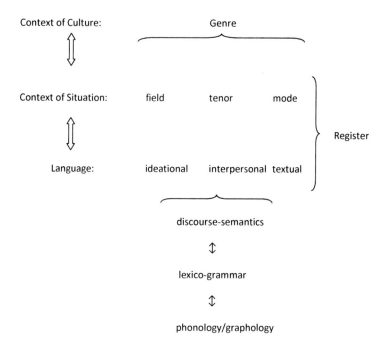

In such a model, genre connects culture to situation, and register connects situation to language, or, as Martin puts it, "register (encompassing field, tenor and mode) contextualizes language and is in turn contextualized by genre" ("Analysing" 37).

Martin's formulation enriches our understanding of genre by showing how social purposes/motives are linked to text structures, and how these are realized as situated social and linguistic actions within register. Indeed, this has been the most common trajectory in SFL genre analysis: Moving from the identification of social purpose as represented in generic structural elements (involving the analysis of what

Hasan calls "generic structure potential"—the range of staging possibilities within a particular genre) (Eggins and Martin 240);[6] to the
analysis of a text's register as represented in field, tenor, and mode; to
language metafunctions; to more micro analyses of semantic, lexico-
grammatic, and phonological/graphological features.

Within Australian genre pedagogy, Martin's view of genre has
been used as part of the influential LERN (Literacy and Education
Research Network) project. The project set out to identify what genres
were the most important within school literacy (and has since been
expanded to include adult migrant ESL settings and workplace settings), and to develop pedagogy to teach those genres most critically
and effectively (Cope and Kalantzis 9). That pedagogy has come to
be known as the "teaching-learning cycle," represented in the shape
of a wheel. The teaching-learning cycle has been adapted by various
researchers (for example, see Macken et al; Hammond et al; Rothery;
Feez and Joyce), but its basic components include three stages: modeling, joint negotiation of text, and independent construction of text.
In the first stage, students are exposed to a number of texts representing a given genre. During this stage, students and teacher identify the
cultural and situational context in which texts in the genre function,
what social purposes they serve, how their structural elements reflect
their functions, and how their language features carry out their functions. As such, the first stage moves from discussion of context and
social purpose to a description/analysis of register and language. In the
second stage, students and teacher engage in the joint negotiation and
then construction of a text within the genre, first conducting research,
developing content knowledge, note-taking, observing, diagramming,
and then working to collaboratively produce a version of the genre.
In the final stage, students independently construct a version of the
genre by conducting research to develop content knowledge, drafting
the text, conferencing with teacher and peers, editing, evaluating, and
publishing their text (Cope and Kalantzis 10-11). The cyclical shape of
the model is meant to reflect its flexibility, so that teachers can enter
into the model at the stage most appropriate to students' level of pre-
paredness (Paltridge, *Genre and the Language Learning Classroom* 30-
31). At the same time, it is meant to reflect how students and teacher
can keep rotating through the cycle as more and more complex genres
are added. The teaching-learning cycle, thus, makes visible to students

the structural and linguistic features of genres, and how these features are connected to social function.

The teaching-learning cycle and the SFL view of genre upon which it is based have not been immune from critique, on either the pedagogical or theoretical fronts. On the pedagogical front, scholars such as Gunther Kress, Bill Cope, and Mary Kalantzis have raised concerns about the degree of formalism exhibited by such an approach, in which generic models and structural analysis are used to teach students how to write texts "correctly" (Cope and Kalantzis 12). Kress also raises concern about the classifying impulse behind Martin et al's approach to genre, in which genres are classified and then modeled to students as though they were givens. By starting with model texts and examining the social purposes embodied within them, such an approach ignores the material/social relations and contexts that may not be visible in the text's structure and features, but that play an important role in how and why the text functions the way it does (Cope and Kalantzis 14). Pedagogically, critics worry that such an approach to genre teaching promotes a "linear transmission pedagogy" in which "textual form is largely presented in an uncritical way at the modeling stage" for students to emulate (Cope and Kalantzis 15). As Cope and Kalantzis explain, "The cycle imagery . . . belies the fact that the underlying pedagogical process is linear. Not only is this a reincarnation of the transmission pedagogy but it also takes genres at their word and posits their powerfulness uncritically, solely on the grounds that they should be taught to groups of students historically marginalized by the school literacy" (15). This approach, they fear, can easily lead to a "cultural assimilationist model of education" (16).

In an updated version of the Teaching Learning Cycle that attempts to address some of these concerns, Feez and Joyce add a separate category called "Building the Context" which precedes text modeling. The context building stage of the cycle employs ethnographic strategies for "learners to experience and explore the cultural and situational aspects of the social context of the target text" (Feez 66). Such strategies include research, interviews, field trips, role-playing, and cross-cultural comparisons.

On the theoretical front, critics have raised concerns about SFL's view of genre and its trajectory, moving as it does from social purpose/text structure to register analysis to linguistic analysis. While Martin is careful to note that genre realizes ideology, which he defines as the

"system of coding orientations engendering subjectivity—at a higher
level of abstraction than genre" ("Analysing" 40), and while Christie
and Martin have acknowledged the role of genre "in the social construction of experience" (*Genres and Institutions* 32), the SFL model,
critics note, does not examine the ways in which genres not only realize but also help reproduce ideology and social purpose. That is, by
taking "genres at their word," such a view of genre also takes social
purposes at their word, thereby ignoring why certain social purposes
exist in the first place as well as what institutional interests are most
served through these purposes and their enactments. According to
Terry Threadgold, genre theory is significant because of the relations
it reveals between genres and institutions, power, the construction of
subjectivity, as well as "the relations it permits/enables/constrains and
refuses between readers and writers, textual producers, and receivers"
(102). Threadgold's critique hinges on SFL genre theory's use of genres
as a starting point for textual analysis while overlooking the "web of
social, political, and historical realities" in which genres are enmeshed
(106). As Threadgold elaborates:

> What we need to know is how institutions and insti-
> tutionalized power relationships and knowledges are
> both constructed by and impose constraints on (and
> restrict access to) possible situation types *and* genres.
> We need to know why certain genres are highly val-
> ued, and others marginalized. We need to under-
> stand the changing history of such valorizations. We
> need to know why some genres are possible, others
> impossible, ways of meaning at given points in his-
> tory. We need to know how and why these factors
> construct identities for social agents . . . and how and
> why some social agents are able to/willing to resist
> and others to comply with existing situational and
> generic constraints. (106)

At the same time, Threadgold, following Derrida, also argues that because texts are always performances of genres, genres are less stable
than SFL approaches imagine: "Genres and system cannot therefore
have static, fixed values, and the extent to which they are predictive of
choices in lexico-grammar is constantly subject to slippage and change
. . ." (116). Indeed, as Brian Paltridge has demonstrated in his anal-

ysis of Environmental Studies research articles, genre identification depends more on contextual cues and interactional and conceptual frames than on structural and linguistic patterns (*Genre, Frames and Writing* 84-85).

While such findings raise questions about SFL approaches to genre pedagogy, the research and debates within SFL genre approaches have been crucial in establishing how genres systemically link social motives/purposes to social and linguistic actions. By arguing for genre as a centerpiece of literacy teaching, SFL genre scholars have debated the ways genres can be used to help students gain access to and select more effectively from the systems of choices available to language users for the realization of meaning in specific contexts. In the next section, we will discuss how scholarship in historical and corpus linguistics has also informed work in genre study.

GENRE AND HISTORICAL/CORPUS LINGUISTICS

Although work in genre within historical and corpus linguistics has not yet had a great impact on rhetorical genre theory and Rhetoric and Composition studies (with the notable exception of Amy Devitt's work), it has much to contribute to research and teaching of genre by accounting for the nature of typology and for language change. In this section, we will examine debates over genre categorization within historical and corpus linguistics, and how such debates might help clarify confusion between genres and modes within Rhetoric and Composition studies. Then we will examine how corpus based studies of genres provide insight into how and why genres change.

According to Hans-Jürgen Diller, the field of historical linguistics became interested in text classification when it expanded its scope of study from sentences to texts (11). Within text linguistics, Diller describes two trajectories of classification: Deductive and Inductive text typologies, which parallel in some ways the difference between what Todorov describes as analytical (or theoretical) versus historical (or empirical) approaches to genre classification, described in Chapter 2. *Deductive* text typologies, which Diller represents through the work of Robert Longacre (*The Grammar of Discourse*), seek to create overarching categories for genre and text classification in a way similar to how Northrop Frye sought to identify universal archetypes in order to classify and describe relations between literary texts. Longacre, for in-

stance, "bases his typology of 'Notional' or 'Deep Structure' text types
. . . on the 'notional categories' which in his view underlie human
language" (Diller 12). The four "notional text types" (or modes) for
Longacre are Narrative, Expository, Behavioral, and Procedural, and
together they overarch and help categorize surface text types which
Longacre calls genres (Diller 12-13). For example, the Narrative mode
overarches genres such as fairy tales, novels, short stories, newspaper
reporting; the Procedural mode includes such genres as food recipes,
how-to books, etc.; the Behavioral mode includes essays and scientific
articles; and the Expository mode includes sermons, pep-talks, speeches, etc. (Diller 13).

Rather than starting with apriori categories, *inductive* text typologies classify text types based on perceived textual patterns. Douglas
Biber's work in corpus linguistics has most influenced such an approach to genre classification. Corpus linguistics, using large scale
electronic text databases or corpora, allow researchers to conduct
systematic searches for linguistic features, patterns, and variations
in spoken and written texts. In *Variation Across Speech and Writing,*
for instance, Biber begins by identifying groups of linguistic features
(what Biber calls "dimensions" such as "narrative versus non-narra-
tive," "non-impersonal versus impersonal style," "situation dependent
versus elaborated reference") that co-occur with high frequency in
texts. Then, applying these dimensions to a statistical analysis of a corpora of twenty-three genres, Biber examined the degree to which these
dimensions appear within various texts in each genre. Based on such
studies, Biber has been able to identify a great deal of linguistic variation within genres, suggesting that genres can be defined in terms of
more or less complexity.[7] (For more on Biber's analysis of textual clus-
ters on the basis of shared multi-dimensional, linguistic characteristics
as well as his historical work mapping the rise and fall of genres, see
*Dimensions of Register Variation: A Cross-Linguistic Comparison; Dis-
course on the Move: Using Corpus Analysis to Describe Discourse Structure;* and *Sociolinguistic Perspectives on Register.*)

This notion of "more or less" has played an important role in historical and corpus linguistic approaches to genre categorization. Based
on Eleanor Rosch's theory of prototypes, which takes a psychological
(as opposed to a classical) view of human categorization, such a typology identifies membership within genre on the basis not of "either-
or" but on the basis of "more-or-less, better and poorer" (Diller 21).

As Brian Paltridge explains, prototype theory describes how people categorize objects according to a prototypical image they have conditioned in their minds by socio-cultural factors, while classical theories describe categorization based on shared, essential properties within objects that result in objective assessment of category membership (*Genre, Frames and Writing* 53). The famous example in this case is the way some birds, such as sparrows, are "birdier" birds than others, such as ostriches. The notion of prototypes, related to Wittgenstein's idea of family resemblances, allows genre researches to define text membership within genres on the basis of how closely their structural and linguistic patterns relate to the genre prototype. Some texts, thus, are closer to their genre prototype while others function more on the periphery of prototypicality, or, more accurately, on the boundaries of different prototypicalities, as in the case of mixed genres. The important point here is that the relation between texts and genres is not simply based on features internal to both, but more powerfully is based on learned, conceptual relations between "memory, context and frames," thus rendering "the notion of prototype as a principle of selection, organization and interpretation of genre frames" (Paltridge, *Genre, Frames and Writing* 62).

Prototype theory has important implications for genre study and teaching. Within SFL genre theory, J.R. Martin has used it to distinguish between typological and topological genre classifications: "For purposes of typological classification, we have to define just what percentage of causal relations is required for a text to qualify [as a member of the genre]. The topological perspective on the other hand allows us to position texts on a cline, as more or less prototypical . . ." ("Analysing" 15). The topological approach thus allows SFL approaches to genre teaching to use the teaching-learning cycle to move students towards more and more prototypical genres through sequenced assignments. At the same time, corpus linguistic-based analyses of genres have allowed researchers and teachers working in English for Specific Purposes (as we will describe in the next chapter) to identify the most and least salient features of different academic and workplace genres so that these can be taught more realistically.

We will conclude this section with a brief discussion of how historical and corpus linguistic approaches to genre have informed the way we understand language change by positing genres as the locus of such change (Diller 31). For example, in his study of the adverbial first par-

ticiple construction in English, Thomas Kohnen describes how that
construction first appeared in and then spread through English via
its use in different genres. The adverbial first participle first appeared
in the English religious treatise and then soon afterward spread to the
sermon (Kohnen 116). What is telling is that the adverbial first participle achieved a certain status by virtue of first appearing in presti-
gious and powerful religious genres, which then acted as catalysts for
linguistic change (Kohnen 111). As Diller explains, "the presence of a
form in a prestigious genre may prompt its reception in other genres
and thus speed up its diffusion throughout the (written) language"
(33). Amy Devitt has likewise demonstrated how genre is a significant
variable in language change (*Writing Genres* 124). In her study of how
Anglo-English became diffused through Scots-English, Devitt found
that Anglicization did not occur evenly throughout Scottish English,
but rather occurred "at quite different rates in different genres" (126).
Anglicization occurred most rapidly, for example, within religious
treatises, and the least rapidly within public records. This suggests
that genres can be understood as sites of contestation within histories
of language change. While religious treatises anglicized more quickly
because of the power of the Church of England, public records, Devitt
explains, were more resistant because they "represent the remnants of
the political power that Scotland until recently had retained within its
own political bodies. The Privy Council may not have much legislative
power anymore, but its records can still reflect that older Scots identity through using its older Scots language" (131). Such studies reveal
the extent to which genres mediate relations of power historically and
linguistically, in ways that enrich the study and teaching of genre. In
the next chapter, we will examine the ways that English for Specific
Purposes has added to the study and teaching of genre by emphasizing
the interaction between discourse community, communicative purpose, and genre.

4 Genre in Linguistic Traditions: English for Specific Purposes

This chapter provides an overview of genre study within English for Specific Purposes (ESP), a field that bridges linguistic and rhetorical traditions. We will begin by defining ESP and identifying key similarities and differences between ESP and Systemic Functional Linguistic (SFL) approaches to genre, and then we will describe how ESP approaches have drawn on linguistic traditions in the process of developing their methods of applied genre study and teaching. We will examine these approaches, track major developments and critiques over the last twenty years, and then conclude by anticipating how ESP genre approaches relate to but also differ from more rhetorical and sociological approaches to genre, the subject of Chapters 5 and 6.

Positioned within the overarching category of Language for Specific Purposes (LSP), English for Specific Purposes focuses on studying and teaching specialized varieties of English, most often to non-native speakers of English, in advanced academic and professional settings. ESP is often used as an umbrella term to include more specialized areas of study such as English for Academic Purposes (EAP), English for Occupational Purposes (EOP), and English for Medical Purposes (EMP). Although ESP has existed since the 1960s and although ESP researchers began to use genre analysis as a research and pedagogical tool in the 1980s, it was John Swales' groundbreaking book *Genre Analysis: English in Academic and Research Settings* that most fully theorized and developed the methodology for bringing genre analysis into ESP research and teaching. It is largely due to Swales' work and the research it has inspired over the last twenty years that ESP and genre analysis have become in many ways synonymous (see Belcher, Cheng).

Swales begins *Genre Analysis* by identifying two key characteristics of ESP genre approaches, namely their focus on academic and research English (which would be expanded to include occupational

English), and their use of genre analysis for *applied* ends. The applied nature of ESP has been a defining feature of the field from its inception. As Swales explains, ESP approaches can be traced to "quantitative studies of the linguistic properties . . . of *registers* of a language" for the purpose of identifying the frequency of occurrence of certain linguistic features in a particular register and then making these features the focus of language instruction (*Genre Analysis* 2). Early work in ESP thus resembled research in corpus linguistics with its quantitative studies of the linguistic properties of language varieties, and to this day research in corpus linguistics continues to influence ESP genre research (Belcher 168; Paltridge, *Genre and the Language Learning Classroom* 119-20). As Swales notes, however, ESP studies since the 1960s have "concomitantly become narrower and deeper" than those early quantitative studies (3). They are *narrower* in the sense that the focus has shifted from broader register categories such as "scientific" or "medical" language to a narrower focus on actual genre varieties used within, say, scientific and medical disciplines (Swales, *Genre Analysis* 3). At the same time, ESP analyses have also become *deeper* in the sense that they not only describe linguistic features of language varieties but also their communicative purposes and effects. This "deeper or multi-layered textual account," Swales explains, signaled an interest in "assessing rhetorical purposes, in unpacking information structures and in accounting for syntactic and lexical choices" (3). It is in their focus on describing and determining linguistic effects that ESP genre approaches help bridge linguistic and rhetorical studies of genre.

ESP and SFL: Similarities and Distinctions

ESP's expanded interest from descriptive analyses of linguistic features to analyses of genres and their communicative functions not only helps distinguish ESP research from corpus linguistics (for more on this distinction, see Tardy and Swales, "Form, Text Organization, Genre, Coherence, and Cohesion"),[8] but also reveals similarities and distinctions between ESP genre analyses and systemic functional linguistic genre analyses. There are several ways in which SFL and ESP genre approaches compare to and differ from one another. They both share the fundamental view that linguistic features are connected to social context and function. And they are both driven by the pedagogical imperative to make visible to disadvantaged students the connections between language and social function that genres embody. Such a "visible pedagogy," according to Ken Hyland, "seeks to offer writers an explicit understanding of how target texts are structured and why they are written the way they are," thereby making "clear what is to be learned rather than relying on hit-or-miss inductive methods" (*Genre and Second Language Writing* 11). Both ESP and SFL genre approaches are also committed to the idea that this kind of explicit teaching of relevant genres provides access to disadvantaged learners. As Hyland elaborates, "the teaching of key genres is, therefore, a means of helping learners gain access to ways of communicating that accrued cultural capital in particular professional, academic, and occupational communities. By making the genres of power visible and attainable through explicit instruction, genre pedagogies seek to demystify the kinds of writing that will enhance learners' career opportunities and provide access to a greater range of life choices" ("Genre-based Pedagogies" 24).

While SFL and ESP genre approaches share analytical strategies and pedagogical commitments, they differ in subtle but important ways. Most obviously, they differ in their applied target audience, with SFL genre approaches generally targeting economically and culturally disadvantaged school-age children in Australia, as we saw in the previous chapter, and ESP genre approaches generally targeting more advanced, often graduate-level, international students in British and U.S. universities, who, as non-native speakers of English, are linguistically disadvantaged. This difference in target audience has important implications for how SFL and ESP approaches perceive and analyze target genres. Because both approaches teach explicitly "genres often assumed to be tacitly acquired via the normal progression of academic acculturation" but denied disadvantaged students (Belcher 169), the question of which genres to teach becomes crucial. Primary and secondary school students are not often, if ever, asked to write in what would be considered disciplinary or professional genres. As a result, SFL scholars and teachers have tended to focus their attention on what Ann Johns, following Swales, calls "pre-genres" such as explanations, recounts, or description (Johns, "Genre and ESL/EFL").[9] For ESP scholars and teachers working with advanced students whose academic disciplines and professional/occupational settings are more bounded and where the genres used within those contexts are more identifiable, the analytical and pedagogical focus has been on actual, community-identified genres used within those disciplinary settings—genres such as research articles, literature reviews, conference abstracts, research presentations, grant proposals, job application letters, academic lectures, various medical texts, legislative documents, and so on.

The differences in target audience and genre focus between SFL and ESP approaches highlight a related difference in understandings of context. Because SFL approaches generally focus on pre-genres, they have tended to define context at a fairly macro level. As we discussed in the previous chapter, SFL genre approaches locate genre at the level of "context of culture." ESP genre approaches, however, locate genres within more specifically defined contexts (what Swales first termed "discourse communities"), where the genres' communicative purposes are more specified and attributable. As we will discuss next, defining genre in relation to discourse community has had important implications for ESP genre approaches, allowing ESP scholars to focus on context and communicative/rhetorical purpose. At the same time, defining genre in relation to discourse community has to some degree also shifted the pedagogical purpose of ESP approaches away from the more overtly political, empowerment-motivated goals of SFL genre-based teaching to a more pragmatic, acculturation-motivated pedagogy aimed at helping advanced non-native English speaking students acquire "knowledge of relevant genres so they can act effectively in their target contexts" (Hyland, "Genre-based Pedagogies" 22).

DISCOURSE COMMUNITY, COMMUNICATIVE PURPOSE, AND GENRE

Three key and inter-related concepts—discourse community, communicative purpose, and genre—frame Swales' approach to genre study. Swales defines discourse communities as "sociorhetorical networks that form in order to work towards sets of common goals" (*Genre Analysis* 9). These common goals become the basis for shared communicative purposes, with genres enabling discourse community members to achieve these communicative purposes (9).

In *Genre Analysis,* Swales proposes six defining characteristics of discourse communities. First, "a discourse community has a broadly agreed set of common public goals" which can either be explicitly stated or tacitly understood (24-25). Second, in order to achieve and further its goals, a discourse community must have "mechanisms of intercommunication among its members" such as meeting rooms or telecommunications technologies or newsletters, etc. (25). Third, membership within a discourse community depends on individuals using these mechanisms to participate in the life of the discourse community (26). Fourth, "a discourse community utilizes and hence possesses one or more genres in the communicative furtherance of its aims" (26). These genres must be recognizable to and defined by members of a discourse community (26). Five, "in addition to owning genres, a discourse community has acquired some specific lexis" which can take the form of "increasingly shared and specialized terminology" such as abbreviations and acronyms (26). Finally, "a discourse community has a threshold level of members with a suitable degree of relevant content and discoursal expertise" who can pass on knowledge of shared goals and communicative purposes to new members (27). As such, genres not only help members of a discourse community to achieve and further their goals; genres also help new members acquire and become initiated into a discourse community's shared goals, hence the value of genre as a teaching tool within ESP.

By proposing that a genre "comprises a class of *communicative events,* the members of which share some set of communicative purposes" (58; emphasis added), Swales defines genres first and foremost as linguistic and rhetorical actions, involving the use of language to communicate something to someone at some time in some context for some purpose. While a communicative event can be random or idiosyncratic, motivated by a unique, distinct purpose, a genre represents a class of communicative events that has formed in response to some shared set of communicative purposes. A genre, therefore, is a relatively stable class of linguistic and rhetorical "events" which members of a discourse community have typified in order to respond to and achieve shared communicative goals.

Swales is careful to note that "exemplars or instances of genres vary in their prototypicality" (49), meaning that a text's genre membership is not defined by "either/or" essential properties but rather along a spectrum of family resemblances, as we discussed in the section on Genre and Historical/Corpus Linguistics in the previous chapter. Since, according to Swales, "communicative purpose has been nominated as the *privileged* property of a genre" (52), a genre prototype is determined by how closely it corresponds to its communicative purpose. From there, as Swales explains, "[o]ther properties, such as form, structure and audience expectations operate to identify the extent to which an exemplar is *prototypical* of a particular genre" (52). As such, it is the rationale behind the genre that "shapes the schematic structure of the discourse and influences and constrains choice of content and style" (58). In short, the rationale determines a genre's allowable range of substantive, structural, syntactic, and lexical choices, and the extent to which a text exists within this range will define its genre membership.

Because a genre's rationale as well as it schematic, syntactic, and lexical conventions are all defined against the backdrop of a discourse community's shared goals, how members of a discourse community define genres is important to how genre analysts understand their function and structure. For this reason, ESP genre analyses, more so than SFL analyses, rely on a discourse community's "nomenclature for genres [as] an important source of insight" (Swales 54). Such naming, as Swales suggests, can provide valuable ethnographic information into how and why members of discourse communities use genres. However, as we will examine later in this chapter, although research such as Ann John's important work combining genre analysis and ethnography (1997) and Swales' "textographic" study of a university building (1998) employ ethnographic strategies, the extent to which ethnographic approaches have played (or should play) a role in ESP genre analyses and the purposes for which such approaches have been used remain subject to debate.

ESP Approaches to Genre Analysis

Because it is communicative purpose (defined in relation to a discourse community's shared goals) that gives rise to and provides the rationale for a genre and shapes its internal structure, communicative purpose often serves as a starting point for ESP genre analyses. A typical ESP approach to genre analysis, for example, will begin by identifying a genre within a discourse community and defining the communicative purpose the genre is designed to achieve. From there, the analysis turns to an examination of the genre's organization—its schematic structure—often characterized by the rhetorical "moves" it undertakes, and then to an examination of the textual and linguistic features (style, tone, voice, grammar, syntax) that realize the rhetorical moves. The trajectory of the analysis thus proceeds from a genre's schematic structure to its lexico-grammatic features, all the while attending to the genre's communicative purpose and the discourse community which defines it. The process is by no means linear or static, but generally speaking, it has tended to move from context to text (Flowerdew 91-92), with context providing knowledge of communicative purpose and discourse community members' genre identifications.

In *Analysing Genre: Language in Professional Settings*, Vijay Bhatia outlines seven steps to analyzing genres, which reflect the trajectory described above. Not all ESP genre researchers will follow all these steps, and not always in the order Bhatia outlines, but together these steps provide insight into the range of ways ESP genre researchers go about conducting genre analyses in academic and professional contexts. The first step involves placing a given genre-text in its situational context. Step two involves surveying the existing research on the genre (22). With the genre identified and contextualized, step three involves refining the researcher's understanding of the genre's discourse community. This includes identifying the writers and readers who use the genre and determining their goals and relationships to one another, as well as the material conditions in which they function—in short, identifying the "reality" which the genre represents (23). Step four involves the researcher collecting a corpus of the genre. Step five introduces an ethnographic dimension, with Bhatia recommending that the researcher conduct an ethnography of the institutional context in which the genre takes place (24) in order to gain "naturalistic" insight into the conditions in which members of a discourse community use the genre. Step six moves from context to text, and involves the decision regarding which level of linguistic analysis to explore: *lexico-grammatical features* (for example, quantitative/statistical study of tenses, clauses, and other syntactic properties, including stylistic analysis) (25-26), *text-patterning* (for example, the patterns in which language is used in a particular genre, such as how and why noun phrases and nominalizations are used in different genres), and *structural interpretation* (for example, the structural "moves" a genre utilizes to achieve its goals, such as the three-move CARS [Creating a Research Space] structure of research article introductions as described by Swales). In the final step, Bhatia advises researchers to seek a specialist informant from the research site to verify findings (34).

While the extent to which step five (conducting an ethnography) is utilized in ESP genre approaches varies both in terms of its frequen-

cy and specificity, in general Bhatia's methodology for genre analysis
describes the trajectory that most ESP genre approaches have taken,
moving from context to textual analysis and, at the textual level, applying various levels of linguistic analyses, from lexico-grammatical
features to language patterns to larger structural patterns. Swales' well-
known and influential analysis of the research article in *Genre Analysis*
generally exemplifies these levels of linguistic, textual, and structural
analyses. For example, in analyzing research article (RA) introductions, Swales first identifies the typical "moves" authors make within
the introduction (Swales and Feak have defined a "move" as a "bounded communicative act that is designed to achieve one main communicative objective" within the larger communicative objective of the
genre) (35): from "establishing a territory" (move 1) to "establishing
a niche" (move 2) to "occupying the niche" (move 3) (141). Within
each of these moves, Swales identifies a range of possible "steps" RA
authors can take, such as "claiming centrality" and "reviewing items
of previous research" in move 1 and "counter-claiming" or "indicating a gap" in move 2. From there, Swales examines steps more specifically by analyzing text-patterning and lexico-grammatical features
within different steps. In analyzing step 3 (reviewing items of previous research) within move 1 (establishing a territory), for instance,
Swales looks at patterns of citation, noting patterns in which RA authors either name the researcher being cited in their citing sentence
or reference the researcher in parenthesis at the end of the sentence or
in end notes. Moving from text-patterning to lexico-grammatical features, Swales then identifies the frequency of "reporting verbs" (such
as "show," "establish," "claim," etc.) that RA authors use "to introduce
previous researchers and their findings" (150).

This general approach to genre analysis within ESP—from identifying purpose to analyzing a genre's rhetorical moves and how these
moves are carried out textually and linguistically—and the research
that has emerged from it has contributed greatly to our knowledge
of discipline-specific genres, notably research articles as well as what
Swales has called "occluded genres" that operate behind the scenes of
research articles (genres such as abstracts, submission letters, review
letters, etc.). Such knowledge has enabled graduate-level non-native
speakers of English to gain access to and participate in academic and
professional discourse communities (Swales, "Occluded Genres" 46).[10]

Recent Developments in ESP Genre Study

Over the past twenty years (see Diane Belcher's "Trends"), ESP genre research has focused on issues related to communicative purpose, context, and the dynamic, intertextual nature of genres. Eleven years after the publication of Swales' *Genre Analysis,* Inger Askehave and John Swales, reflecting on the notion of "communicative purpose" in light of more complex, dynamic understandings of context and cognition, wonder if "'communicative purpose' has assumed a taken-for-granted status, a convenient but under-considered starting point for the analyst" (197). They point to research that "has, in various ways, established that . . . purposes, goals, or public outcomes are more evasive, multiple, layered, and complex than originally envisaged" (197), and note how genre researches such as Bhatia had already recognized that while genre conventions constrain "allowable contributions in terms of their intent, positioning, form, and functional value, . . . these constraints . . . are often exploited by the expert members of the discourse community to achieve private intentions within the framework of socially recognized purpose(s)" (Bhatia 13). Askehave and Swales acknowledge that "we are no longer looking at a simple enumerable list or 'set' of communicative purposes, but at a complexly layered one, wherein some purposes are not likely to be officially 'acknowledged' by the institution, even if they may be 'recognized'—particularly in off-record situations—by some of its expert members" (199).

In an effort to account for the complexity of communicative purpose, Askehave and Swales suggest that researchers begin with a provisional identification of genre purpose and then "repurpose" the genre after more "extensive text-in-context inquiry" (208). For example, in his recent study of research genres, Swales examines the use of humor in dissertation defenses, arguing that the use of humor enables the achievement of the more serious purposes of the dissertation defense: The purpose and use of humor helps to "lubricate the wheels of the genre" and enables the participants in the defense to proceed "in an informal atmosphere of solidarity and cooperation" (Swales, *Research Genres* 170). More recently, Sunny Hyon has examined the multi-functionality of communicative purposes in university retention-promotion-tenure (RPT) reports. Analyzing how report writers use playfulness and inventiveness in RPT reports, Hyon suggests that while not overturning the reports' official communicative purposes, "the inventiveness . . . may *add* unofficial purposes to these reports" ("Convention and Inventiveness in an Occluded Academic Genre" 178). Likewise, Ken Hyland has recently analyzed the strategies that academic writers use in different academic communities to construct themselves and their readers. Focusing on "stance" and "engagement," Hyland examines how writers insert their personality into their texts through the use of hedges, boosters, and attitude markers, and how they construct their readers through the use of questions, reader pronouns, and directives (Hyland, "Stance and Engagement"). Hyland's research demonstrates that, within the conventions of disciplinary discourses, individual writers can "manipulate the options available to them for creative and rhetorical purposes of their own" (Johns et al., "Crossing the Boundaries" 238).

In recognizing the complexity of communicative purpose and broadening the range of analysis to include "sets of communicative purposes," recent ESP approaches to genre study acknowledge the dynamic, interactive nature of genres. In addition to analyzing occluded genres that function behind the scenes of more dominant genres, ESP genre researchers have begun also to attend to what Swales calls "genre chains," whereby "one genre is a necessary antecedent for another" (Swales, *Research Genres* 18). Attending to networks of genres reveals that genre competence involves knowledge not only of individual genres, but also of how genres interact with one another in complex ways to achieve dynamic purposes. Bronia P.C. So has explored the implications of this complex set of relations for ESP genre pedagogy, concluding that: "To enable students to cope with a wide range of genres in today's world, it is important to help them acquire not only the knowledge of the rhetorical context, audience, generic conventions, as well as overlaps and distinctions, but more importantly also the knowledge and understanding of intertextuality and interdiscursivity in genre writing" (77).

To examine genre intertextuality, some ESP researchers have emphasized ethnographic approaches to genre study. Ann Johns, for example, has promoted the idea of students as both genre researchers and genre theorists to help bridge the gap between what genre researchers know about genres (as complex, dynamic entities) and what student are often taught about genres (as static, fixed forms) in literacy classrooms (Johns, "Destabilizing and Enriching" 237-40; see also Johns, "Teaching Classroom and Authentic Genres"). In *Text, Role, and Con-*

text: Developing Academic Literacies, Johns invites students to become ethnographers of the academic contexts in which they are learning to write, including the values and expectations underlying the genres they are asked to write and what role these genres play in their academic contexts. In "Destabilizing and Enriching Novice Students' Genre Theories," Johns shifts the analysis to students' own theories of genre in the context of a "remedial" EAP course, inviting students to reflect on the (often limited and limiting) theories of genre they bring with them and encouraging them "to broaden their concepts of genre and their genre repertoire" at the same time as they acquire new academic genres (244). This more auto-ethnographic approach enables students to become more "aware of the interaction between process, intertextuality, and products, and the variation among texts even within what is assumed to be a single pedagogical genre such as the research paper or five-paragraph essay" (246).

Brian Paltridge has recently described the use of ethnography in a writing course for second language graduate students at the University of Sydney, in which students interview their professors in order to find out why they want students to write in certain genres and what purposes these genres serve within the discipline. In so doing, students can deploy their "thicker" understanding of genres within their disciplinary setting in order to "negotiate the boundaries, values, and expectations of the disciplines in which they are writing" (Johns et al., "Crossing the Boundaries" 236). Such ethnographic approaches in ESP genre teaching signal a recognition among ESP genre researchers of the deeply social nature of genres, not only in the sense that genres are embedded in social contexts such as discourse communities, but also in the sense that genres help shape social contexts—a view of genre acknowledged by Ken Hyland when he writes: "It is through this recurrent use of conventional forms and communicative practices that individuals develop relationships, establish communities, and get things done. Genres therefore not only embed social realities but also construct them" (Johns et al, "Crossing the Boundaries" 237). As Swales puts it is in his "textographic" study of a university building (1998), genres help connect "lifeways" and "textways" (*Other Floors*).[11]

Despite recent attempts to bring a more dynamic, complex understanding of genre into ESP classrooms, ESP genre approaches have been subject to critique by scholars who contend that such approaches are often subject to a pedagogy of accommodation, prescriptiveness, and genre competence rather than genre performance. To counterbalance these motivations, some ESP scholars have called for a more critical approach to genre study and teaching within ESP.

ESP AND CRITICAL APPROACHES TO GENRE

Sarah Benesch was one of the first EAP scholars to point out the ideological consequences of giving non-native English speaking students access to academic and professional discourse communities through explicit teaching of genre conventions (see *Critical English* and "ESL, Ideology, and the Politics of Pragmatism").[12] By ignoring the ideological implications of such a pedagogy of accommodation, Benesch argues, EAP teachers unwittingly reproduce the very academic cultures of power that exclude non-native speaking students in the first place. As such, "EAP's accommodation to traditional academic practices" may actually "limit the participation of nonnative-speaking students in academic culture" (Benesch, "ESL, Ideology, and the Politics of Pragmatism" 713). Benesch has not been alone in questioning the implications of what Pennycook has called ESP's "vulgar pragmatism." As noted in Belcher, Peter Master has called on ESP to be more self-reflective about its role both in spreading global English and in helping language learners meet the needs of institutions and workplaces without questioning what and whose interests these needs represent (Master 724). Likewise, Alan Luke explains that a "a salient criticism of the 'genre model' is that its emphasis on the direct transmission of text types does not necessarily lead on to a critical appraisal of that disciplinary corpus, its field or its related institutions, but rather may lend itself to an uncritical reproduction of discipline" (314).

Such critiques do not reject an accomodationist approach entirely, but call instead for what Pennycook calls a "critical pragmatism," one that still aims to provide non-native speakers of English with access to genres of power and opportunity but that does so more critically. The difference between Pennycook's "vulgar" and "critical" pragmatism hinges on what ESP researchers and teachers mean by "explicit" analysis and teaching of genres. The kind of explicit analysis and teaching called for by critical pragmatism would go beyond explicating genre patterns and features to include an analysis of the ideologies, identities, and power relations embedded in and reproduced by these patterns and features. As Brian Paltridge explains, a critical perspective on genre "might explore the connections between discourse, language learning, language use, and the social and political contexts" while providing "students with the tools they need to succeed" (*Genre and the Language Learning Classroom* 121). Such an approach argues that effective participation within a discourse community requires more than just the ability to follow genre conventions as these relate to communicative purposes; it requires the ability to know why genres and purposes exist, whose interests they serve and whose they exclude, what they make possible and what they obscure, and so on. This more critical approach to genre, its proponents argue, shifts the focus from a pedagogy of cultural accommodation to what Pennycook calls a "pedagogy of cultural alternatives" (264), whereby students can potentially adapt genre conventions in order to represent alternative purposes and/or their own cultural perspectives.

Related to the critique of ESP's pedagogy of accommodation has been a concern with ESP's potentially prescriptive view of genre. Christine Casanave has warned, for example, that ESP genre-based approaches can privilege "a socially situated product perspective" (82), while Kay and Dudley-Evans observe that ESP approaches tend to focus on the teaching of "conventionalized lists of genre-identifying features" which can lead to "an imposed rather than a responsive notion of text" (311). The result can be characterized as a competence-based rather than performance-based acquisition of genres, in which students recognize and reproduce a genre's constitutive conventions but are not as able to apply and adapt these genre conventions in response to actual communicative goals and situations.

In "Understanding Learners and Learning in ESP Genre-based Writing Instruction," An Cheng takes up the distinction between "noticing" and "performing" genre (86). Cheng critiques ESP genre approaches for focusing too exclusively on examining target genres, and calls for more learner-and-context-focused research that "examines learners' learning of genre and their development of generic/rhetorical consciousness" (77). The slighting of learners and learning in ESP genre approaches (a charge that could also be leveled against rhetorical genre approaches) raises important questions about what it means to use genres. To what extent does genre competence (knowledge of genre conventions) translate into genre performance? Is knowledge of genre conventions enough, or does genre performance require inter- and extra-textual knowledge that exceeds the ability of text-based genre analyses to deliver? If genre knowledge involves more than just knowledge of genre conventions, then what does genre knowledge entail? And how do genre researchers and teachers access and identify that knowledge? Questions such as these push at the disciplinary edges of ESP genre approaches, bringing us to the boundaries and debates between ESP and Rhetorical Genre Studies (RGS) approaches.

The way that RGS scholars have taken up the above questions reveals important differences between ESP and rhetorical genre approaches, having to do with the sociological nature of genres and the extent to which genres can and should be taught explicitly. While both ESP and rhetorical genre scholars acknowledge the dynamic relationship between texts and contexts, and while both recognize genres as situated rhetorical and linguistic actions, RGS has tended to understand genres not only as situated within contexts such as discourse communities, but also as constitutive of contexts—as symbolic worlds readers and writers co-construct and inhabit. That is, for RGS, context provides more than valuable background knowledge regarding communicative purpose(s), discourse community members, genre nomenclature, or even genre chains and occluded genres—significant as these are. Generally speaking, then, while ESP genre scholars have tended to understand genres as communicative tools situated within social contexts, rhetorical genre scholars have tended to understand genres as sociological concepts embodying textual and social ways of knowing, being, and interacting in particular contexts.

Even when more recent ESP genre research has acknowledged the sociological nature of genres, such as when Ken Hyland, cited earlier, describes how genres "not only embed social realities but also construct them," the emphasis of ESP genre analysis has remained on explicating genre conventions (schematic and lexico-grammatic) against the *backdrop* of the genre's social context.[13] So while both ESP and Rhetorical genre approaches recognize genres as relating texts and context, the point of emphasis and analytical/pedagogical trajectory of each approach has differed, so that, generally speaking, in ESP genre study, context has been used to understand texts and communicative purposes while in Rhetorical Genre Studies, texts have been used to study contexts and social actions—in particular, how texts mediate situated symbolic actions.

The difference in emphasis between communicative purpose and social action not only reflects different analytical trajectories between ESP and rhetorical genre approaches; it also underscores different pedagogical philosophies and goals. Rhetorical genre researchers, for example, tend to question whether explicit teaching of genre is enough, arguing instead for a more immersion- and ethnographic-based pedagogy in which students encounter, analyze, and practice writing genres in the contexts of their use. Such an approach, RGS researchers argue, allows students to get at some of the inter- and extra-textual knowledge that exceeds knowledge of genre conventions and that genre users must possess in order to perform genres effectively. Around the time of Swales's *Genre Analysis,* Charles Bazerman was describing this rhetorical/sociological view when he suggested that writing instruction should go beyond "the formal trappings" of genres and instead help make students aware that "the more [they] understand the fundamental assumptions and aims of [their] community, the better able [they] will be . . . to evaluate whether the rhetorical habits [they] and [their] colleagues bring to the task are appropriate and effective" (*Shaping* 320, 323). As Mary Jo Reiff recently put it, "Making genre analysis the focal point of ethnographic inquiry . . . ties communicative actions to their contexts and can illustrate to students how patterns of linguistic and rhetorical behavior . . . are inextricably linked to patterns of social behavior" (Johns et al, 243).

The debate between explicit and more sociological approaches to genre teaching is not absolute, of course, and many genre scholars and teachers employ hybrid models that cross boundaries of the debate, as we will examine in the next two chapters and in Chapters 10 and 11. But as Diane Belcher explains, "for learners faced with linguistic and literacy barriers . . . ESP proponents contend that immersion is not enough" (171). Christine Tardy, while acknowledging genres' complexity (as a "kind of nexus among the textual, social, and political dimensions of writing"), likewise advises that, given the non-native English speaking population most often targeted in ESP genre approaches, it is necessary to compartmentalize genres. As Tardy writes, "some of the advanced ESL writers I observed, for example, had difficulty analyzing genres from a linguistic *and* rhetorical perspective and then drawing links between these features and the rhetorical scene. They found little relevance in such analysis and at times saw the complexities of genre as too abstract to be of use. Perhaps at some stages and for some learners, more filtered or compartmentalized views of genre are also necessary" (Johns et al, 239).

This pedagogical debate and the set of theoretical questions that inform it bring us to the permeable yet dividing boundaries between not only ESP and rhetorical genre approaches, but between linguistic and rhetorical traditions in genre study. In Chapter 5, we will explore rhetorical genre theory, tracing its roots, current theories and approaches, and its analytical and pedagogical possibilities, and in Chapter 6, we will examine how these theories and approaches have informed the study and teaching of genre within Rhetorical Genre Studies.

5 Genre in Rhetorical and Sociological Traditions

At the end of Chapter 4, we began to draw some general distinctions between linguistic (particularly English for Specific Purposes) and rhetorical genre approaches, having to do with differences between their communicative and sociological emphases, and with the extent to which genres can and should be taught explicitly. Both linguistic and rhetorical approaches to genre—whether in the form of Systemic Functional Linguistics, English for Specific Purposes, or Rhetorical Genre Studies—share a fundamental understanding of genre as inextricably tied to situation. As Aviva Freedman recently put it, "both insist on the limitations of traditional conceptions of genres which focused only on recurring textual features. Both stressed the need to recognize the social dimensions of genre. . . . Both approaches emphasize the addressee, the context, and the occasion" ("Interaction" 104). Yet while both linguistic and rhetorical genre approaches recognize genres as connecting texts and contexts, the point of emphasis and analytical/ pedagogical trajectory of each approach has differed, as Freedman and others have noted (see especially Hyon, "Genre in Three Traditions"; also Hyland, "Genre-Based Pedagogies" and Paltridge, *Genre and the Language Learning Classroom*), and these differences have had significant implications for how each tradition recognizes the work that genres do, how genres can be studied, and the ways genres can be taught and acquired.

In the case of English for Specific Purposes (ESP) and Rhetorical Genre Studies (RGS), the differences in emphasis and trajectory can be traced to each field's guiding definitions of genre and the traditions that inform them. Following John Swales, ESP genre approaches have generally defined genres as communicative events which help members of a discourse community achieve shared communicative purposes. As such, genres are *forms of communicative action*. Within RGS, and following Carolyn Miller, genres have been defined as *forms of social action*. The next chapter will explore in greater detail what it means to think of genres as forms of social action and its implications for the researching and teaching of genres within RGS. But first, in this chapter, we will compare RGS's and ESP's guiding definitions of genre in order to clarify their communicative and sociological emphases. Then we will situate RGS's guiding definition of genre within the rhetorical, phenomenological, and sociological traditions from which it grew. We will conclude the chapter by describing recent genre scholarship in Brazil, which has synthesized the sociological, rhetorical, and linguistic traditions (while also drawing on French and Swiss genre pedagogic traditions) in ways that reveal the possible interconnections between these traditions.

COMMUNICATIVE AND SOCIOLOGICAL ORIENTATIONS TO GENRE

Within ESP genre approaches, the aims of genre analysis have generally been to examine what a discourse community's goals are and how genre features (structurally and lexico-grammatically) embody and help its members carry out their communicative goals. Thus, as generally understood in ESP genre research, it is communicative purpose (defined in relation to a discourse community's shared goals) that both gives rise to and provides the rationale for a genre, and shapes its internal structure. It is communicative purpose that often serves as a starting point for ESP genre analyses, which then proceed toward an analysis of a genre's rhetorical moves and steps, then to textual and linguistic features that carry out the moves and steps. Because ESP approaches have tended to define genres as forms of communicative action that help members of a discourse community carry out its work, the trajectory of inquiry has tended to go from context to text. That trajectory has been used to great effect by scholars and teachers to help, in particular, graduate-level, international, non-native speakers of English gain access to and participate more effectively within various academic contexts by explicating and teaching the genres that coordinate the work of these contexts. Significantly, such an internal, linguistic trajectory has tended to take the existence of a discourse community and its goals as a given—a starting point for the identification and analysis of genres.

Rhetorical Genre Studies has tended to focus more on how genres enable their users to carry out situated symbolic actions rhetorically and linguistically, and in so doing, to perform social actions and relations, enact social roles, and frame social realities. At the same time, RGS has also focused on how genres, through their use, dynamically maintain, reveal tensions within, and help reproduce social practices and realities. For RGS, then, context provides more than valuable background knowledge regarding communicative purpose(s), discourse community membership, genre nomenclature, or even genre chains and occluded genres—significant as these are. Rather, within RGS context is viewed as an ongoing, intersubjective performance, one that is mediated by genres and other culturally available tools (Bazerman, "Textual Performance" 387). The focus of genre analysis within RGS has thus been directed toward an understanding of how genres mediate situated practices, interactions, symbolic realities, and "congruent meanings" (380): in short, the role that genres play in how individuals experience, co-construct, and enact social practices and sites of activity. So while ESP genre scholars have tended to understand genres as communicative tools situated within social contexts, RGS scholars have tended to understand genres as sociological concepts mediating textual and social ways of knowing, being, and interacting in particular contexts. In RGS, understanding contexts (and their performance) is both the starting point of genre analysis and its goal.

Such a performative, sociological view is captured in Charles Bazerman's often-cited description of genre:

> Genres are not just forms. Genres are forms of life, ways of being. They are frames for social action. They are locations within which meaning is constructed. Genres shape the thoughts we form and the communications by which we interact. Genres are the familiar places we go to create intelligible communicative action with each other and the guideposts we use to explore the unfamiliar. ("The Life of Genre" 19)

From this perspective, genres can be understood as both habitations and habits: recognizable sites of rhetorical and social *action* as well as typified ways of rhetorically and socially *acting*. We inhabit genres (genre as noun) and we enact genres (genre as verb). Elaborating on what it means to think of genres as nouns and verbs, Catherine Schryer explains: "As discourse formations or constellations of strategies, genres provide us with the flexible guidelines, or access to strategies that we need to function together in the constant social construction of reality. They guide us as we together and 'on the fly' mutually negotiate our way from moment to moment and yet provide us with some security that an utterance will end in a predictable way. They are, as Lemke suggested, 'trajectory entities,' structured structures that structure our management of time/space" (Schryer, "Genre and Power" 95). As such, Schryer goes on to explain, genres "are profoundly ideological" (95). At the same time, as Bazerman has emphasized, genres are profoundly socio-cognitive. They are "meaning landscapes" that "orient us toward shared mentally constructed spaces" (Bazerman, "Textual Performance" 385) as well as "tools of cognition" connected to "repertoire[s] of cognitive practices" (Bazerman, "Genre and Cognitive Development" 290) that contribute to our "sense-making" (Bazerman, *Constructing Experience* 94).

The focus in RGS on the study of genres as forms of situated cognition, social action, and social reproduction has come somewhat at the expense of the more precise linguistic analyses performed in ESP and Systemic Functional genre research. This in part has to do with the traditions (rhetoric, sociology, phenomenology, philosophy, psychology [particularly sociocultural psychology], communication, semiotics, technical and professional communication, Writing in the Disciplines) that have informed research in RGS, as well as the disciplines from which RGS scholars are generally trained, mainly areas such as English, communication, education, technical communication, and less so, linguistics. But equally, it has to do with a different theoretical orientation to genre. RGS did not emerge out of a pedagogical imperative as Systemic Functional and ESP approaches did. Although RGS scholars early on recognized genre's pedagogical possibilities and took those up in the context of Writing Across the Curriculum and academic writing (see for example, Elaine Maimon's "Maps and Genres," Bazerman's *The Informed Writer* and *The Informed Reader,* and Amy Devitt's "Generalizing"), the turn to pedagogy within RGS has remained a subject of debate. As we shall see, the theoretical, historical, and ethnomethodological studies of genre that established the field of RGS developed an understanding of genre as rhetorically and socially dynamic, "stabilized for now" (Schryer, "Genre and Power"), ideological, performative, intertextual, socio-cognitive, and responsive to and also constructive of situations. Such an understanding of genres suggests that they cannot be explicated, explained, or acquired only through textual or linguistic means; they also cannot be abstracted from the contexts of their use for pedagogical purposes. Because learning genres is about learning to inhabit "interactionally produced worlds" (Bazerman, "Textual Performance" 386) and social relationships, to think and act and recognize situations in a particular way, and to orient oneself to particular goals, values, and assumptions, some RGS scholars have questioned the value of explicit genre teaching, while others have more recently sought to develop pedagogical approaches based in genre awareness, ethnography, and situated apprenticeship. RGS continues to work through what it means to teach genres in ways that honor the field's understanding of them as complex, dynamic socio-cognitive actions. At the same time, recent work among genre scholars in Brazil offers possibilities for synthesizing the various pedagogical approaches.

RHETORICAL CRITICISM AND GENRE

"If I had to sum up in one word the difference between the 'old' rhetoric and a 'new,'" Kenneth Burke wrote in 1951, "I would reduce it to this: The key term for the old rhetoric was *persuasion* and its stress was upon deliberate design. The key term for the new rhetoric would be *identification,* which can include a partially 'unconscious' factor in appeal" ("Rhetoric—Old and New" 203). This shift in the understanding of rhetoric—from persuasion to identification—has had a great impact on what it means to study and teach rhetoric, starting in the early to mid-twentieth century.

According to Burke, rhetoric is a form of symbolic action; it is "the use of language as a symbolic means of inducing cooperation in beings that by nature respond to symbols" (*Rhetoric of Motives* 43). Rhetoric allows human beings to function within and construct social reality—to use language symbolically to establish identification and induce cooperation. At the same time, rhetoric is also contingent and dynamic as language users vie for and negotiate identifications (how they identify themselves and others against how they are identified), how they establish and change affiliations, and so on. David Fleming has described this view of rhetoric in anthropological terms as the condition of our existence—as a way of being, knowing, organizing, and interacting in the world (176). Not only has the notion of rhetoric as symbolic action thus expanded our understanding of the work that rhetoric performs; it has also expanded the realm of rhetorical scholarship to include the study of rhetoric in areas that were once thought outside the purview of rhetoric, areas such as the rhetoric of science and rhetoric of economics. Such an expanded view of rhetoric would come to play an important role in the understanding of genres as complex forms of rhetorical and social action.

RGS has contributed to the work of new rhetoric by examining how genres—as typified rhetorical ways of acting within recurring situations—function as symbolic means of establishing social identification and cooperation. In her groundbreaking and influential 1984 article "Genre as Social Action," Carolyn Miller drew on and built connections between new rhetorical conceptualizations of rhetoric as symbolic action and scholarship in rhetorical criticism and sociology that focused on rhetorical and social typification. The notion of *typification* (socially defined and shared recognitions of similarities) would prove central to a view of genre as social action.

Rhetorical criticism, since at least the work of Edwin Black and Lloyd Bitzer in the 1960s, has recognized genres as fundamentally connected to situation types. Black, for instance, critiqued traditional (Neo-Aristotelian) rhetorical criticism for being too focused on singular rhetorical events and strategies. Such a focus on singularity, Campbell and Jamieson explain, "did not, and perhaps could not, trace traditions or recognize affinities and recurrent forms" (14). For Black, a recognition of traditions and recurrence enables rhetorical criticism to examine why and how certain rhetorical forms and strategies, over time, become habitual and influential (35). That is, such traditions allow rhetoricians to study how habitual rhetorical forms and strategies come to shape the ways we recognize and are inclined to act within situations we perceive as similar. From this understanding, Black proposed a generic perspective on rhetorical criticism based on the premises that "there is a limited number of situations in which a rhetor can find himself;" "there is a limited number of ways in which a rhetor can and will respond rhetorically to any given situational type;" and "the recurrence of a given situational type through history will provide the critic with information on the rhetorical responses available in the situation" (133-34).

Around the same time as Edwin Black, Lloyd Bitzer had also begun to develop a theory of rhetoric as conventionally bound to situation. In "The Rhetorical Situation," Bitzer describes a rhetorical situation as not merely a backdrop to rhetorical action but rather as a precondition for it. Bitzer acknowledges that all discourse takes place in context, but the distinguishing characteristic of *rhetorical* discourse is that it emerges from and responds to a perceived *rhetorical* situation. The same exact utterance will be rhetorical in one situation and not rhetorical in another, depending on whether it takes place in a rhetorical situation or not. One of Bitzer's central claims is that rhetorical discourse achieves its status *as* rhetorical discourse not by virtue of inherent, formal characteristics nor even by virtue of an individual's persuasive intentions, but rather by the nature of the situation that calls it into being. A rhetorical situation, thus, calls forth rhetorical discourse.

Bitzer defines rhetorical situation as "a complex of persons, events, objects, and relations presenting an actual or potential exigence which can be completely or partially removed if discourse, introduced into the situation, can so constrain human decision or action as to bring about the significant modification of the exigence" (304). In general terms, an exigence is characterized by an urgency: a need or obligation or stimulus that calls for a response. In Bitzer's formulation of rhetorical situation, however, certain conditions must obtain for an exigence to be rhetorical—that is, for an exigence to invite a rhetorical action. For one thing, an exigence must be capable of being modified or else it cannot be considered a rhetorical exigence (304). (For example, an earthquake is an exigence, but it is not a rhetorical exigence because it cannot be altered through the use of rhetoric. However, an earthquake can create a rhetorical exigence when a governor, say, calls for emergency funding to rebuild infrastructure in an earthquake's aftermath.) Likewise, for an exigence to be considered rhetorical, it must be capable of being modified by means of discourse, and not through other non-discursive means such as the use of material tools (in the above case, the Governor would use speeches to make the case for emergency funding). Finally, for an exigence to be considered rhetorical, it needs to occur within a situation comprised of individuals who are capable of being acted upon by the discourse so as to modify the exigence (the need for federal government officials who have access to emergency funding).

In developing her theory of genre as social action, as we will describe, Carolyn Miller would later challenge some of Bitzer's assumptions regarding the nature of rhetorical situations, but Bitzer's work, along with Edwin Black's, would provide some important foundations for RGS. For one thing, by positing rhetorical situation as generative of rhetorical action, Bitzer recognized the "power of situation to constrain a fitting response" (Bitzer 307). Using as an example the related situations generated by President Kennedy's assassination, Bitzer describes how the range of rhetorical responses were constrained by the nature of the situations (first the need for information, then the need for explanation, then the need to eulogize, then the need to reassure the public) as well as by the expectations of the audience, so that "one could predict with near certainty the types and themes of forthcoming discourse" (306). The rhetor's intentions to act in certain ways, at certain times, using certain types of discourse were largely determined by the kinds of situations for which they were perceived as fitting (306-07).

Another of Bitzer's contributions, which would prove influential to RGS, was his acknowledgement that some situations recur, giving rise to typified responses:

> From day to day, year to year, comparable situations occur, prompting comparable responses; hence rhetorical forms are born and a special vocabulary, grammar, and style are established. This is true also of the situation which invites the inaugural address of a President. The situation recurs and, because we experience situations and the rhetorical responses to them, a form of discourse is not only established *but comes to have a power of its own*—the tradition itself tends to function as a constraint upon any new response in the form. (309; emphasis added)

Here, Bitzer not only describes how recurring situations give rise to rhetorical forms (such as genres); he also suggests (following Black's notion that rhetorical conventions can predispose future audience expectations) that the rhetorical forms can come to have a power of their own in shaping how individuals recognize and respond to like situations. That is, the socially available rhetorical forms come to influence how subsequent rhetors define and experience recurrent situations as typically requiring certain kinds of rhetorical responses. Indeed, as Miller and other RGS scholars would later elaborate, the forms of discourse and the situations to which they respond are bound together in ways that make it difficult to establish a cause-effect relationship between them.

Another influence from rhetorical criticism on RGS has been the work of Karlyn Kohrs Campbell and Kathleen Hall Jamieson. In *Form and Genre: Shaping Rhetorical Action*, Campbell and Jamieson extend Black and Bitzer's work by recognizing genres as "stylistic and substantive responses to perceived situational demands" (19). Campbell and Jamieson begin by arguing that situational demands (not theoretical, apriori categories) should serve as the basis for how we identify and define genres.[14] Instead of starting with apriori genre categories, Campbell and Jamieson advocate for a more inductive approach, whereby genres are identified as emerging in dynamic relationship to historically grounded, perceived situations. What gives a genre its character is the "fusion" or "constellation" of substantive and stylistic forms that emerge in response to a recurring situation. As Campbell and Jamieson put it, "a genre is composed of a constellation of recognizable forms bound together by an internal dynamic" (21). "These forms, *in isolation,* appear in other discourses. What is distinctive about the acts in a genre is the recurrence of the forms *together* in constellation" (20). It is this "dynamic constellation of forms" (24) within a genre that functions to produce a particular rhetorical effect in a recurrent situation.

According to Campbell and Jamieson, the constellation of forms that constitutes a genre not only creates a typified alignment of meaning and action; it also functions as a cultural artifact—an ongoing record of how individuals draw on and combine available forms in order to respond to the demands of perceived situations. As a result, genre criticism enables rhetoricians to study how "rhetoric develops in time and through time" (26). As Campbell and Jamieson explain: "The critic who classifies a rhetorical artifact as generically akin to a class of similar artifacts has identified an undercurrent of history rather than comprehended an act isolated in time" (26). As such, "the existence of the recurrent provides insight into the human condition" (27). This sense of genre as both a site of typified rhetorical action and a cultural artifact would provide a significant foundation for RGS and its study of genres as social actions.

SOCIAL PHENOMENOLOGY AND TYPIFICATION

In establishing the idea of genres as "typified rhetorical actions based in recurrent situations" in her article "Genre as Social Action," Carolyn Miller also drew on the work of sociologist Alfred Schutz, whose philosophy of social science and notion of *typification*, grounded in phenomenology, provides another important influence on Miller's and subsequent RGS scholars' understanding of genre as social action.

Phenomenology is a philosophical tradition that began at the beginning of the twentieth century in Germany with the work of Edmund Husserl and later expanded through the work of Martin Heidegger (for an accessible historical review, see Sokolowski). Generally speaking, phenomenology emerged as a challenge to the Cartesian split between mind and world, the internal and the external. It rejected the idea that consciousness is self-contained, interiorized, and solitary (Sokolowski 216)—something privately held and formed through mental associations and introspective awareness. Instead, Sokolowski explains, "Phenomenology shows that the mind is a public thing, that it acts and manifests itself out in the open, not just inside its own confines" (12). As such, phenomenology seeks to account for how things manifest themselves to us and how we experience these manifestations—how, that is, objects in the world become available (are given) to our consciousness.

At the heart of phenomenology's outer-directed view of consciousness and experience is the notion of *intentionality*, understood not as a practical act (as in, "I intend to go shopping for groceries this afternoon," or "I intend to have a beer on the deck before dinner") but as a cognitive, sense-making act (as in, I intend grocery shopping or I intend a beer on the deck). In the former examples, intentionality is a plan for action (a description of what one intends to do), but in the latter, phenomenological, understanding of intention, intentionality is an act of object-directed cognition (Sokolowski 34-35), an act of making something available to our consciousness. When we intend grocery shopping, we connect our consciousness and experience to the objects of grocery shopping: parking lots, grocery carts, the making of shopping lists, the categorization of food in different aisles, the use of coupons, standing in the check-out line, and so on.[15] The phenomenological notion of intentionality would prove to be significant for RGS. In the same way that intentions bring objects to our consciousness, genres bring texts and situations to our consciousness. Genres inform our intentionalities.

Another key concept within phenomenology that would influence RGS, and one intimately related to the notion of intentionality, is *life-world*. The life-world is the "world of common experience," the "world as encountered in everyday life" (Gurwitsch 35). We carry out and make sense of our lives and social activities within the life-world, which becomes the taken-for-granted world of shared intentionalities. In bringing phenomenology to bear on sociology, Alfred Schutz contributed to an understanding of the life-world as a fundamentally intersubjective and social phenomenon in which human experience and activity are learned, negotiated, and distributed in mutually construed, coordinated ways. As Schutz explains, "the life-world . . . is the arena, as well as what sets the limits, of my and our reciprocal action. . . . The life-world is thus a reality which we modify through our acts and which, on the other hand, modifies our actions" (Schutz and Luckmann 6, 7). Such an understanding of the life-world would come to inform Bazerman's notion of genre systems and would be compatible with current work in genre and Activity Systems theory (Russell, "Writing in Multiple Contexts"), which we discuss in Chapter 6.

Central to the construction and experience of the life-world are what Schutz calls the "stocks of knowledge" which mediate our apprehension of objects. Our perceptions of things (the way that things are manifest to our consciousness) are mediated by our stocks of knowledge, which are socially derived and confirmed rules, maxims, strategies, and recipes for behaving and acting in typical situations (Gurwitsch 49-50). According to Schutz, *typifications* constitute a major part of our stocks of knowledge that mediate our experiences of the life-world. Typifications are the stocks of knowledge that derive from situations that we perceive as similar and that are "constituted in inferences from . . . previous direct experiences" (Schutz and Luckmann 74). Typifications are related in fundamental ways to situations (99), and are based on the experience and assumption that what has worked before in a given situation is likely to work again in that situation. Typifications are part of what Schutz calls our habitual knowledge (108); they are the routinized, socially available categorizations of strategies and forms for recognizing and acting within familiar situations. Motivation and typification go hand in hand. Schutz, for example, describes how we develop "in order to" motives that are related to typifications: In order to achieve this particular result (get groceries) in this particular situation (at the grocery store), I must (or should or might or could) do this (make a grocery list). In short, we define ourselves, our actions, and others in the world "by way of typifications and constructions, modes of how 'someone' traditionally behaves or is expected to behave in certain situations" (Natanson 118).

Since we encounter and negotiate the life-world as a series of situations (some more and some less routine than others), typifications play a crucial role in how we recognize and act within the life-world (Schutz and Luckmann 113). Yet while typifications help arrange our subjective experiences of the life-world within certain structures (Schutz and Luckmann 92), typifications are not static or completely determinative. Rather, they are subject to (or brought into contact with) unique, immediate experiences and "biographical articulations" (78), which then modify our typifications. As Schutz explains, typifications are "enlivened . . . arranged and subordinated to the living reality" of our immediate experiences (Schutz and Luckmann 77). Our encounters with situations are thus defined by the contact between our concrete experiences/unique biographies and the socially derived, intersubjective typifications available to us for acting in recognizable situations. This contact allows for the possibility for new typifications to emerge: "a type arises from a situationally adequate solution to a problematic situation through the new determination of an experience which could not be mastered with the aid of the stock of knowledge already at hand" (Schutz and Luckmann 231). This understanding of how types emerge would prove influential to RGS's understanding of how genres emerge and come to shape social action within recurrent situations.

Schutz's key contribution to RGS, as Miller would articulate it, is that in order to act in a situation, we must first determine it (Schutz and Luckmann 114). And our ability to determine a situation, as Miller would emphasize, is related in fundamental ways to socially available typifications. As such, how we determine a situation is based not so much on our direct perception of the situation but more so on our ability to define it by way of the available typifications, which then shape our perceptions of how, why, and when to act. Interpretation, meaning, and action are thus interconnected for Schutz. We act within contexts of meaning that we interpret via available typifications, and our actions become meaningful and consequential to others within these contexts of meaning. Miller's key move within RGS was to recognize genres as such typifications.

GENRE AS SOCIAL ACTION

In developing the idea of genres as social actions, Carolyn Miller drew on the work of Burke, Black, Bitzer, and Campbell and Jamieson in rhetorical criticism and connected that to Schutz's work in social phenomenology to arrive at an understanding of genres as socially derived, intersubjective, rhetorical typifications that help us recognize and act within recurrent situations. This understanding is captured in her famous definition of genres "as typified rhetorical actions based in recurrent situations" ("Genre as Social Action" 31). Miller's crucial contribution to RGS is her formulation that genres need to be defined not only in terms of the fusion of forms in relation to recurrent situations (described within rhetorical criticism), but also in terms of the typified actions produced by this fusion (described within social phenomenology). Miller's focus on *action* and the idea that actions are "based in recurrent situations" have had important implications for RGS, particularly for the way that scholars in RGS understand genre's dynamic relationship to exigencies, situations, and social motives— in short, genre's relationship to how we construct, interpret, and act within situations.

In "Genre as Social Action," Miller begins where Campbell and Jamieson leave off, by arguing against theoretical, deductive genre approaches and instead for an understanding of genre based on the actions produced in recurrent situations—an inductive approach that emerges from "the knowledge that practice creates" (27). Miller advocates for what she calls an "ethnomethodological" approach, which is best suited to allow genre researchers to identify and locate genres in the environments of their use, as well as to describe the actions genres help individuals produce in these environments.[16]

An ethnomethodological approach also enables researchers to examine another of Miller's important contributions: How genres participate in the construction of the situations to which they respond. In defining rhetorical situations, Bitzer, as we saw earlier, emphasized their ontological status. A rhetorical situation exists apriori to rhetorical discourse and rhetors, and the exigence which characterizes a rhetorical situation is likewise materialistic and apriori in nature, defined as "an imperfection marked by urgency; . . . a defect, an obstacle, something waiting to be done, a thing which is other than it should be" (Bitzer 304). For Miller, "what is particularly important about rhetorical situations for a theory of genre is that they recur, as Bitzer originally noted, but in order to understand recurrence, it is necessary to reject the materialist tendencies in situational theory" (28). Without considering its implications, Bitzer himself seems at least to have acknowledged this more sociological view of recurrence at the end of his essay, where he explains that as situations recur, the rhetorical forms that emerge in response to them come to have a power of their own in shaping how individuals recognize and respond to these situations. These forms come to mediate how individuals perceive and respond to recurrent situations.

Informed by the work of Alfred Schutz, Miller recognizes the mediated relationship between situations and responses, and therefore the social construction of recurrence. As Miller argues, "situations . . . are the result, not of *'perception,'* but of *'definition'*" (29; emphasis added), meaning that our recognition of a situation as calling for a certain response is based on our having defined it as a situation that calls for a certain response. "Before we can act," Miller explains, "we must interpret the indeterminate material environment" (29). It is our shared interpretation of a situation, through available typifications such as genres, that makes it recognizable as recurrent and that gives it meaning and value. Actions are inextricably tied to and based in interpretations. As such, defining genres as rhetorical actions means recognizing genres as forms of social interpretation that make possible certain actions.

From her understanding of rhetorical situation as a social construct, Miller reconceptualizes the notion of exigence in likewise important ways. An exigence does not exist as an ontological fact, something objectively perceivable by its inherent characteristics. Instead, the social construction of situation is bound up in the social construction of exigence. How we define and act within a situation depends on how we recognize the exigence it offers, and this process of recognition is socially learned and maintained. As Miller explains, "Exigence is a form of social knowledge—a mutual construing of objects, events, interests and purposes that not only links them but makes them what they are: an objectified social need" (30). What we perceive as an exigence requiring a certain response is predicated on how we have learned to construe it as such.

The process that leads to the mutual construing of exigence starts quite early in one's life. When she was three years old, Anis' daughter was at an outdoor concert where she noticed a young boy dressed in a princess costume. Enamored of princesses and princess paraphernalia, she was eager to talk to the boy about his dress. Later, when her parents noted how wonderful it was that there was a boy wearing a princess costume, she insisted that the boy was a girl, secure in her knowledge that only girls wear princess costumes. No matter the attempts, she would not concede that the child was in fact a boy. Her socially learned gender definitions in this case had already begun to inform her recognition or construal of objects, persons, and events in the world. Her socially learned and shared typifications had already begun to be formed. While this may be an example of an extreme case, it does underscore the degree to which our ability to recognize, make sense of, and respond to exigencies is part of our social knowledge, and part of how we come to shared agreements on what situations call for, what they mean, and how to act within them. Even in cases where the situation clearly originates in a material reality (the death of a President, a severe flood, the birth of a child, etc.) how we make sense of that situation—the kind of urgency and significance with which we mark it, what it occasions us to do, who it authorizes to act and not act—is part of our social knowledge and mutual construing of typifications. While exigencies are not objective in the sense that they exist in and of themselves, they do become "objectified" as over time their mutual construal renders them as habitual, even inevitable, social needs to act in particular ways in particular situations.

As Miller argues, genres play an important role in mediating between recurrent situations and actions. In positioning genre as operating between socially defined situation types (forms of life) and recognizable symbolic acts (forms of discourse), Miller shows how the existence of genres both helps us recognize situations as recurrent and helps provide the typified strategies we use to act within them (35). Charles Bazerman makes the connection between genres and Schutz's notion of typification explicit: "typifications of situations, goals, and tasks can be crystallized in recognizable textual forms, deployed in recognizable circumstances—or genres. . . . The textual features of genres serve as well-known solutions to well-known rhetorical problems arising in well-known rhetorical situations" (*Constructing Experience* 18). Because genres are how we mutually construe or define situations as calling for certain actions, they help supply what Miller calls social motives: "[A]t the level of genre, motive becomes a conventionalized social purpose, or exigence, within the recurrent situation" (35-36). By associating social purposes with recurrent situations, genres enable their users both to define and to perform meaningful actions within recurrent situations. As Amy Devitt elaborates, "Genre not only responds to but also constructs recurring situations" ("Generalizing" 577). Part of the actions that genres perform, through their use, is the reproduction of the situations to which they respond.

For Miller, then, genres must be defined not only in terms of the fusion of substantive and formal features they embody within recurrent situations, but also by the social actions they help produce. Within recurrent situations, genres maintain social motives for acting and provide their users with typified rhetorical strategies for doing so. This is why genres not only provide typified ways of acting within recurrent situations, but also function as cultural artifacts that can tell us things about how a particular culture defines and configures situations and ways of acting. Anticipating the research and pedagogical implications of such an understanding of genre, Miller concludes,

> [W]hat we learn when we learn a genre is not just a pattern of forms or even a method of achieving our own ends. We learn, more importantly, what ends we may have: we learn that we may eulogize, apologize, recommend one person to another, instruct customers on behalf of a manufacturer, take on an official role, account for progress in achieving goals. We learn to understand better the situations in which we find ourselves and the potential for failure and success in acting together. As a recurrent, significant action, a genre embodies an aspect of cultural rationality. For the critic, genres can serve both as an index to cultural patterns and as tools for exploring the achievements of particular speakers and writers; for the student, genres serve as keys to understanding how to participate in the actions of a community. (38-39)

The tenets and implications embodied in Miller's notion of genre as social action have helped shape the field of RGS, enabling researchers to study cultural patterns and practices while also challenging researchers to consider how genres might best be used to help students understand and participate in social actions.

As we will examine in more detail in the next chapter, Miller's phenomenologically informed understanding of genre as social action has been taken up and expanded by RGS scholars over the last twenty-five years to include the idea of genre systems as well as Vygotsky's Activity Theory and theories of social cognition. David Russell has recently pointed out how a phenomenological/sociological view of genre is "deeply compatible with Vygotsky's [psychological] view of mediated action" that informs current RGS research on genre and activity systems ("Writing in Multiple Contexts" 357). Early on in his research on genre, Charles Bazerman had already begun to articulate the connections between socio-rhetorical approaches to genre and implications for socio-cognitive development (more recently, Bazerman has described genres as "psycho-social recognition phenomena" ["Speech Acts, Genres, and Activity Systems" 317] and as "tools of cognition" ["Genre and Cognitive Development"]). As Bazerman explains in *Constructing Experience,* "the typifications of situation, intentions and goals, modes of action, and textual genres that the writer applies to the situation create a kind of habitat for the writer to inhabit both psychologically and socially. That is, typifications give writers symbolic means to make sense of things; in turn, those means of sense-making help set the stage and frame possible action" (19). At the same time, genre-based typifications also help establish sites of shared cognition wherein our sense-making procedures interact with others' sense-making procedures (94).

Such social grounding of cognition can be seen in what Bazerman calls "the mutual creation of social moments" (*Constructing Experience* 174) that we inhabit by way of genres and that help orient our understanding of where we are and what we can do (Bazerman 94). Bringing a sociologically-based understanding of genre to bear on the classical rhetorical notion of *kairos,* Bazerman explains how genres help us create, recognize, inhabit, and act within moments of opportunity and significance (178). By learning genres, "we are learning to recognize not only categories of social moments and what works rhetorically in such moments but also how we can act and respond" (178). At the same time, we are learning how to negotiate our typifications with those of others in "ways that are compatible or at least predictably conflictual . . . for us to meet in mutually recognized moments" (184). Through such "kairotic coordination" (how we interact with each other in shared moments), "we learn the elements of timing and the appropriate responses and the genres of communication; even more, through that learning we discover how we may participate in these forums and sort out how and whether such participation will meet our goals" (181). Through his reinterpretation of *kairos,* Bazerman thus elaborates on the sociological and psychological implications of genre: both as a way in which "we imagine and thereby create social order" (188) and as a way in which we cognitively reflect on, anticipate, and make sense of our placement and interactions within social order.

We will discuss how genres symbolically coordinate spatial and temporal relations in more detail in the next chapter. But here it is worth noting Bazerman's observation of the ways that genres abstract and reorient situations and actions within various genres' symbolic environments ("The Writing of Social Organization" 223). In his historical research, Bazerman describes how a number of written genres originated as "overt representations of social situations, relationships and actions," such as letters and transcriptions (225)—see for example Bazerman's study of the evolution of the experimental article in science, which began as correspondence reports read at Royal Society of London meetings ("The Writing of Social Organization" 228-29; *Shaping Written Knowledge*). Eventually, the genre of the experimental article would shift from indexing situated interactions that occurred at a meeting of the Royal Society to establishing its own forms of organization and symbolic interaction that writers and readers of experimental articles would inhabit: "Simultaneous with the emergence of the format, contents, and style of the experimental article, the scientific community developed roles, values, activities, and intellectual orientations organized around the production and reception of such articles" (228). Here once again we see how genres symbolically create social order and coordinate social actions.

THE FRENCH AND SWISS GENRE TRADITIONS
AND THE BRAZILIAN GENRE SYNTHESIS

Genre research in Brazil has been especially instructive for the way it has synthesized the linguistic, rhetorical, and social/sociological traditions that we have been describing in the last three chapters, while also drawing on the French and Swiss genre traditions. In so doing, Brazilian genre studies offer a way of seeing these traditions as compatible with one another and as providing analytical and theoretical tools by which to understand how genres function linguistically, rhetorically, and sociologically.

The French and Swiss genre traditions, particularly the theory of "socio-discursive interactionism" that informs them, draw on theorists such as Bakhtin, Vygotsky, Wittgenstein, Foucault, and Habermas, all of whom are familiar to RGS scholars. Yet the theory of socio-discursive interactionism itself has not had much direct influence on North American RGS, although its Vygotskian conceptualization of activity and action clearly parallels RGS's adaptation of Vygotsky's Activity Theory, as we will see in the next chapter. Insofar as it is grounded in sociological, linguistic, and rhetorical traditions, however, and has proven to be influential to Brazilian genre studies, socio-discursive interactionism deserves mention here as a theory of human action based in social and discursive contexts and grounded in genre.

Developed by Jean-Paul Bronckart, Joaquim Dolz, Bernard Schneuwly, and others (see Bronckart; Bronckart et al; Dolz and Schneuwly), socio-discursive interactionism (SDI) "postulates that human actions should be treated in their social and discursive dimensions, considering language as the main characteristic of human social activity, since human beings interact in order to communicate, through collective language activities and individual actions, consolidated through texts of different genres" (Baltar et al. 53). Within SDI, genres are considered both "as products of social activities . . . and as tools that allow people to realize language actions and participate in different social activities" (Araújo 46). The influence of Bakhtin is evident in SDI's focus on language-in-use and genres as typified utterances. Likewise, the influence of Vygotsky is also evident in SDI's key distinctions between *acting, activity,* and *action.* The term "acting" describes "any form of directed [i.e., motivated] intervention;" it is the motivated doing of something. The term "activity" refers to the shared, socially defined notion of acting in particular situations. The term "action" refers to the interpretation of "acting" on an individual level; it involves an individually carried-out activity (Baltar et al. 53).

Individual *action* is thus framed within socially defined *activities.* Such socially defined activities give recognizable meaning to individual actions at the same time as they associate actions with particular individuals who are authorized to enact the activities at certain times, in certain contexts. As such, we are constantly negotiating between, on the one hand, the socially sanctioned activities which supply social motives and authorize certain roles and, on the other hand, our immediate, situated actions (Baltar et al. 53-54). Within this framework, SDI pays attention to actors' *motivational plans* (their reasons for acting), *intentional plans* (their purposes for acting), *and available resources and instruments* (habitual strategies, familiar tools) (Baltar et al. 54).

In the same way that social actions involve a negotiation between socially defined activities and individually instantiated actions, Baltar et al. explain, so too language actions involve a social dimension (a context that defines an activity) and a behavioral or physical dimension (the act of making an utterance or text or discourse) (54). Language actions thus involve an *act* of enunciation/text/discourse as defined in relation to an *activity* that "predetermines the objectives that can be wished for and that gives the sending and receiving actants a specific social role" (Baltar et al. 54). Within SDI, genres play a mediating role between the social and behavioral dimensions of language (the activity and action).

SDI has been used to develop both analytical and pedagogical models for genre study. Analytically, the model "consists of examining: (a) the content with which, the place where, and time when the participants engage in interaction; (b) the participants in their physical space; (c) the social place in which the interaction takes place; (d) the participants' social roles; and (e) the writing effects" (Araújo 46). Pedagogically, the model has provided a way for language teachers to teach writing at a textual rather than grammatical level, and to situate the teaching of writing within genres and their contexts of use. Towards that end, Dolz, Noverraz, and Schneuwly describe what they call a "didactic sequence" which facilitates genre acquisition via "a set of school activities organized, in a systematic way, around an oral or written genre" (97). SDI allows teachers to situate students' writing within social activities that define it as meaningful and consequential social-discursive actions. We will discuss the pedagogies growing out of the Brazilian tradition in Chapters 10 and 11.

It is especially worth noting the way that Brazilian genre studies have synthesized various traditions: the French and Swiss genre pedagogical traditions, European philosophical traditions, Critical Discourse Analysis, the Systemic Functional Linguistic genre tradition,

English for Specific Purposes, and RGS (see Araújo; also Bazerman, Bonini, and Figueiredo). Araújo's study of genre research in Brazil from 1980 to 2007 reveals that while the focus of genre investigation remains predominantly on the description of genre features, 20% of the studies utilized some kind of ethnographic, action-research, or case study approaches to get at richer genre contexts (50-51). At the same time, while socio-discursive interactionism is the most preferred theoretical approach for analyzing genres, that approach is often combined with a number of perspectives that are used to describe structural and lexico-grammatical aspects of genres (51). The Brazilian synthesis suggests that rhetorical and sociological genre traditions need not be incompatible with linguistic traditions, and that when interconnected, these traditions can provide rich insight into how genres function and can be taught at various levels.

In the next chapter, we will examine the major developments that have informed and emerged from work in RGS over the last twenty-five years, including notions of genre and activity systems that parallel research in SDI. The emphasis within RGS has been to show that genres are not only communicative tools. Genres are also socially derived, typified ways of knowing and acting; they embody and help us enact social motives, which we negotiate in relation to our individual motives; they are dynamically tied to the situations of their use; and they help coordinate the performance of social realities, interactions and identities. To study and teach genres in the context of this socio-rhetorical understanding requires both a knowledge of a genre's structural and lexico-grammatical features as well as a knowledge of the social action(s) a genre produces and the social typifications that inform that action: the social motives, relations, values, and assumptions embodied within a genre that frame how, why, and when to act.

6 Rhetorical Genre Studies

In this chapter, we will examine how the understanding of genres as social actions (as typified ways of acting within recurrent situations, and as cultural artifacts that can tell us things about how a particular culture configures situations and ways of acting) has developed within Rhetorical Genre Studies (RGS) since Carolyn Miller's groundbreaking article "Genre as Social Action," discussed in Chapter 5. Along the way, we will examine how key RGS concepts such as uptake, genre systems and genre sets, genre chronotope, meta-genres, and activity systems have enriched understandings of genres as complex social actions and cultural objects. And we will consider the implications and challenges for genre research and teaching that arise from such understandings, which Parts 2 and 3 of the book will take up in more detail.

GENRES AS FORMS OF SITUATED COGNITION

In "Rethinking Genre from a Sociocognitive Perspective," Carol Berkenkotter and Thomas Huckin examine the socio-cognitive work that genres perform within academic disciplinary contexts. Building on the idea that knowledge formation, genre formation, and socio-historical formation are interconnected (see Bazerman, *Shaping Written Knowledge; Constructing Experience*), Berkenkotter and Huckin take as their starting point the notion that genres dynamically embody a community's ways of knowing, being, and acting. "Our thesis," they write, "is that genres are inherently dynamic rhetorical structures that can be manipulated according to the conditions of use and that genre knowledge is therefore best conceptualized as a form of situated cognition embedded in disciplinary activities. For writers to make things happen, that is, to publish, to exert an influence on the field, to be cited, and so forth, they must know how to strategically use their understanding of genre" (477).

Several important genre claims emerge for RGS from this thesis. First is the notion that "genres are dynamic rhetorical forms that develop from responses to recurrent situations and serve to stabilize experience and give it coherence and meaning" (479). Within disciplinary contexts, for instance, genres normalize activities and practices, enabling community members to participate in these activities and practices in fairly predictable, familiar ways in order to get things done. At the same time, though, genres are *dynamic* because as their conditions of use change—for example because of changes in material conditions, changes in community membership, changes in technology, changes in disciplinary purposes, values, and what Charles Bazerman describes as systems of accountability (*Shaping* 61)—genres must change along with them or risk becoming obsolete. (For example, in his study of the evolution of the experimental article from 1665 to 1800, Bazerman describes how the genre changed [in terms of its structure and organization, presentation of results, stance, methods, etc.] in coordinated emergence with changes in where and how experiments were conducted, where and how they were made public, and how nature was viewed (*Shaping* 59-79). Furthermore, as Berkenkotter and Huckin note, variation is an inherent part of recurrence, and so genres must be able to accommodate that variation. Beyond being responsive to the dynamics of change and the variation within recurrence, genres also need to be responsive to their users' individually formed inclinations and dispositions (what Pierre Bourdieu calls "habitus")—balancing individuals' "own uniquely formed knowledge of the world" with "socially induced perceptions of commonality" (481). For genres to function effectively over time, Berkenkotter and Huckin surmise, they "must accommodate both stability and change" (481). Catherine Schryer has captured this dynamic in her definition of genres as "stabilized-for-now or stabilized-enough sites of social and ideological action" ("The Lab vs. the Clinic" 108).

Another of Berkenkotter and Huckin's contributions to the development of genre as social action is that genres are forms of situated cognition, a view that Carolyn Miller had suggested when she theorized exigence as a form of genre knowledge and that Charles Bazerman suggested when he connected genre knowledge with mutually recognized moments (see Chapter 5). For genres to perform actions, they must be connected to cognition, since how we know and how we act are related to one another. Genre knowledge (knowledge of rhetori-

cal and formal conventions) is inextricably linked to what Berkenkotter and Huckin describe as procedural knowledge (knowledge of when
and how to use certain disciplinary tools, how and when to inquire,
how and when to frame questions, how to recognize and negotiate
problems, and where, how, and when to produce knowledge within
disciplinary contexts). Genre knowledge is also linked to background
knowledge—both content knowledge and knowledge of shared assumptions, including knowledge of *kairos,* having to do with rhetorical
timing and opportunity (487-91). As forms of situated cognition, thus,
genres enable their users not only to communicate effectively, but also
to participate in (and reproduce) a community's "norms, epistemology,
ideology, and social ontology" (501).

Berkenkotter and Huckin, continuing to draw on the sociological
tradition that first informed RGS, turn to the work of sociologist Anthony Giddens and his notion of "duality of structure" to describe how
genres enable their users both to enact and reproduce community.[17]
In *The Constitution of Society: Outline of the Theory of Structuration,*
Giddens examines how structures are constantly being reproduced as
they are being enacted. Giddens rejects, on the one hand, the idea that
structures always already exist ontologically, and that we are passively
subject to them. On the other hand, he also rejects the idea that we are
originating agents of our reality. Instead, Giddens describes a recursive
phenomenon in which, through our social practices, we reproduce the
very social structures that subsequently make our actions necessary,
possible, recognizable, and meaningful, so that our practices reproduce the very structures that consequently call for these practices. As
Berkenkotter and Huckin note, genres play an important role in this
process of structuration.

For example, a classroom on a university campus is a physical space
made meaningful by its location in a university building on campus.
But the classroom can be used for different purposes, not just to hold
courses; it can be used for a department meeting, a job talk, a col-
loquium, and so on. We turn the physical space of a classroom into
a course such as a graduate seminar on rhetorical theory, a biology
course, or a first-year composition course through various genres, ini-
tially through the course timetable, which places courses within different rooms on campus, but then later through genres such as the
syllabus, which begin the process of transforming the physical space
of a classroom into a socially bounded, ideological space marked by

course goals, policies, assignments, and course schedule. Many other genres work together to construct the classroom as a particular course and to coordinate its work. In terms of Giddens' structuration theory, the genres provide us with the tools and resources to perform certain actions and relations in a way that not only confirms, within variation, our sense of what it means to be in a course such as this (a graduate seminar, for example), but also, through their use, help us define and reproduce this course as a certain kind of recurrent structure.

This process of social enactment and reproduction is not nearly as smooth as the above characterization suggests, however. Within any socio-historically bounded structure or system of activity there exist competing demands and goals, contradictions, tensions, and power relations that shape which ideologies and actions are reproduced. Defining genres as "stabilized-for-now or stabilized-enough sites of social and ideological action" (108), Catherine Schryer draws on her research into veterinary school medical genres in "The Lab vs. the Clinic: Sites of Competing Genres" to reveal how genres reflect and maintain socio-historically entrenched hierarchies between researchers and clinicians, a hierarchy reflected in other academic disciplines as well. The way that veterinary students are trained, what they come to value, how they recognize problems and go about solving them, the degree of ambiguity they are willing to tolerate along the way, the roles they perceive themselves performing, and the contributions they see themselves making—all these are "deeply embedded within the profession's basic genres" (113), particularly the "experimental article genre" (IMRDS—Introduction, Methods, Results, Discussion, Summary) and the "recording genre" (POVMR—Problem Oriented Veterinary Medical record). Schryer's analysis of these two genres reveals differences in how each coordinates and orients the activities of its users in terms of purpose, representation of time and activity, addressivity, and epistemological assumptions (119-21). These differences, Schryer argues, are associated with status and power within the discipline, and as such they position their users at different levels of hierarchy within veterinary medicine. For example, the IMRDS genre and its users have higher status largely because the genre's typified strategies more closely resemble and "instantiate the central ideology of science—the need to order and control the natural world" (121). Because the work it enables more closely reflects dominant scientific practices, the researchers who are socialized into and use the IMRDS hold higher status than the clinicians who are socialized into and use the POVMR. The genres thus become forms of cultural capital, valued differently within the system of values and relations that comprises the veterinary academic community.

These competing genres and the ideologies they embody reflect ongoing, socio-historically saturated tensions and power relations within veterinary medicine. Even if there was a concerted interest among members of the community to alleviate these tensions, Schryer speculates, doing so will take a long time, not only because the genres "deeply enact their ideology" (122), but also because the genres do not function in isolation; they relate to other more and less powerful genres. At the same time, the genres are part of a complex socialization process that includes methods of training and labeling students, in ways that are connected to but also exceed the genres.

Such a multi-dimensional and complex understanding of genre— as a dynamic concept marked by stability and change; functioning as a form of situated cognition; tied to ideology, power, and social actions and relations; and recursively helping to enact and reproduce community—challenges RGS to consider how genre knowledge is acquired, and raises questions as to whether genre knowledge can be taught explicitly, in ways advocated within ESP and SFL genre approaches. Since their research led them to conclude that "genre knowledge is a form of situated cognition, inextricable from . . . procedural and social knowledge," Berkenkotter and Huckin offer that these levels of knowledge can only be acquired over time, "requiring immersion into the culture, and a lengthy period of apprenticeship and enculturation" (487). Situating and then explicating textual features gets us closer to but not close enough to understanding genres as social actions, in ways valued in RGS.[18] Further complicating matters is the recognition, articulated by Freadman ("Anyone"), Devitt ("Intertextuality"), Bazerman (*Constructing;* "Systems"), and Orlikowski and Yates, that genres do not exist in isolation but rather in dynamic interaction with other genres. In order to understand genre as social action, thus, we need to look at the constellations of genres that coordinate complex social actions within and between systems of activity.

UPTAKE AND RELATIONS BETWEEN GENRES

In Chapter 2, we described Mikhail Bakhtin's contributions to literary genre study, especially his understanding of the complex relations within and between genres. In one set of relationships, Bakhtin describes how complex "secondary" genres such as the novel absorb and transform more simple "primary genres" (genres that Bakhtin describes as being linked immediately to their contexts). A secondary genre re-contextualizes primary genres by placing them in relationship to other primary genres within its symbolic world (see Bazerman's "The Writing of Social Organization" and *Shaping Written Knowledge* for how scientific articles re-contextualize situated interactions within their genred symbolic worlds). As such, "the primary genres are altered and assume a special character when they enter into complex ones" (Bakhtin, "Problem" 62). At the same time, Bakhtin also describes a more horizontal set of relationships between genres, in which genres engage in dialogic interaction with one another as one genre becomes a response to another within a sphere of communication. For example, a call for papers leads to proposals, which lead to letters of acceptance or rejection, and so on. Such an intertextual view of genres has been central to RGS's understanding of genres as complex social actions.

Bakhtin defines genres as "relatively stable types of . . . utterances" (60) within which words and sentences attain typical expressions, relations, meanings, and boundaries (87), and within which exist "typical conception[s] of the addressee" (95) and typical forms of addressivity (99). Genres help frame the boundaries and meanings of utterances, providing us with conceptual frames through which we encounter utterances, predict their length and structure, anticipate their end, and prepare responsive utterances (79). In short, genres enable us to create typified relationships between utterances as we organize and enact complex forms of social interaction. As typified utterances, genres are dialogically related to and acquire meaning in interaction with other genres.[19]

Anne Freadman, in two important essays, "Anyone for Tennis?" and "Uptake," turns to the notion of "uptake" to describe the complex ways genres relate to and take up one another within systems of activity. Using a game of tennis as an analogy, Freadman describes how utterances play off of (or take up) each other in a way similar to how shots in a tennis match play off of each other. Freadman begins by distinguishing between a ball and a shot. A ball is a physical object that becomes meaningful when it is played—that is, when it becomes a shot. A shot, therefore, is a played ball, in much the same way that an utterance is a played sentence in Bakhtin's formulation. Tennis players do not exchange balls, Freadman explains; they exchange shots ("Anyone" 43). But for shots to be meaningful exchanges, they need to take place within a particular game. "Each shot is formally determined by the rules of the game, and materially determined by the skill of the players, and each return shot is determined by the shot to which it is a response" (44). Within the context of a game of tennis, shots become meaningful because they are played within certain rules and boundaries (if the shot lands inside the line it means something, whereas if it falls outside, it means something else) by players capable of exchanging them.

So shots become meaningful because they take place within a certain game. The game itself, according to Freadman, becomes meaningful because it takes place within a certain "ceremonial." If the same exchange of shots happens on a tennis court at a neighborhood park or on a court in Wimbledon, England, the rules of the game remain the same, but because of the different ceremonials, the games themselves have different meanings and values. As Freadman puts it, ceremonials provide "the rules for playing" of games: "Ceremonies are games that situate other games: they are the rules for the setting of a game, for constituting participants as players in that game, for placing and timing it in relation with other places and times. They are the rules for playing of a game, but they are not the rules of the game" ("Anyone" 46-47). In the case of Wimbledon, for instance, it is the ritual and the system of signs that define it as a ceremonial: It is the strawberries and cream, the tea and scones, the royal family box, the tradition of center court, the player rankings, the dress code, the prize money, etc. It is the entire system of signs that goes into making the ceremonial what it is and that gives meaning and value to the games and shots that take place there.

Freadman uses this tennis analogy to describe how genres are both meaningful in and relate to one another within ceremonials. Genres are "games" that take place within "ceremonials." And within ceremonials, genres constitute the rules for play for the exchange of texts, or "shots." In short, ceremonials are the rules for playing, genres are the rules for play (for the exchange of texts), and texts are the actual exchanges—the playing of the game. We cannot really understand a particular exchange of texts without understanding the genres, and we cannot understand particular genres without understanding how they are related to one another within a ceremonial.

Ceremonials contain multiple genres. For example, Freadman describes the ceremonial of a trial, which consists of several related genres: the swearing in of the jury, the judge's instructions, the opening statement, calling of witnesses, cross-examination, jury deliberations, the reading of the verdict, etc. (59). "Each of these moments is a genre, though it may be occupied by several texts, and each of the texts will deploy a range of tactics. . . . To understand the rules of the genre is to know when and where it is appropriate to do and say certain things, and to know that to say and do them at inappropriate places and times is to run the risk of having them ruled out. To use these rules with skill is to apply questions of strategy to decisions of timing and the tactical plan of the rhetoric" (59). Within the rules of the ceremonial, the various genres play off of each other in coordinated, consequential ways. And within the rules of the genre game, every text is a situated performance in which its speaker or writer plays off of the typified strategies embodied in the genre, including the sense of timing and opportunity.[20]

The ability to know how to negotiate genres and how to apply and turn genre strategies (rules for play) into textual practices (actual performances) involves knowledge of what Freadman refers to as *uptake*. Within speech act theory, uptake traditionally refers to how an illocutionary act (saying, for example, "it is hot in here" with the intention of getting someone to cool the room) gets taken up as a perlocutionary effect (someone subsequently opening a window) under certain conditions. In her work, Freadman applies uptake to genre theory, arguing that genres are defined in part by the uptakes they condition and secure within ceremonials: for example, how a call for papers gets taken up as proposals, or, as in Freadman's more consequential example, how a court sentence during a trial gets taken up as an execution. For example, in a classroom setting, some genres function mainly within intra-classroom relations, such as when the assignment prompt creates the conditions for the student essay, while other genres function directly and indirectly in relation to genres outside of the classroom, such as the way that class rosters and grade sheets connect students in the classroom to a system of genres, including transcripts, at the registrar's office and, beyond that, to genres such as resumes and letters of recommendation that draw students into larger economic relations. Together, these inter- and intra-generic relations maintain the conditions within which individuals identify, situate, and interact with one another in relations of power, and perform meaningful, consequential social actions—or, conversely, are excluded from them. Uptake helps us understand how systematic, normalized relations between genres coordinate complex forms of social action—how and why genres get taken up in certain ways and not others, and what gets done and not done as a result.

As Freadman is careful to note, uptake does not depend on causation but on *selection*. Uptake, she explains, "selects, defines, or represents its object. . . . This is the hidden dimension of the long, ramified, intertextual memory of uptake: the object is taken from a set of possibilities" ("Uptake" 48). Uptakes, Freadman tells us, have memories (40). What we choose to take up and how we do so is the result of *learned recognitions of significance* that over time and in particular contexts become habitual. Knowledge of uptake is knowledge of what to take up, how, and when, including how to execute uptakes strategically and when to resist expected uptakes. Knowledge of uptake, as Freadman puts it, is knowledge of "generic boundary" (43) or what Bawarshi has described as a genre's "uptake profile" ("Genres as Forms of In[ter]vention" 81), which delimits the range of ways, from more to less prototypical, that a genre can be taken up within a particular context. As such, knowledge of uptake is knowledge of when and why to use a genre; how to select an appropriate genre in relation to another or others; where along the range of its uptake profile to take up a genre, and at what cost; how some genres explicitly cite other genres in their uptake while some do so only implicitly, and so on. Such genre uptake knowledge is often tacitly acquired, ideologically consequential, deeply remembered and affective, and quite durable, connected not only to memories of prior, habitual responses to a genre, but also memories of prior engagements with other, related genres. Genre uptake knowledge is also bound up in memories of prior experiences, relations with other users of the genre, and a sense of one's authority within a ceremonial.

Since, according to Freadman, ceremonials, genres, and uptakes are connected, and since "knowing a genre is . . . knowing how to take it up" ("Anyone" 63) within a system of relations, we cannot fully understand genres as social actions without accounting for uptake. And this creates another challenge for RGS researchers to consider when thinking about the pedagogical implications of genre teaching: How does one teach a largely habitual, meta-cognitive process mostly acquired through socialization? Freadman explains, for example, that when a genre is abstracted from its context of use and taught explicitly in the context of a classroom, or when a genre from one disciplinary or public context is simulated in another context, say, a classroom, the genre has been severed from its semiotic environment, and the pairing of the explicated or simulated genre "with its appropriate uptake has been broken" ("Anyone" 48). Like Berkenkotter and Huckin, Freadman recommends an apprenticeship-based genre approach along with teaching students how to recognize a genre's context and its relationship to other genres within and between systems of activity.

GENRE SETS AND GENRE SYSTEMS

Over the past fifteen years, RGS scholars have developed several useful concepts to describe the complex ways in which related genres enable their users to perform consequential social actions. In *Writing Genres,* Amy Devitt distinguishes between "context of genres" ("the set of all existing genres in a society or culture") (54), "genre repertoires" ("the set of genres that a group owns, acting through which a group achieves all of its purposes, not just those connected to a particular activity") (57; for an additional discussion of genre repertoires, see also Orlikowski and Yates), "genre systems" (the "set of genres interacting to achieve an overarching function within an activity system") (56), and "genre sets" (the "more loosely defined sets of genres, associated through the activities and functions of a collective but defining only a limited range of actions") (57). While the four categories describe different levels of genre relationships (Clay Spinuzzi has defined another category he calls "genre ecology" to describe the contingent, mediated, interconnected, and less sequenced relationships among genres within and between activity systems—see *Tracing Genres*), we will focus on genre systems and genre sets, since these are most associated with specific, bounded social actions. In fact, part of what defines a genre system or genre set as such are the actions that these genres, working in dynamic interaction with each other, enable individuals to perform over time, within different contexts of activity. By studying genre systems and genre sets, researchers can gain insight into social roles and relationships, power dynamics, the distribution of cognition and activities, and the social construction of space-time (what Bakhtin calls "chronotope") within different contexts.

   The notion of genre set was first introduced by Amy Devitt to describe the set of genres used by tax accountants to perform their work
("Intertextuality"). Expanding the notion of genre sets, Charles Bazerman introduced the idea of genre systems to describe the constellation
of genre sets that coordinate and enact the work of multiple groups
within larger systems of activity ("Systems"; see also Bazerman's earlier
discussion of genre systems in *Constructing Experience,* 31-38).[21] Using
U.S. patent applications as his case study, Bazerman traces the system
of interrelated genres that connect patent applications to patent grants,
including the application, letters of correspondence, various forms, appeals, and potential court rulings, as well as the patent grant. The
patent grant subsequently connects to other genre systems, such as
funding corporations, and so on. "What we have, in essence," Bazerman explains, "is a complex web of interrelated genres where each participant makes a recognizable act or move in some recognizable genre,
which then may be followed by a certain range of appropriate generic
responses by others" ("Systems" 96-97). As Bazerman's study suggests,
a genre system includes genres from multiple genre sets, over time, and
can involve the interaction of users with different levels of expertise
and authority, who may not all have equal knowledge of or access to all
the genres within the system. Yet the relationship of the genres to one
another, coordinated through a series of appropriately timed and expected uptakes, enables their users to enact complex social actions over
time—in this case, enabling the approval or denial of a patent grant.
   Genre sets are more bounded constellations of genres that enable
particular groups of individuals to accomplish particular actions within a genre system. Anthony Paré, for example, has described the genre
set used by hospital social workers, which includes referral forms, initial assessments, ongoing assessments (progress reports), and closing/
transfer reports ("Writing as a Way into Social Work" 156). Likewise,
Bazerman describes the various genre sets available within a classroom. A teacher's genre set can include writing the syllabus, developing assignments, preparing lesson plans, sending announcements to
the class, replying to student questions, providing feedback on student
papers, and submitting grade sheets. Students' genre set can include
class notes, reading notes, e-mail queries to the instructor, essays, an-
swering exam questions, and so on ("Speech Acts, Genres, and Activity Systems" 318). Within a classroom, genre sets can also include
groupings of genres that enable specific actions, such as the genre set

of peer review or teacher feedback in response to student writing. To-gether, these genre sets form an interactive genre system, which helps teacher and students organize and carry out the work of the course in a coordinated, sequenced way.

The teacher and students do not have equal access to all these genres, and they do not have equal authority to determine when these genres can be used, which is what helps establish power relationships. For example, the teacher may have access to grading rubrics that are invisible to students, yet these rubrics work behind the scenes (as what Janet Giltrow has described as meta-genres, which we will dis-cuss shortly) to mediate between the genre of a student's paper and its uptake in the genre of the instructor's feedback on the student's paper. But because the work of the course is organized and carried out through its genre system, its genre sets are interdependent and must interact within appropriately timed uptakes in order to produce recog-nizable, consequential social activities within the classroom. As Paré explains in regard to hospital social workers, "the social work new-comer must learn how to participate in the social work community's genre set and learn how that set is influenced by and fits into the larger institution's genre system" ("Writing" 159).

The classroom genre system functions in relation to other genre systems. The system of genres that enables a student to register for a class (on-line registration, course descriptions, time schedule, forms for paying tuition, financial aid applications, etc.) is related to the class-room genre system that eventually enables a teacher to provide feed-back on a student paper. Likewise, if the student lodges a complaint about his or her grade, then the student must participate in another related system of genres, that might include writing a grade complaint e-mail first to the teacher and eventually to the writing program direc-tor, submitting a formal letter of grade appeal that makes a case for a higher grade, meeting with the director, having the director potential-ly submit a change of grade form, etc. Genres do not exist in isolation, and neither do genre systems and genre sets.

As Bazerman's research on patents reveals, genre systems help maintain and enact social intentions:

> [T]he genres, in-so-far as they identify a repertoire of
> actions that may be taken in a set of circumstances,
> identify the possible intentions one may have. Thus
> they embody the range of social intentions toward

> which one may orient one's energies. . . . That is:
> the intention, the recognition of the intention, the
> achievement of that intention with the coparticipa-
> tion of others, and the further actions of others re-
> specting that achievement . . . all exist in the realm
> of social fact constructed by the maintenance of the
> patent system and the communicative forms (genres)
> by which it is enacted. ("Systems" 82)

Our experience with a genre system and its genre sets habituates what
Freadman describes as our uptake memory, informing our expectations and intentions as we encounter, experience, and negotiate the
seams between genres.

GENRE AND DISTRIBUTED COGNITION

Part of how genre systems and their genre sets coordinate complex
social actions within systems of activity is by supplying intentions,
distributing cognition, and shaping our notions of timing and opportunity (what Greek rhetoricians called *kairos*). Genre systems do not
just sequence activities; they also sequence how we relate to and assign
roles to one another, how we define the limits of our agency, how we
come to know and learn, and how we construct, value, and experience
ourselves in social time and space—what Bakhtin refers to as "chronotope" (see *Dialogic Imagination* 84-258). Aviva Freedman and Graham
Smart have applied theories of "distributed cognition" (Salomon; Cole
and Engeström) to genre systems in order to describe how "within specific activities, thinking, knowing, and learning are distributed among
co-participants, as well as mediated through the cultural artifacts in
place" ("Navigating" 240). Genre systems and sets help to mediate and
distribute cognition within systems of activity by allowing us to think
"in conjunction or partnership with others" (Salomon xiii). In terms of
hospital social workers, Paré explains: "By learning to use [their genre
set]—that is, by learning the questions to ask during interviews, by
learning the appropriate stance to take toward information and readers, by learning how to organize their observations of the world under
the categories offered by the texts—[social work] students are joining
in socially shared cognition" ("Writing" 154). If, as Berkenkotter and
Huckin describe, genres are forms of situated cognition, then genre

systems and genre sets are the means by which cognition is distributed among participants across time and space.

Genre systems and genre sets organize and distribute cognition, in part, by shaping our sense of timing and opportunity—when, where, why, how, and by whom we expect actions to take place (Yates and Orlikowski, "Genre Systems" 106). Yates and Orlikowski, in their research on the function of chronos and kairos in communicative interaction, describe how genre systems choreograph a time and place for coordinated social interaction among participants and activities chronologically (by way of measurable, quantifiable, "objective" time) and kairotically (by way of constructing a sense of timeliness and opportunity in specific situations) (104, 108). Part of participating in a genre system is knowing strategically when, how, and where to use certain genres in relation to other genres. As Yates and Orlikowski conclude, "Understanding the role of *chronos* and *kairos* in the unfolding enactment of a genre system can help us understand conditions under which actors exercise discretion about whether and when to take certain communicative actions" (118-19). As such, knowledge of a genre's rhetorical conventions must be accompanied by knowledge of its placement and timing within a system and set of genres.

Bawarshi, for example, has described how assignment prompts in a writing classroom choreograph both chronological and kairotic time for the production of student writing. Chronologically, the writing prompt assigns a specific time sequence for the production of the student essay, often delimiting what is due at what time and when. At the same time, the writing prompt also establishes a kairotic relationship by providing the student essay with a timeliness and an opportunity that authorizes it. Participating within this kairotic interplay between two genres, students must discern the opportunity granted by the prompt and then write an essay that defines its own opportunity in relation to the prompt. In so doing, students negotiate a complex kairotic relationship in which they are expected to take up the opportunity discerned in the writing prompt without acknowledging its presence explicitly in their essay (*Genre and the Invention of the Writer* 133-41). This uptake between the opportunity discerned in one genre and the opportunity defined or appropriated by students in another genre reveals how genre systems shape what Bazerman has called "*kairotic* coordination," which leads to "the kinds of shared orientations to and shared participations within mutually recognized moments"

(*Constructing Experience* 110). By choreographing mutually recogniz-able moments for acting and interacting, genres systems enable the distribution of cognition across time and space.

Schryer has likewise described how genres are strategies "that we use to mutually negotiate or improvise our way through time and space" ("Genre and Power" 74). Drawing on Bakhtin's notion of chro-notope, Schryer explains that "genres express space/time relations that reflect current social beliefs regarding the placement and actions of human individuals in space and time" (75). Specifically, she focuses on the power dynamics that emerge from the way genres position their users within space/time relations (76). Schryer's research on veterinary school genres, described earlier, reveals how the genre sets used by clinicians and researchers function in hierarchical relationship to one another within the larger genre system, and position their users in rela-tions of power within that system. Devitt's research on tax accountants likewise illustrates the conflicts and differences in ideology embodied within and across different tax accounting genres ("Intertextuality" 84-85), while Paré's research on hospital social workers demonstrates the competing values and uneven status of genres and their users with-in a hospital's genre system. Working in a context in which medicine predominates, hospital social workers have a lower disciplinary status than doctors and psychiatrists, and their genres reflect that status. Not only do social work genres exist to serve the needs of the more presti-gious members of the hospital, but they also must accommodate those needs in terms of adopting cognitive strategies that are more prized in medicine, such as objectivity and factuality (Paré, "Writing" 160). As Paré describes it, "Social work newcomers learn to collaborate in com-munity knowledge-making activities, or genre sets, that are shaped by levels of power and status within the larger genre system" (160).

All of which is to say that cognition is not distributed evenly within genre systems, nor is it distributed arbitrarily. Instead, how we nego-tiate the various genres within a system of genres depends on what we described earlier as our uptake knowledge—our ideologically-in-formed, learned, and remembered knowledge of when, why, where, and how to take up a genre in relation to other genres within a system of activity. Carol Berkenkotter, for example, has demonstrated how psychotherapists and their clients engage in a series of uptakes that synchronizes their activities and interactions ("Genre Systems"). Dur-ing the course of a psychotherapy session, therapists and clients participate in a number of genres, including the "client's narrative during the therapy session," the "therapists' notes" (which are taken during the session), and the "psychosocial assessment" (which the therapist writes after the session). The movement between these genres is guided by what Berkenkotter calls a process of "recontextualization," in which the therapist re-contextualizes the patient's narrative from one genre to the next.

Recontextualization—the taking up of information from one genre to another—is akin to translation, as "the therapist must translate into psychiatric nomenclature the information the client provided during the initial interview" ("Genre Systems" 335). But as Berkenkotter's analysis makes clear, the therapist is not simply putting into a different language and genre (for example, in his or her therapist's notes and then later in his or her psychosocial assessment report) what the client has reported in an earlier genre (what the client reports in his or her narrative during the therapy session). During the process of genre recontextualization, the client's narrative is transformed and resituated into what Bazerman has called different "social facts" ("Speech Acts" 311), in each case becoming imbued with a different ideological use and exchange value, setting up different social relations, and performing different social actions within the genre system that leads eventually to a diagnosis. The process of moving from client narrative to therapist diagnosis, Berkenkotter explains, is guided by the psychotherapy genre system, which is connected to other genres systems, such as when insurance companies use the psychosocial assessment report to determine coverage and reimbursement.

Most striking from Berkenkotter's analysis is the role played by the *DSM IV* (*Diagnostic and Statistical Manual of Mental Disorders*) during the process of recontextualization. Therapists rely on the *DSM IV* to help them define, categorize, and diagnose mental disorders; as such, it informs the therapist's uptake knowledge by shaping how the therapist encounters and recognizes moments of significance in the client's narrative and then how the therapist begins to recontextualize those moments into a diagnosis first within the genre of therapist notes and then within the "psychosocial assessment."

META-GENRES

In mediating between the client's narrative and the therapist's notes, the *DSM IV* (Berkenkotter, "Genre Systems" 339) functions as what

Janet Giltrow has called a "meta-genre" that teaches and stabilizes
uptakes. Giltrow defines meta-genres as "atmospheres surrounding
genres" ("Meta-genre" 195). Like genres, meta-genres have "semiotic
ties to their contexts of use" (190), but their function is to provide
shared background knowledge and guidance in how to produce and
negotiate genres within systems and sets of genres. Meta-genres can
take the form of guidelines or manuals for how to produce and use
genres—genres about genres (190)—but they can also take the form
of shared discourse about genres. For example, Giltrow points to how
academics have shared language to talk about academic writing, words
such as "argument" (and its collocations, "logic" and "evidence"), "spe-
cifics," and "detail" (193-94). A syllabus, thus, can perhaps be defined
as a meta-genre, as can a writing program's learning outcomes, which
supply the shared vocabulary for assigning, producing, reflecting on,
and assessing student writing. Some communities will have more defined, explicit meta-genres that guide their genre systems while other
communities will have tacitly agreed upon meta-genres. In either case,
meta-genres help teach and stabilize uptakes, and knowledge of meta-
genres can signal insider and outsider status. As Giltrow observes,

> meta-genres flourish at those boundaries, at the
> thresholds of communities of discourse, patrolling
> or controlling individuals' participation in the col-
> lective, foreseeing or suspecting their involvements
> elsewhere, differentiating, initiating, restricting, in-
> ducing forms of activity, rationalizing and represent-
> ing the relations of the genre to the community that
> uses it. This representation is not always direct; often
> it is oblique, a mediated symbolics of practice. (203)

As Giltrow also notes, meta-genres can be quite durable (199),
sometimes working against attempts to change genres within a genre
system, sometimes carried consciously or unconsciously by individuals
beyond the contexts of their use and affecting how individuals engage
with genres in different systems of activity. In any case, meta-genres
form part of our genre and uptake knowledge, and hence play a role in
distributing cognition and shaping how we navigate genre systems and
their genre sets in order to enact meaningful, consequential actions.

In the next section, we will illustrate how the key concepts we have
discussed in this chapter—genres as situated and distributed cogni-

tion, genre systems and sets, uptake, genre chronotope, and meta-genre—interact within Activity Systems.

GENRE AND ACTIVITY SYSTEMS

As we have been suggesting so far, genre systems, genre sets, meta-genres, and the habitual uptakes that mediate interactions within and between them all take place and become meaningful within contexts. Scholars have described these contexts as ceremonials (Freadman), discourse communities (Swales), spheres of communication (Bakhtin), and communities of practice (Lave and Wenger), all of which reiterate the idea that genres situate and distribute cognition, frame social identities, organize spatial and temporal relations, and coordinate meaningful, consequential actions within contexts. As we saw in Giddens' theory of structuration, however, these contexts are not merely back-drops or frames within which genres and actions take place. Instead, contexts exist in a dynamic, inter-dependent, mutually-constructing relationship with the genre systems they situate so that through the use of genres and other mediational means, we enact context as we function within it. Synthesizing Yrjo Engeström's concept of activity system with Bazerman's concept of genre systems, David Russell turns to activity systems as a way to account for these dynamic, ecological interactions between genres and their contexts of use.

In their systems version of Vygotskian activity theory, Engeström, and Engeström and Cole propose a view of context defined by and emerging from mediated, interactive, multiply shared, often competing, and motivated activities. As Engeström explains, within an activity system, the subjects or agents, the objectives, and the mediational means function inseparably from one another ("Developmental Studies" 67). As such, context becomes "an ongoing, dynamic accomplishment of people acting together with shared tools, including—most powerfully—writing" (Russell, "Rethinking Genre" 508-09). At the same time, Engeström notes, an "activity system is not a homogeneous entity. To the contrary it is composed of a multitude of often disparate elements, voices and viewpoints" (68).

In "Rethinking Genre in School and Society: An Activity Theory Analysis," and following Engeström and Cole and Engeström, David Russell defines an activity system as "any ongoing, object-direct-ed, historically conditioned, dialectically structured, tool-mediated human interaction" (510). As figure 6.1 illustrates, an activity system is comprised of "subjects," "mediational means," and "objects/motives," which interact to produce certain outcomes. This interaction is supported by "rules/norms," "community," and "division of labor." Subjects are the individuals, working individually or in groups, who carry out an activity; mediational means are the material and semiotic "tools in use" that enable subjects to carry out their work; and the object/motive is the focus of the action—that to which the subjects apply their mediational means in order to accomplish an outcome. As Russell explains, object/motives constitute both "the *object of study* of some disciplines (e.g., cells in cytology, literary works in literary criticism)" as well as "an overall direction of that activity, a (provisionally) shared purpose or motive (e.g. analyzing cells, analyzing literary works)" (511). Supporting and informing the interaction between subjects, motives, and objects/motives are rules/norms, community, and division of labor. As Engeström describes them, rules/norms "refer to the explicit and implicit regulations, norms and conventions that constrain actions and interactions within the activity system"; community "comprises multiple individuals and/or sub-groups who share the same general object and who construct themselves as distinct from other communities"; and "division of labor refers to both the horizontal division of tasks between the members of the community and to the vertical division of power and status" (*Learning by Expanding* 78).

For example, within the activity system of a first-year writing classroom, the subjects would include teacher and students; the object/motive would be the production and improvement of student writing in relation to defined course outcomes, which students are required to meet in order to complete the course; and the mediational means include the physical space of the classroom (desks and chairs, dry-erase boards, technological equipment, etc.) as well as, importantly, the various genre sets described earlier that define the genre system of the classroom—from meta-genres such as the writing program's outcomes statement and the course syllabus, to the related genres that distribute cognition and coordinate the work of teacher and students, such as assignment prompts, the various genres of student writing, peer review sheets, teacher end comments, student-teacher conferences, class discussions, student course evaluations, grade sheets, and so on. Genre systems mediate the work of activity systems by maintaining stabilized for now, normalized ways of acting and interacting that subjects use

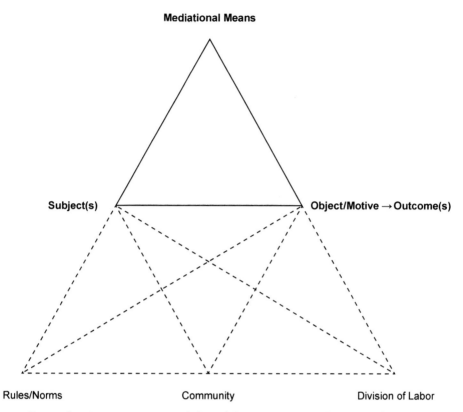

Figure 6.1: An activity system (adapted from Engeström, "Activity Theory" 31).

in order to produce consequential, recognizable outcomes. Underscoring the interaction between students/teacher, genre system, and object/ motive are the rules and norms of school culture, the sense of academic community, and the division of labor that create hierarchies between teacher and students.

As Russell notes, "[d]issensus, resistance, conflicts, and deep contradictions are constantly produced in activity systems" as subjects may have different understandings of the motives, and as the division of labor will create hierarchical differences and power relations (511). As we discussed earlier in terms of the classroom genre system, students and teacher do not have equal access to all the genres, and the different genre sets within which they participate position them in various relations of power. At the same time, while the overarching outcome of the activity system may be students' ability to demonstrate the course outcomes, some of the genres within the classroom genre system might create conflict for the teacher, as she or he uses some genres to assume the role of coach to student writing while other genres require the teacher to assume the role of evaluator of student writing. Nonetheless, in the coordinated, complex activities and relations they help their users enact, genre systems not only "operationalize" (Russell 513) activity systems, but also maintain and dynamically re-create them (Russell 512).

Figure 6.2 illustrates the multiple genre sets and their genre system that interact to enable subjects within an activity system to accomplish their objective(s). In the case of the classroom activity system, these genre sets operationalize the micro-level activities that together operationalize the macro-level activities of the classroom. As such, there are both intra- and inter-genre set uptakes. The arrows in Figure 6.2 describe the uptake relations between genres within a genre set *and* between genre sets within a genre system. Within the genre set of the peer review, for instance, the assignment prompt, student texts, and peer review worksheet will mediate how students take up each other's work. At the same time, the genre set of peer review is also connected to the genre set of teacher feedback. And as we discussed earlier, within the activity system of the classroom, meta-genre(s) inform genre knowledge and guide uptakes.

As Figure 6.2 also suggests, genres not only coordinate the work within an activity system, but also between activity systems. Within the genre set of teacher feedback, for example, the teacher end comment is connected to the genre of the grade sheet, which then connects the classroom activity system to another activity system within the university, the registrar's office, where student grades enter into a different genre system that leads to transcripts, affects financial aid, determines entry into different majors and disciplines, and so on. As Russell elaborates, "classroom genres are linked intertexually to written genres of the university activity system: Student papers are commodified into grades placed on student papers, which then are further commodified in grade reports, which are collated into transcripts, and so on. . . . Thus, the system of written genres extends beyond the classroom, spatially and temporally, as transcripts, diplomas, and other documents become tools for helping students select—and to select students for—further, deeper, and more powerful involvements" in other

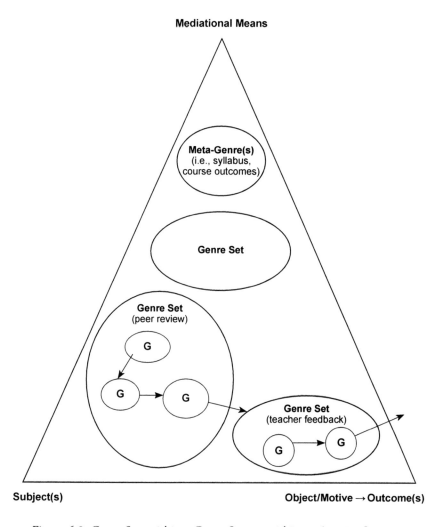

Figure 6.2. Genre Sets within a Genre System within an Activity System.

activity systems (530-31). In this way, activity systems and the genres that operationalize them are always connected to other activity systems and genre systems.

As illustrated in Figure 6.3 (adapted from Russell, "Rethinking Genre"), the multiple activity systems branch out and connect to one another in a rhizome-like way. In a large activity system like the university, some activity systems (departments, classrooms, research labs,

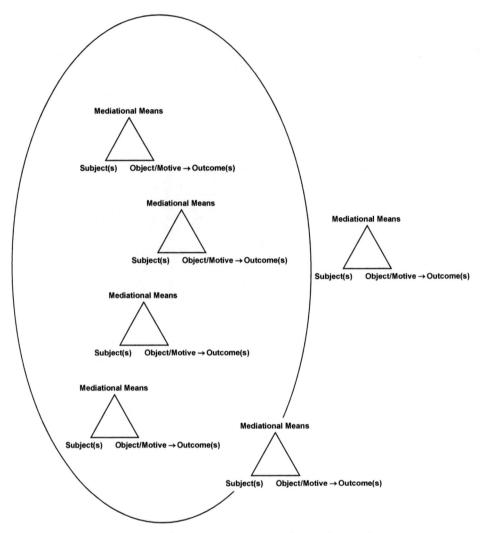

Figure 6.3: An overarching activity system made up of multiple activity systems, some of which connect the overarching activity system to external activity systems (adapted from Russell, "Rethinking Genre" 526).

etc.) are more centrally related to the overall outcomes and motives; others such as financial aid offices, the registrar's office, athletic departments, and the office of development exist on the peripheries and boundaries connecting the overarching activity system to other activity systems. While the inter-relations between activity systems enable individuals to perform and navigate complex social activities and relations over time and space, they also, as Russell describes, create conflicts and contradictions as individuals "are pulled between the object/motives of the multiple activity systems with which they interact" (519). This is often the case with the tension between athletics and academics on university campuses, and also the case as private industry increasingly funds academic research. As Russell has more recently explained, "to theorize the ways texts mediate activity across different contexts, one must theorize the relations of all these elements in multiple activity systems, what Engeström et al. call polycontextuality" ("Writing in Multiple Contexts" 358-59).

Part of the work meta-genres perform, existing as Giltrow explains on the boundaries between activity systems, is to smooth over some of the tensions individuals experience within and between activity systems by rationalizing the contradictions and conflicts. At the same time, however, these tensions can also lead to resistance and change, as individuals bring knowledge from one activity system to another (Russell, "Rethinking Genre" 522), which affects how they use and take up genres (uptake memory can traverse activity systems). Likewise, as individuals encounter greater tensions within and between activity systems (because of changes in technology, access to genres, the presence of newcomers, cultural differences, etc.) the genres begin to reflect those tensions as they take hybrid forms (Russell 523).[22]

Charles Bazerman's *The Languages of Edison's Light* provides one of the fullest accounts of the way multiple activity systems evolve, are mobilized, and interact in complex projects—in this case, in the invention of the incandescent light bulb. Bazerman's research reveals how Thomas Edison and his colleagues actively mobilized various activity systems in order to create the conditions as well as the social need that eventually made incandescent light and central power a reality. That is, before Edison and his colleagues made incandescent light and central power a technological reality, they had to make them a social and discursive reality. They did so, in part, by relying on networks of information, particularly newspapers. As Bazerman details, changes in journalism and the wider circulation of newspapers not only helped establish Edison as a celebrity, which in turn gave him the credibility to win financial backers to support his research, but also helped capture the public imagination: "Edison's use of the public stage to gain public

attention for his inventions culminated when he announced the per-
fection of the incandescent light in such a way that it seemed the fulfillment of many social needs and dreams" (38). Bazerman's research
reveals the interdependencies among systems of activity as financial
markets and capital investment, patent systems, newspapers, fairs and
exhibitions, and urban politics came to bear on the invention and do-
mestication of incandescent light. But equally significant, Bazerman's
research also reveals the agency involved in mobilizing these multiple
realms. For example, the Menlo Park Notebooks, which helped to coordinate Edison's and his colleagues' laboratory research, were also
frequently annotated after the fact to index the formal legal record
and granted patents. In this way, "these raw working documents were
transformed into legal records for circulation in other communicative
and documentary systems beyond the laboratory" (Bazerman 66). At
the same time, drawings that first appeared in the notebooks would
later be "re-presented in advertisements, publicity, and newspaper articles" (76). Here, we see how mediational means such as the notebooks
served different objects/motives as they were recontextualized in different activity systems.

As a conceptual and an analytical tool, the notion of activity systems has contributed much to RGS. It has allowed genre scholars to
illustrate the dialectical relationship between genres, individuals, activities, and contexts. It has also helped genre scholars map the complex relations (what Spinuzzi and Spinuzzi and Zachry call "genre
ecologies") within and between genre systems, as these operationalize constellations of activity systems. It has allowed genre scholars to
bring together several key concepts and to show how they co-operate:
genre systems, genre sets, meta-genre, and uptake. It has enabled genre
scholars to more fully describe tensions within genres as individuals negotiate multiple, competing goals. It has helped genre scholars
trace individual and group cognitive development as these are mediated by activity system-specific genres (Bazerman, "Genre and Cognitive Development" 295). It has helped to articulate further some of
the challenges of teaching genres. And it has provided genre scholars
with a flexible analytical tool for studying varying dimensions of activity. Since larger activity systems will often contain multiple activity
systems and be connected to multiple other activity systems, a genre
researcher can adjust her or his analytical frame in order to study varying levels of activity. However, no matter the size of the activity system

framework under study, the concept of activity system will compel the researcher at least to recognize and acknowledge the interdependencies between what is happening in one activity system and its genres with what is happening in related ones.

CONCLUSION

Since part of what defines a genre is its placement within a system of genre relations within and between activity systems, genres cannot be defined or taught only through their formal features. This brings us back to the pedagogical quandary RGS has faced. For example, if students perceive a task as serving a certain function within an activity system, they will likely select a mediational means (a genre or set of genres) that is appropriate to their understanding of the objective. They will also assume a subjectivity compatible with that understanding. Some students may recognize the object/motives but may not have access to the appropriate mediational means, or they may not feel they have the requisite authority (subjectivity) to accomplish the task even though they understand the object/motives and have access to the mediational means. How we understand the object and outcomes determines what mediational means we use and how we use them. Likewise, how we recognize the object and motives to act depends on our subject position.

In *Building Genre Knowledge,* Christine Tardy follows the development of four international graduate students (two MA and two PhD) as over time they learn the genres of their disciplines. The four students took a graduate level writing course, which was explicitly about teaching disciplinary genres (the mediational means), but outside of the object/motive context of their particular activity systems. What Tardy found was that genre knowledge is not fully activated or learned until the object/motives are acquired and become real for their users. Students can be taught to write a conference proposal or abstract, but until the stakes or outcomes are real, formal knowledge of the mediational means is not enough. What Tardy also found is that the task might be real and the formal genre knowledge mastered, but if the student does not feel authorized—does not feel that she or he has the authority to contribute to the objectives of the discipline—then the other knowledges are incomplete. Meta-knowledge of mediational means without access to task and authorizing subjectivity is incomplete. One's subjectivity is defined in part by one's relationship to and understanding of the object/motive, and how to manipulate the mediational means in terms of the object/motive. As such, subjectivity and identity are bound up in genre knowledge and performance, as we are constantly accomplishing ourselves and our objectives/motives as we enact them through our mediational means.

A rhetorical and sociological understanding of genre has revealed genre as a rich analytical tool for studying academic, workplace, and public systems of activity, but it has also left RGS researchers with questions about the pedagogical implications of teaching genres. Clearly, genres are part of how individuals participate in complex relations with one another in order to get things done, and how newcomers learn to construct themselves and participate effectively within activity systems. But how we can teach genres in ways that honor their complexity and their status as more than just typified rhetorical features is the question RGS continues to face. In Part 2 of the book, we will next explore the range of ways genre researchers have studied how genres are acquired and used in academic, workplace, public, and new media environments. And then in Part 3, we will examine genre's pedagogical possibilities for the teaching of writing.

Part 2: Genre Research in Multiple Contexts

7 Genre Research in Academic Contexts

Complementing the largely theoretical perspectives discussed in Part 1 is an international body of empirical research on genre—systematic observations of genres within their settings of use—that has contributed to reconceptualizations of genre and our understanding of genre as a dynamic discursive formation and site for interaction. Research studies on genre—ranging from case studies of legal genres, to examination of the historical evolution of the experimental article, to participant-observer explorations of veterinary records—seek to describe how genres are learned and acquired, how genres evolve and change, and how genres function as discursive actions within particular social, historical, and cultural contexts. This chapter and the others in Part 2 survey research studies on genre that have sought to explore, empirically, how genres function as sites of interaction that enable access to, structure, and frame participants' actions within groups or organizational contexts. Aviva Freedman, in *Rhetorical Genre Studies and Beyond* (with Natasha Artemeva), captures this interactive relationship between theory and empirical data, noting that "the data flesh out and specify the theory, modifying, elaborating, and necessarily shaping it in the context of what is observed" (101-02). Working in relationship to theoretical perspectives on genre as a dynamic social action, empirical studies seek to test and contribute to theoretical assumptions by exploring the complex interplay between texts and their social contexts.

Further reflecting on the interaction between theoretical and empirical inquiries (and between social actions and individual actors), Charles Bazerman, in a recent methodological article, defines "theories of the middle range" or empirically grounded theories that grow out of historical research and "can build a systematic and principled picture of contemporary and future writing practices" ("Theories of the Middle Range" 302). Historical genre studies, because they are

grounded in broader social and cultural theories while simultaneously examining particular textual phenomena and individual processes,
can mediate between the abstract and the particular. This historical
research is exemplified by studies across a range of genres, from the
scientific article (Bazerman, *Shaping Written Knowledge*, "How Natural Philosophers Can Cooperate"; Selzer; Gross, Harmon and Reidy),
to letters (Barton and Hall), to business correspondence (Yates, *Control through Communication*), to economic discourse (McCloskey, *The
Rhetoric of Economics*) to political genres (Campbell and Jamieson,
Form and Genre; *Deeds Done in Words*). Walking readers through his
own processes of methodological reasoning and investigation in his
rich and varied historical work, Bazerman describes how the balance
of theoretical concepts and empirical details contributed to identification of different levels of research questions (from more "universal"
questions to site-specific ones), to locating a strategic research site, to
formulating a method of data gathering (locating archives and focusing a research corpus). Historical inquiry brings into interaction theoretical and empirical inquiry; thus, "theory and concepts are heuristics
for finding and seeing things in the world; conversely, noticing what
exists in the world is heuristic for conceptual development" (315).

   With its focus on inquiry into communal literacy practices, historical research on genre is in dialogue with multiple types of inquiry,
from sociological research to linguistic research to psychological or
cognitive empirical work. Indeed, research studies from a genre framework have ranged from cognitive studies of genre acquisition and
genre knowledge—such as Aviva Freedman's work on the "felt sense"
of genre—to linguistically-oriented work, such as Swales' groundbreaking work on the rhetorical moves of the empirical research article
(see Tardy and Swales for a further overview of genre research from
linguistics, language and discourse studies). While more recent studies
examine the social contexts shaping genres and the social actions that
genres enable, Bazerman has recently called for "a renewed sociocognitive research program in writing to learn" ("Genre and Cognitive
Development" 287). Indeed, genre research forms a rich site for interdisciplinarity, with Amy Devitt arguing, in her conclusion to *Writing
Genres*, that further research on genre is needed, including cognitive
studies, historical studies, and collaborative research between sociologists and genre theorists (218). Joining this call, Bazerman argues
for forging links in our research on genre with methods arising from

related fields and disciplines, such as discourse analysis and ethno-methodology (as we noted at the end of Chapter 5, genre research in Brazil has embodied such interdisciplinarity). Research that draws on multiple methods "holds much promise for drawing humanities' understandings of the workings of language into relation with the social sciences' understandings of human relations, behavior, and consciousness" ("The Life of Genre" 23). In this way, genre studies can benefit not only from research studies of how genres are learned, performed, and situated, but genre analysis itself can be used as a research methodology and "can play a major role in the current investigations into the communicative grounds of social order" (23).

Genre analysis, located between textually oriented and socio-cultural methods, enables a pluralistic methodology, integrating multiple methods and data sources in the study of genre. However, while genre analysis is a useful analytic approach for studying texts as meaningful social actions, Bazerman acknowledges the "methodological dilemma" of trying to "make sense out of the complexity, indeterminacy, and contextual multiplicity that a text presents us with" (321). Without access to the immediate evidence of the readers' uptakes of a genre or to the immediate contexts in which genres are used, researchers often have to rely on their intuitions about a text, creating a related methodological challenge—the challenge of achieving a kind of critical distance or reflexivity and moving beyond a "'naturalized' user's view of genres and activity systems to a more carefully researched, observed and analyzed knowledge" ("Speech Acts" 321). In addition, with the focus on regularized features of texts, genre analysis can limit our observations of the complexity and multiplicity of texts and the ways in which they differ and change. In order to address this methodological dilemma, Bazerman suggests employing a variety of methods when conducting genre analysis: 1) Examine less obvious patterns or features of texts; 2) Extend the sample to include a larger number and range of texts from different social and historical contexts; 3) Gather other people's understanding of genres via interviews and observations; and 4) Conduct ethnographic research of how texts are used in social organizations—particularly within genre sets, genre systems, and activity systems (321-22, 326). The genre-based research studies surveyed in this chapter and the chapters that follow (Chapters 8 and 9), while by no means exhaustive, illustrate multiple methods for "gather[ing] information not just about the texts but about other people's understanding of them" (325), beginning with a focus in this chapter on genre research in academic contexts.

Research on Genre Learning and
Acquisition in Academic Contexts

In a 1993 special issue of *Research in the Teaching of English,* Aviva Freedman illustrates well how empirical research is necessary in backing up theoretical and pedagogical claims and assumptions about genre. She introduces a key theoretical debate regarding the explicit teaching of genre and draws on research to support her claims, first taking up the Strong Hypothesis—that explicit teaching of genres is neither necessary nor productive since students acquire genre tacitly. Freedman cites an earlier large-scale research study she conducted ("Development in Story Writing") in 1987, which examines the narrative structure in the writings of 7,500 students in grades 5, 8, and 12. Results indicated that students were able to perform a narrative structure without being taught the stages or structural organization. A "plausible interpretation," argues Freedman, is that students learned to perform narrative genres through reading narratives or hearing stories told orally, leading her to conclude, "This schema was internalized, without evidence of any prior explicit teaching and was brought to bear as tacit, shaping knowledge in the course of their writing in the context of the elicited task" ("Show and Tell" 227). To further test this premise, Freedman devised an ethnographic study of students in an undergraduate class in law, a broader study that ultimately focused on the case studies of six students. Freedman and her research associates conducted in-class observations, weekly interviews with students, interviews with instructors, and analyses of students' logs of law-related activities, notes, and drafts for all writing in the law course. Based on analysis of this data, they discovered that these six students produced distinctive subgenres of academic writing—lexically, syntactically, structurally, and rhetorically—despite the lack of explicit instruction. Freedman notes that in comparison to other academic writing produced by these same students, these essays "evinced a very distinct mode of argumentation" ("Learning to Write Again" 99). The students, however, consulted no models, were given no explicit instructions about writing legal essays, and made no attempt to formulate the rules underlying the genre in the course of drafting and revising. How, then, did they acquire a new genre? According to Freedman's study, learners used the following model for acquisition:

> Learners approach the task with a 'dimly felt sense' of the new genre they are attempting. They begin composing by focusing on the specific content to be embodied in this genre. In the course of the composing this 'dimly felt sense' of the genre is both given form and reshaped as a) this 'sense,' b) the composing processes, and c) the unfolding text interrelate and modify one another. Then, on the basis of external feedback (the grade assigned), the learners either confirm or modify their map of the genre. (101)

The felt sense is, as Freedman describes it, a generalized sense of academic discourse that is modified based on inferences writers made from writing assignments, feedback on assignments, class discussions, lectures, and readings. Students learned the genres, then, through active performance, and intuitively acquired new genres, making explicit methods unnecessary.

Despite her conclusion that *"Clearly, explicit teaching may not be necessary for the acquisition of even very sophisticated school genres"* ("Show and Tell" 230), Freedman grants that the research evidence from genres studies is "scanty and suggestive rather than conclusive" (241), and she poses a Restricted Hypothesis, which "does allow for certain limited conditions under which explicit teaching may enhance learning" (241). These conditions might include contextualized learning (where, for instance, students are reading the genres they will be asked to write) and engagement in an authentic task, where students are able to clearly see how genre is tied to social motive. But such instruction, according to Freedman, is dependent on the accuracy of the teacher's explicit knowledge of genre, the learning style of the student, and the time period between exposure to context and application of knowledge; thus, questions remain about the effectiveness of explicit teaching of genre. Freedman concludes by issuing a call for further research that will help answer some of the lingering issues and questions:

> . . . [M]y presentation of the two hypotheses is intended to point to the necessity for further study. . . .
> Further research and further observation may be able
> to provide substantive evidence for one or the other of

these hypotheses. Certainly, experimental procedures
can be designed to find out whether and to what degree the exemptions specified in the Restricted Hypothesis hold—and importantly, for whom. It is
likely that different learning styles, different matura-
tional stages, and (or) different socio-cultural experiences may require different teaching strategies. (245)

In response to Freedman (in the same 1993 issue of *RTE*), Joseph
Williams and Gregory Colomb cite earlier research studies that, while
not specific to genre approaches, confirm the effectiveness of explicit
teaching within contextualized learning (Hillocks) and the necessity
of explicit teaching in secondary education (Fraser et al; Walberg).
To support their "case for explicit teaching," Williams and Colomb
cite data from their educational research at the University of Chicago,
which explored students' perceptions of writing abilities in order to
argue that students value and profit from explicit instruction. Their
study examined 400 students enrolled in advanced academic and
professional writing courses who received explicit teaching of the features of genres, including syntactic, lexical, discursive, and rhetorical features. Students saw as particularly valuable explicit teaching
of problem formulation, introductions, organization, and verbs and
nominalizations, and their perceived usefulness of these strategies cor-
responded with their evaluation of their writing abilities. Based on
their findings, Williams and Colomb argue for explicit teaching of
"prototypical features" or the central constitutive features of genres,
which can help students gain access to knowledge of context:

When students practice explicit features *even before
they are fully socialized,* they are compelled to focus
on, perhaps even to generate the knowledge for those
generic moves. When we learn social context, we are
also learning its forms; but when we learn forms, we
may also be learning their social contexts. Generic
forms may be more generative than Freedman realizes. In any event, we have a chicken-and-egg problem
that only research will unscramble. (262)

While Williams and Colomb posit that explicit teaching of generic
forms may help students generate genre knowledge, their study is limited to a focus on how explicit teaching of generic forms leads to learning

of generic forms, rather than to the broader rhetorical understanding of genres as responses to situations. As a result, they call for more research to "unscramble" this interaction between explicit teaching and implicit learning and between generic patterns and social patterns. In her rejoinder to Williams and Colomb, Freedman acknowledges that learners participating in authentic contexts of communication can develop a genre awareness or raised consciousness of specific features that will, in turn, lead to acquisition. However, Freedman joins in the call for further research, ending her response to Williams and Colomb with an "Invitation to the Community": "It should not be the task of the skeptics to argue against a pedagogic strategy but rather the work of the proponents to bring forward convincing research and theoretical evidence. . . . The relevant research and theory-building need to be undertaken" (278).

Taking up the Call for Research on Genre Knowledge and Learning

Freedman's call for further research on genre has been taken up by researchers over the past two decades who are interested in the question of how students acquire genre knowledge, how teachers can facilitate genre learning, and how this learning translates to performance. The question of what it means to learn genres has been central to researchers examining early childhood writing development. Contesting Freedman's above claim that research on genre acquisition has been inconclusive, Marilyn Chapman notes that "research studies of young children's writing have shown that learning genre is part of children's literacy development" ("Situated, Social, Active" 472). In their comprehensive review of research studies on children's genre knowledge, Carol Donovan and Laura Smolkin summarize the three major research questions addressed by research on children's understanding of genre: 1) What is the nature of children's genre knowledge and their developing understanding of genre? 2) In what ways do different tasks and other methodological choices reveal differences in children's genre knowledge? and 3) How can teachers best support young children's writing development in different genres? (135-36). In response to the first question, a large strand of research has focused on children's ability to acquire and perform in narrative genres (Langer, *Children Reading and Writing*; Donovan, "Children's Story Writing,"

"Children's Development and Control"; Pappas, "Is Narrative 'Primary'?"; Kamberelis and Bovino) or to transfer knowledge of narrative genres to informational or persuasive genres (Chapman, "The Emergence of Genres"; Donovan, "Children's Development and Control"; Langer, "Reading, Writing, and Genre Development"; Troia and Graham). Other studies, in response to the third question, have focused on pedagogical approaches that support genre acquisition, such as reading or rereading genres (Pappas, "Young Children's Strategies in Learning"), providing explicit genre instruction (Duke and Kays; Fitzgerald and Teasley), and situating approaches to teaching genre (Chapman, "Situated, Social, Active"). And in response to the second question, regarding methodological choices used to study children's genre knowledge, Donovan and Smolkin argue that careful attention must be given to methods employed to study children's processes of learning genres, particularly since the majority of studies on genre knowledge are descriptive and qualitative in nature.

Many studies of genre knowledge at all levels of education draw on Freedman's model of genre acquisition as a basis for data-gathering, which was one of the first to propose multiple research methods: 1) exploring past and current readings of genres, 2) analyzing previous writing experiences, 3) collecting assignments from instructors, 4) observing talk about writing, or 5) analyzing class discussion. Drawing on these methods and data sources, researchers seek to more clearly define what Freedman describes as a "felt sense" or sense of genre, a recognition that students' initial "broad schema for academic discourse"—their "sense of shape, structure, rhetorical stance, and thinking strategies"—must be modified when confronted with new genres in response to particular disciplines or assignments ("Learning to Write Again" 104).

At the University of Washington and the University of Tennessee, the authors of this book along with their research teams conducted a cross-institutional study to determine what types of genre knowledge student writers enter college with and the extent to which that prior knowledge helps or hinders their abilities to learn new academic discourse conventions. Drawing on research methods that explore modes of acquisition defined by Freedman (surveys that ask students to report on previous literacy experiences, instructor syllabi and assignments, examination of texts produced in class, interviews with students), the focus of our research is on student writers' previous experiences with genres, participation in rhetorically situated language use (including written, oral and digital communication), and familiarity with typical ways of responding to communicative situations. The study addresses the following research questions: What genres (written, oral, digital) do students already know when they arrive in first-year composition courses? How do students use their prior genre knowledge when writing new genres for first-year composition courses? To what extent does this prior knowledge help or hinder the student's ability to gain access to academic discourse? And what factors contribute to how and why students transform prior genre knowledge into new genre knowledge?

To answer these questions, we asked participants to respond to a survey describing past literacy experiences (reading, writing, digital literacy), both in school and out of school. In addition, we invited students to participate in discourse-based interviews that pose questions based on early texts students have produced in their first-year composition (FYC) courses (a beginning-of-term writing sample and Paper 1), with the purpose of reflecting on how they called on previous discursive resources in order to write their first paper in FYC. We also collected and analyzed all writing produced in FYC in order to deepen our understanding of the evolution of students' genre knowledge and how, over time, that either helps or hinders their ability to approximate academic discourse. Finally, to contextualize this analysis, we also collected the syllabi and assignments that prompted the students' writing.

While the study is still in progress at the time of this writing, preliminary findings back up some of Freedman's earlier findings, namely that composing processes are important in formulating and modifying a felt sense of genre (for more on preliminary findings from this study, see http://utuwpriorgenre.blogspot.com/). According to Freedman's study, as students write in a new genre, they employ a number of subprocesses to carry out their purpose, and "in the course of composing, there is a shuttling back and forth between this felt sense and the unfolding text, each modifying the other as the text unfolds" ("Learning to Write Again" 102). Nearly half of the UT respondents (46%), for example, reported drawing on familiar writing process skills or habits (invention, brainstorming, freewriting, drafting, revision) when facing a new writing task or new genre. Freedman's study underscores that invention methods, in particular, can assist not only in generating ideas but can also suggest and limit the range of possible rhetorical strategies, thus helping students formulate a clearer sense of genre. Freedman's acquisition model also emphasizes the importance of previous writing experiences, and students in the UT/UW study did, in fact, indicate the influence of their high school writing courses and AP courses. These responses reinforce the complex activities and interactions that Freedman describes that constitute a "felt sense" of genre: "students begin with a broad schema for academic discourse—a schema that has itself been inferred in the course of their previous performances, their previous creations of such discourse" ("Learning to Write Again" 104). A number of students from both UT and UW indicated the significance of these previous genre performances, with 34% of UW students and 31% of UT students noting the importance of genres written in high school, such as research and persuasion papers, critiques, essays, and reports. Bazerman notes,

> Genre is a tool for getting at the resources the students bring with them, the genres they carry from their educations and their experiences in society, and it is a tool for framing challenges that bring students into new domains that are as yet for them unexplored, but not so different from what they know as to be unintelligible. ("The Life of Genre" 24)

Through studies of classroom genres and students' generic productions, we can explore the complex interaction of psychological, social, and institutional factors within the classroom setting and can draw on students' prior genre knowledge to inform strategies for teaching students to enter new realms of discourse.

The cross-institutional research at UT/UW sought to replicate and extend findings from a research study exploring students' prior genre knowledge and the effect on learning new academic genres that was conducted at the University of Kansas. Using teacher-research methods, Amy Devitt conducted research on how students' antecedent genres influence their writing of new genres in first-year composition, posing the following questions: "What genres do first-year students in my own writing course already know when they arrive at my class? And how do those students use their known genres when writing new genres for my class?" ("First-year Composition and Antecedent Genres"). Based on questionnaires and collection and analysis of student writing, the preliminary results indicated that "students do use the genres they already know when writing for new situations, whether or not they report knowing or enjoying that genre" ("First-year Composition"). Backing up Freedman's finding that a student's "broad schema for academic discourse" is "inferred in the course of their previous performances, the previous creations of such discourse" and is modified for particular assignments and disciplinary expectations, Devitt's findings suggest that new academic genres are defined against prior or antecedent genres:

> Students may be assessing the similarity of rhetorical situations between the known and new genres and making decisions about how to adapt the known genre to the new situation, or they may be acting less consciously but merely grounding themselves in what they know in the face of a new and difficult task. ("First-year Composition")

Devitt cites the example of "Nathan," who does not report writing academic genres but uses academic genre conventions in his writing. While Nathan reports on the questionnaire that he did not write many papers in high school, "the papers he wrote for his college composition course consistently drew on traditional thesis-support papers, especially the five-paragraph theme, genres he did not report knowing" ("First-year Composition"). While this case seems to demonstrate Freedman's claim that genre knowledge exists on an unconscious level, Devitt's study challenges Freedman's claim that there are no benefits to explicit teaching and proposes teaching "genre awareness" explicitly—an approach that both recognizes that genre knowledge is tacit but also emphasizes the importance of contextualized approaches to explicit teaching of genres. She develops this claim more fully in her book *Writing Genres*, arguing that students can acquire an awareness of how genres function rhetorically and socially—"a critical consciousness of both rhetorical purposes and ideological effects of generic forms" (192).

This claim for the importance of both implicit teaching—through immersion in writing situations (for instance, through classroom discussions or assignment sequences)—and explicit instruction is backed up by a qualitative study done by Mary Soliday in collaboration with a colleague in science, David Eastzer. The study focused on a science course taught by Eastzer at City College in New York. Researchers used surveys, conducted interviews with students, observed and audiotaped classes, and gathered course documents in order to respond to the following research questions, which sought to unpack the interaction between implicit and explicit methods: What genres did David ask students to produce in his course? How did David convey genre knowledge to the students? How did students approach those requirements to produce written genres? How did David judge whether a students' writing fulfilled his expectations for genre? (66).

Researchers discovered that David "mapped out genre both implicitly and explicitly" (68). He immersed students in the genre they were asked to produce through sequencing of assignments, lectures, class discussion, assigned readings, and conferences. He also explicitly mapped out his genre expectations in course documents, assignment sheets, and model texts. While "this qualitative research provides some evidence that writers acquire genre knowledge both consciously and unconsciously" (66), the findings also confirm Freedman's hypothesis that the success of explicit versus implicit teaching may depend on individual learning styles. One student, Jonathan, conforms to the explicit expectations outlined by David while also reworking and revising the genre expectations, using a comparative analysis of two scientific newspaper articles to insert his own judgment about the journalists' scientific knowledge. Another student, Carson, uses his prior genre knowledge to acquire the new genre and relates the writing assignment in the science course to a similar essay he wrote for his law class. However, a third student, Dawn, demonstrates "a weaker grasp of the genre of the case study" (78) and does not seem to have the same genre repertoires as Jonathan and Carson: "Her approach to genre was more closely tied to the texts, the assignment sheets, and to what she heard in class—she did not accent the genres with her own preferences as freely as did Jonathan or Carson" (78). In other words, Dawn did not bring her prior genre knowledge into engagement with the new genres she was learning. Dawn's case, in particular, may confirm Freedman's claim that the success of explicit teaching may depend on whether or not the student is at the appropriate stage of development as a writer or may depend on "the congeniality of the student's learning style" (244).

Based on these findings, Soliday concludes that, because learning genres is based on both individual genre knowledge and communal expectations, students benefit from both implicit and explicit approaches to teaching genre, a finding similar to Devitt's conclusions. In addition, just as Devitt and others (see Richard Coe, "Teaching Genre as

Process") have suggested teaching genre awareness by having students practice writing alternative genres or "reinventing" genres, Soliday argues that writers are able to assimilate genres when they "rework the voice of the other, the communal form, into their own individual words, intentions, and worldviews" (82).

Freedman's earlier research suggests that a key factor in the acquisition of genres and developing awareness of communal expectations is a dimension of collaboration—feedback from other writers or the instructor (the final stage of her acquisition model), where students can make adjustments to their writing and refine their rhetorical choices and sense of genre. This role that feedback plays in genre acquisition is explored in a study by Elizabeth Wardle. Wardle explores the relationship of peer response to genre knowledge and authority, arguing that students' interactions with peers can help them begin to learn new genre conventions and gain academic literacies. Drawing on participant/observer research (which involved observation of both classroom and workshop talk), collection of peer critiques, and interviews with students, Wardle observed how 26 students in an intermediate college writing course "wrestled with" and "began to learn" new genre conventions. When confronted with writing new genres, students tended to work through their genre confusion in workshop discussion, suggesting that it might be more effective for students to write out their critiques following the discussion. While none of the students, in their peer critiques, offered any explicit genre feedback, the peer groups created an opportunity for "immersion" in the class context, leading Wardle to conclude that "genre knowledge may at least partially be gained through participating in the work of creating a new genre with the help of a community of supportive peers" ("Is This What Yours Sounds Like?'" 101).

An additional finding in Wardle's study is that, despite poorly articulated genre expectations on the part of instructors, students still managed to gain genre knowledge while sharing papers in groups. Soliday's above study further reinforces the challenge of negotiating individual and communal expectations when there is a gap between instructor's knowledge of genre and explicit instructions to students. Some of the struggling writers she studied "were those who haven't learned to translate a teacher's requirements for genre into their own words" (81). This issue is taken up more formally in a study by Anne Beaufort and John Williams called "Writing History: Informed or Not by Genre

Theory?" They report on a longitudinal case study of students' undergraduate work in six history courses taken from freshman through junior years, with Beaufort providing the compositionist perspective and Williams the historian perspective. One of their findings is that the instructor's tacit genre knowledge makes it difficult to clearly articulate explicit genre expectations. Their research report focuses on the case of Tim, who—by the end of his senior year—could not articulate genre conventions and could recall no explicit instructions on writing history genres. Beaufort and Williams argue that many of Tim's essays were less successful over his career due to his lack of understanding of genre conventions. After discourse-based interviews, analysis of twelve papers, and interviews with history instructors, they list a number of problems related to students' vague awareness of genre expectations and what they call "genre confusion," including, most significantly, a lack of a clear "framework of analysis" and conscious understanding of the connection between rhetorical purpose and disciplinary expectations, a "crucial aspect of genre knowledge [that] is often overlooked" (53-54). Without explicit instruction on how to apply an analytic framework—a metacognitive awareness of how genres function rhetorically and socially—Tim reported difficulty in making clear rhetorical choices regarding structure, style, ethos and authorial stance.

Beaufort's collaborator on the research project and a faculty member in history, John Williams, simultaneously reported on his teacher-research experiment, which focused on using an explicit genre approach to teaching writing in history. Williams experimented with an assignment that specified genre in his junior-level history course. From the 90 student papers he read, Williams concluded that the emphasis on genre in the assignment did help students write better and more convincing papers, and it "pushed [him] to think further about the characteristics of the historical essay" (61). Together, the student perspective (Tim's) and the faculty perspective (John's) lead Beaufort and Williams to conclude the following: "The tacitly held conventions of historical discourse, and the difficulty of articulating them for students, lies at the center of this problem of expectations" (63). In other words, because genre awareness is tacit, instructors have difficulty articulating explicit features, a problem that Freedman earlier alludes to when she notes that the success of contextualized teaching of genre "depends on the accuracy of the teacher's explicit knowledge" (244).

Even if teachers can articulate clear genre expectations, students' tacit genre knowledge may conflict with the teachers' genre knowledge. This finding is backed up by a study conducted by Janet Giltrow and Michele Valiquette called "Genres and Knowledge: Students Writing in the Disciplines," a study that explored the question of how members of a community conserve genre knowledge and how newcomers to the community acquire that genre knowledge. Giltrow and Valiquette conducted think-aloud protocols with experienced Teaching Assistants from two different disciplines: Psychology and Criminology. As TAs read aloud from student texts that they had already marked, they were asked to interrupt their reading to add commentary, which "a) identified discourse features that triggered evaluation, and b) expressed the discursive principles with which the student was either complying or failing to comply" (50). As TAs read students' papers and paused to reflect on meaning and conventions, it became clear that there were very different presuppositions regarding genre expectations and what shared knowledge can be assumed. As predicted by Giltrow and Valiquette, student writers attempting classroom versions of the academic genres they were asked to produce in each discipline were challenged by the task of estimating shared knowledge. Genre competence, then, and genre performance, rely not just on disciplinary knowledge, but also "knowledge about this knowledge"—a type of insider knowledge that helps writers judge how much background information to include and how much explanation of concepts is needed.

While Giltrow and Valiquette explored the conflicting genre expectations of students and Teaching Assistants, Pat Currie, in a study entitled "What Counts as Good Writing?" explored the different genre expectations of professors and TAs who are team-teaching a course. The study focused on the graded assignments and written feedback of non-native English writers in a business course and compared TA's evaluations with the professor's evaluation. When students wrote narrative genres, there was much agreement about genre expectations among students, TAs, and professors. However, when writers shifted to argument, "Neither the NNES students nor the assistant controlled the genre of argument expected: major problems were evident in terms of all components—claims, warrant, backing, and grounds" (74), leading to different responses and evaluations from the TA and professor. Currie concludes by arguing for further research that explores the articulation of conventions and expectations of various communities students seek to enter. In addition, in order to measure the relation-ship between expectations and results, she argues for more research into genre performance—"research into both the skills and strategies" of successful and less successful students (77). The next section high-lights research studies that focus on this connection between genre knowledge and genre performance.

RESEARCH ON HOW GENRE KNOWLEDGE
TRANSLATES TO PERFORMANCE

Taking up Currie's call (as discussed in the previous section) for further research into the skills and strategies of successful and less successful student writers, a study done by Sally Mitchell and Richard Andrews, "Learning to Operate Successfully in Advanced Level History," charts the transition of students from writing historical narrative to more complex cognitive and rhetorical tasks of writing historical analysis. Confirming previous studies, such as Bereiter and Scardamalia's ob-servation of a class in which students' ability to specify features of an argument did not translate to writing effective arguments, Mitchell and Andrews argue that teaching explicit features of argumentative essays did not result in successful arguments. The focus of their study was the Cambridge History Project, a British secondary education project that focuses both on historical knowledge and disciplinary skills. Taking up Freedman's claim that explicit teaching of genre and successful acquisition of genre are dependent on cognitive maturity and skill level, the researchers examined history essays that grew in-creasingly complex (following Bloom's cognitive levels) with each as-signment. They concluded that genre practice is tied to disciplinary genre knowledge and that genre conventions, such as structure and arrangement, cannot be taught apart from issues of context and mean-ing. "Planning an essay," they argue, "is not the same as engaging in an argument" (95). In other words, genre knowledge—knowledge about the typified conventions of an argument—is not the same as genre performance—being able to produce argument genres. This critical engagement with genre is possible only if instructors and students understand that genre conventions generate thought and argument, a finding that supports Devitt's approach to teaching "genre awareness." Instructors can avoid teaching genres as forms by constantly linking form to context and by having students explore how formal features are tied to rhetorical and social actions, a type of teaching that better ensures the transfer of genre knowledge to performance of genres in the same context or new contexts.

In "Transferability and Genres," Devitt notes that genre knowledge gives writers "a place to start, a location, however different, from which to begin writing;" however, she also notes that "drawing from known genres in new locations results in mismatches as well" (220). In their study on "Teaching and Learning a Multimodal Genre in a Psychology Course," Chris Anson, Deanna Dannels, and Karen St. Clair discovered that the tacit, prior genre knowledge that students bring to a new assignment may make it difficult to get outside the framework of traditional, single mode genres, thus negatively affecting performance of new genres. Anson et al. used a teacher-research approach and conducted surveys and observations to study the nature of genre acquisition and performance in a 200-level psychology course. The researchers hypothesized that when faced with a new genre—such as a "studio book" that included writings, artifacts, and visuals—students would "apply broad schematic representations to the genre first, placing it into the best-matching 'metagenre' category—general discursive types they have experienced before, often repeatedly" (174). They also acknowledged that, for the students, "acting on such generalized knowledge, however, is not enough to guarantee them a successful performance" (175). When it came to multimodal or hybrid genres that combine writing and speaking, for instance, students tended to interpret these multimodal genres as separate genres and had difficulty seeing them outside of the scripted classroom genres they were more familiar with. Based on these performances and students' "difficulty seeing genres outside of their traditional instantiations" (189), Anson et al. recommend more fully supporting students in their acquisition of strategies and skills for communication.

Devitt's study, too, explores the effects of previous genre knowledge on performance in new genres as demonstrated by a student, Mason, whose genre repertoire is dominated by personal narrative. Even when an assignment explicitly asked for an analytic paper, Mason wrote a personal narrative in response, leading Devitt to conclude, "Clearly, the personal narrative constitutes a strong antecedent genre for Mason, one that overpowered the assignment's call for analysis papers that all other students in the class heeded" ("First-year Composition"). Mason did, eventually, adapt the elements of the personal narrative to new genres, like analysis papers. As a result, while both Devitt's study and Anson et al's study show that prior genre knowledge may hinder, as well as help, genre performance, Devitt convincingly concludes that "writers use the genres they know when faced with a genre they do not know," and while these genres may not meet the needs of the new situation, "as antecedent genres, they help writers move into a new genre; they help writers adjust their old situations to new locations" ("Transferability and Genres" 222).

In the UT/UW cross-institutional study mentioned previously, we were interested not just in what prior genre knowledge students bring to first-year writing but also their perceptions of what genres they have performed most or least successfully and how these previous performances enabled and/or limited their access to college-level writing. When students were asked the question, "What do you consider your most successful piece of writing?" students from both UT and UW identified research papers and a range of creative genres as their most successful genres. Students' reasons for success were related to their interest in and investment in a topic they could choose as well as the investment of time in an extended project like the research paper. Students also linked their successful performance in a genre to their knowledge of rhetorically effective strategies, with a clear majority of students identifying rhetorical effectiveness and understanding of genre conventions as the reason for their successful performance. A preliminary finding from the study is that genre type does not predict success, but that success is dependent upon how the genre gets taken up and the social and rhetorical actions that it performs. Furthermore, preliminary results from the interviews suggest that it is not so much prior knowledge of genre that informs successful performance, but rather how and when students feel they can deploy that prior genre knowledge. Confirming Devitt's conclusions noted above, successful performance seems to depend on the flexible use of prior genre knowledge. Some students clung too closely and too long to prior genres even when the situations and tasks did not call for them. Others began to show an ability to abstract strategies from prior genres and reformulate them to new situations and tasks.

Students may be more likely to transfer genre knowledge from one situation to another if they have an understanding of the flexible, dynamic nature of genres. For example, an additional finding from Mitchell and Andrews' study (described above) is that explicit teach-

ing and cultivation of genre knowledge—in order to lead to successful genre performance—must include critical awareness of alternative
genre responses:

> Researchers such as ourselves and many teachers
> often seem to be caught in a dilemma: we want on
> the one hand to encourage and explore new and al-
> ternative forms of thinking and writing, and on the
> other we want to help students achieve as highly as
> possible within existing conventions. Too often the
> result is an overemphasis on conventional form as if
> repeated practice in that area will lead to the evidence
> of thought and engagement we are hoping for. (99)

These tensions between successfully performing within the conventions of genre while also using individual genre knowledge to challenge conventions are explored in Peter Medway's case study of six
architecture students' sketchbooks and his finding that students can
successfully negotiate a genre without being confined to following
shared knowledge and conventions. He found, based on individual
and changeable exigencies, that there was much variation in the sketchbooks that students wrote; therefore, if the sketchbook is defined as a
genre, it is a very loose and "fuzzy" genre, with multiple functions of
recording and preserving ideas, analyzing and developing arguments,
and preparing actions. Based on his analysis, Medway finds that "each
sketchbook is a unique composition individually improvised, sometimes from specific strategies known from particular genres, but also
from rhythms and tonalities that have been 'caught' from a range of
genres that are more generally and diffusely 'out there' in the culture"
(149). What made the sketchbooks successful was some combination
of students following genre conventions while also improvising and
challenging conventions.

This negotiation between genre choice and constraint and between
individual agency and social convention is the subject of study by Bill
Green and Alison Lee entitled "Writing Geography: Literacy, Identity,
and Schooling." This study focused on two cases that are part of a larger corpus of data and research collected for a project examining gender
politics of school writing, a curriculum informed by the Australian
systemic functional genre application of explicit teaching of genre. In
studying the essays of two students, "Kathryn" and "Robert," research-

ers noted that Robert's text fits more the conventional genre form, whereas Kathryn's departs from those conventions. Compared to Robert's factual discourse with highly technical language, Kathryn's language is more qualified, her subject position more pronounced, and her discourse less focused on the presentation of facts than on the call for action. Noting that Robert's text is "situated within a dominant techno-scientific mode of representation of the world, a mode of representation extensively critiqued by feminists as hegemonically masculinist," the researchers found that the texts they studied "enact[ed] a significant gender difference" (214). They concluded that "genre is a category inescapable from the politics and problematics of gender, among other forms of social difference and power" (208). These forms of social difference and power that shape and are shaped by genre are the subject of the studies in the following section, which explore the negotiation of cultural identities and genre expectations and examine how the transfer from genre knowledge to performance is culturally mediated.

INTERCULTURAL RESEARCH ON GENRE
WITHIN ACADEMIC SETTINGS

In their introduction to *Genres in a Changing World,* a volume featuring studies from the 4th International Symposium on the Study of Textual Genres (SIGET), Charles Bazerman, Adair Bonini, and Débora Figueiredo note that genre "has been researched in the social histories of many countries and has been creatively applied in many different educational settings internationally" (ix). Several presentations from SIGET, which was held in Tubarão, Brazil, focused on the genre-based approach to the Brazilian system of education, and many of these studies were later featured in a special issue of the journal *L1: Educational Studies in Language and Literature.* In one of those studies, Vera Lúcia Lopes Cristovão reported on her study of 4th and 5th graders who received genre instruction as they wrote in multiple genres—memories, opinions, and poems. She analyzed 230 memory texts (on the topic "The Place Where I Live"), randomly selected from 6500 texts total, and also observed students as they were led through a "didactic sequence" that first defines the features of the genre, then provides examples of genres, then asks students to read, analyze and finally produce the genre. She found that this approach to genre, based in critical analysis and production, can empower students, "providing contact with their cultural anchorage and respect to their sociocultural settings" (23).

Another study appearing in the special issue of *L1* found that, regardless of social environment, genre instruction can be effective. Ana Maria de Mattos Guimarães conducted a study of two fifth grade classes in Brazil, one a public school for low-income students, and the other a private school with students from a higher socio-economic class. Both schools implemented a "didactic sequence," which begins with early production of the genre based on the prior knowledge of students. The didactic sequence then consists of reading and analyzing the genre, identifying the characteristic traits, defining the communicative situation, and finally producing the genre. After analyzing student texts and interviewing students at both schools, the researcher found improved final texts following genre instruction and analysis, particularly improvement in student writers' abilities to mobilize thematic content and to organize material. Guimarães concluded that her study "reveals the importance of consistent work on genre teaching in schools" (31) and demonstrates that the method was effective, regardless of students' social environment.

However, other studies have found the socio-economic class level can, in fact, play a significant role in the development of genre knowledge. Alina Spinello and Chris Pratt conducted research on the genre knowledge of two groups of Brazilian elementary school children— one group of middle-class and one group of working class students who had lived on the street at least one year. All participants were interviewed and were asked to produce the genres of narrative, letter, and newspaper article. They then read a text and were asked to identify genre and justify their response. Several weeks later the researchers met with some of the children for informal discussion with them about their exposure to stories, letters, and newspaper articles at home, school and on the streets. Middle-class children were able to identify and produce genres (particularly stories and letters) more successfully than working class students. They also were aware of the linguistic conventions and formal structures of stories and letters and displayed more of a "meta-textual awareness" or genre knowledge. However, street children were less familiar with "school" genres and more familiar with newspaper articles, leading the researchers to conclude that

different "literacy environments" in which children from different sociocultural groups interact account for differences in genre knowledge.

Shifting from groups of Brazilian children to British children,
Debra Myhill also investigated the influence of sociocultural background on genre acquisition, arguing that middle-class children are
better positioned for acculturation to academic genres. Myhill was
interested in how students' prior genre knowledge—defined as sociocultural conventions for organization, meaning, and formal features—affects their ability to produce school genres. From a large
corpus of essays written in response to national tests and representing
varied age levels and sociocultural groups, the texts were quantitatively
and qualitatively analyzed. Backing up studies like Freedman's and
Devitt's, Myhill found that young writers draw on their prior knowledge of the narrative genre, based on broad cultural experiences of narrative. However, they struggled more with genres for which they had
no prior sociocultural knowledge (much like the children in the above
study by Spinello and Pratt). Students' sociocultural prior knowledge
of genre enabled them to produce genres with a fuller understanding
of how form and content, text and context, interrelate—an understanding of genres as dynamic cultural forms. Myhill concludes, "It is
necessary that we help teachers develop strategies to assist all children
in learning how to balance the expectations of the school context with
their own social and cultural experiences of written genres" (136).

Further exploring the issue of class and genre performance is a
study done by Rochelle Kapp and Bongi Bangeni. Arguing for both
explicit and implicit approaches to teaching genre, Kapp and Bangeni
conducted a case study of 20 first-year students in the humanities at
the University of Cape Town, South Africa. These were mainly black,
working-class students and were nearly all first-generation college students; in addition, most studied through the medium of English (their
second language). They argue that "While a genre approach is a key
resource for providing metaknowledge of discourse conventions, it
does not provide the . . . writing space to enable students from outside the dominant discourse to become critical participants" (110-11).
The researchers focused on how teaching the genre of the social sciences essay can help students navigate their entry into the discipline.
They were interested in a genre approach in which explicit teaching
coincides with "acquisition"—a more unconscious process (113) and
in which students learn formal features alongside the form of the aca-

demic conversation. Through conscious learning of genre and immersion in reading and writing genres of the culture, students "were able to articulate and demonstrate metalevel understanding of the genre of the social science essay" (125). Findings included the claim that while students can learn from explicit teaching of forms, acquiring genre knowledge and discourse knowledge takes time (126).

While the previous study makes a claim for both explicit and implicit approaches, Sunny Hyon makes a case for explicit teaching, particularly for students from different cultural and linguistic backgrounds. Hyon studied the role of genre in a course taken by 11 students—8 graduate and 3 undergraduate—representing a range of cultural and linguistic backgrounds (five from East Asia, three from the Middle East, one from Latin America, one from Puerto Rico, and one from Africa). The students were enrolled in an ESL Reading course that focused on four genres—a hard news story, a feature article, a textbook, and a research article—that were discussed in terms of content, structure, language style, and purpose. Hyon's method of instruction included "explicit discussion, modeling, and analyses of genres" ("Genre and ESL Reading" 126). While conceding Freedman's point that students might have eventually developed genre awareness tacitly on their own, she found that "ESL university students may be among the 'some' for whom explicit genre-based teaching is helpful, as they have often not had as much tacit exposure to English-language genres as their L1 counterparts" (136).

Research on Genres and Advanced Academic Literacies

The studies described above primarily focus on children's literacies and the literacies of first-year college students; however, other studies of second-language learners have focused on genre as a component of advanced academic literacy. Solange Aranha, drawing on methods from Swales' approach to genre analysis, studied a genre-based writing course for graduate students in two fields, Genetics and Dentistry, at São Paulo State University in Brazil. Through participant-observation of classes and discourse analysis of student texts, she found that "the act of recognizing (reading) is different from the act of producing (writing) academic genres" (487). She concludes by distinguishing between the writers' genre awareness and their "reflexive awareness" or sense of ownership of and investment in the genre.

Interested in the cultural factors influencing genre awareness and expertise, Ann Beer conducted a study entitled, "Diplomats in the Basement: Graduate Engineering Students and Intercultural Communication," using the framework of intercultural communication to explore the complexity and the challenge of negotiating different genres (63). She studied international graduate students in Engineering in a Canadian University and examined how their diverse languages, differences in levels of English proficiency and cultural backgrounds affected their ability to "reposition" with regard to cultural genre differences. Based on her examination of documents, observations of and interviews with the graduate students, Beer found that "success for these graduate students depends to a large extent on their language and genre competence in the new culture" (73).

Examining the development of genre competence in a new culture, Christine Tardy carried out a two-year case study of two graduate students and their writing in the disciplines ("It's Like a Story"). Tardy conducted interviews with and collected writing from two students: Paul, a computer science major and native of the People's Republic of China, and Chatri, an engineering student and native of Thailand. Focusing on Paul's master's thesis and Chatri's research papers, Tardy found that, as these writers engaged in high-stakes writing tasks, their rhetorical and genre knowledge became more explicit and more sophisticated. In part, this knowledge was influenced by disciplinary participation, including mentoring and feedback from expert members of the community. Tardy expands on this research in her recent book *Building Genre Knowledge*, a longitudinal study of four multi-lingual graduate students in engineering and computer sciences. Through multiple methods of class observation (including a genre-based graduate-level class), analysis of written texts, interviews with the graduate students, and feedback from their professors, Tardy tracks the development of students' genre knowledge and their increasing competence in performing genres of their disciplines as evidenced through formal, content, process, and rhetorical dimensions of genre knowledge.

Research studies in ESL and ESP make cultural background a significant variable in their research, necessitating more "cross-talk" between researchers across educational levels and across subdisciplines (such as Composition and Rhetoric and Linguistics or ESL). In "Crossing the Boundaries of Genre Studies: Commentaries by Experts," a step was taken in this direction recently as Ann Johns invited

the authors of this book to join with experts from a number of traditions—Systemic Functional Linguistics, English for Special Purposes, and the New Rhetoric—to discuss genre theory and research as it
crosses L1 and L2 writing. Drawing on her research (described above)
of ESL graduate students, Christine Tardy described the multi-dimensional features of genre that interest all of us as teachers and researchers, including domains of formal knowledge, rhetorical knowledge,
subject-matter knowledge, and procedural knowledge. Drawing on
Ann Johns' work on ethnography, Brian Paltridge examined the use
of ethnographies in L2 graduate courses and teacher education programs, while Reiff examined approaches to ethnography in FYC (see
also Reiff, "Mediating Materiality and Discursivity"). Ken Hyland reported on his linguistic research on the writer's stance, drawing on his
research of 240 research papers from eight different disciplines, while
Bawarshi reported on the intersection of rhetorical genre analysis and
the writer's invention process. Richard Coe and Ann Johns concluded
the article by synthesizing the various perspectives, with Johns noting
that, while all of the contributors emphasize different aspects of genre
(text or context), speak in different disciplinary vernaculars, and draw
from different traditions (linguistics, rhetoric, English, education),
"there is also considerable overlap in the commentaries, indicating
continued efforts to encompass in theory and practice the complexities of texts, contexts, writers and their purposes, and all that is beyond a text that influences writers and audiences" (247). Given this
overlap in interests and research efforts, further dialogue among genre
researchers "in linguistic and non-linguistic camps" (Johns et al. 234)
and from a variety of scholarly traditions, as modeled by recent genre
scholarship in Brazil, is needed. With this cross-dialogue in mind, the
next chapter focuses on research carried out by genre scholars with
interests in technical and professional communication, fostering an
important dialogue among researchers interested in the interaction of
genres in multiple social contexts, whether academic or workplace, disciplinary or professional.

8 Genre Research in Workplace and Professional Contexts

In addition to the growing body of empirical research on genre in academic contexts is a wide range of research studies that investigate professional and workplace genres. Parallel to the interest (described in the previous chapter) in how novice writers gain access to academic discourse and learn new genres, a rich body of research examines how novices learn new genres in the workplace and use those genres to carry out the social goals of the organization. Catherine Schryer notes, "Although some composition researchers have brought genre theory into university classrooms, it has been empirical researchers in professional communication who have most profited from and most developed [Carolyn] Miller's linking of genres to social contexts" ("Genre and Power" 77). Like those who conduct research on academic genres, those who study workplace genres are interested in writers' processes of learning genres and initiation into the community, their use of genres in the production and transmission of knowledge, and the ways in which genre constrains or enables the social actions of participants in professional organizations.

Moving the debate defined by Freedman regarding tacit learning or explicit instruction of academic genres to new contexts, workplace researchers are similarly interested in what aspects of genre can be taught explicitly and which learned through "immersion" or participation in a workplace community. Further deepening this connection between learning of academic genres and learning of workplace genres, a number of recent studies seek to explore how genre knowledge transfers from university to workplace settings. In *Worlds Apart: Acting and Writing in Academic and Workplace Contexts,* Patrick Dias, Aviva Freedman, Peter Medway and Anthony Paré carry out a multisite, comparative, longitudinal (seven-year) study of writing in different university courses and corresponding workplaces: law and public administration courses and government institutions; management courses and financial institutions; social work courses and social work agencies; and architecture courses and architecture firms. Rhetorical Genre Studies informs the research project, serving as "the main conceptual frame for inquiry" (23). After selecting four matching university and professional settings, researchers conduct an inventory of genres in each domain, track documents, conduct reading protocols, carry out ethnographic observation and interviews, and ask for participant validation of results. While the study reinforces the idea that learning to write in the community's genres is a means by which individuals are socialized into particular goals, activities, identities, and ideologies, the researchers also found that work and school comprised very different genre systems (223), with more flexibility for innovation in workplace genres (230). For instance, school texts and workplace texts differed in terms of reading practices, with workplace texts having multiple readers (rather than the teacher as reader) and fulfilling a different purpose or function for readers, outside of the "epistemic motive and need to rank" (224). Workplace genres also have more "intertextual density" and are situated in "a complex multi-symbolic communicative web," with functions that differ from academic genres, such as recording information or performing an action (224-25).

This conclusion that academic and workplace settings are "worlds apart" is backed up by the findings of research reports collected in a book by Patrick Dias and Anthony Paré entitled *Transitions: Writing in Academic and Workplace Settings,* a book that "grows out of a long-term study of writing in certain academic disciplines and their related workplace settings" (1). In a chapter from the book entitled "Write Where You Are: Situating Learning to Write in the University and Workplace Settings," Aviva Freedman and Christine Adam seek to differentiate processes of novices learning to write in the workplace from processes of students learning new genres in university courses. They studied seven MA students involved in full-time internships organized by a Canadian University's school of public administration, in which the students spent a semester working in paid, full-time public sector jobs. They compared these to a second set of subjects—3 students in an upper-level undergraduate course in financial analysis. Through visits to the respective classroom and workplace sites, observations, interviews, and collection of texts, they found that the goals of academic and workplace writing differed significantly. Whereas learning was the goal of academic writing, action and policy setting were the goals of workplace writing. Freedman and Adam concluded, "When students leave the university to enter the workplace, they not only need to learn new genres of discourse, they need to learn new ways to learn such genres" (56) since the complex and dynamic rhetorical setting of the workplace cannot be replicated in the classroom.

Freedman's and Adam's conclusion is reinforced by Jane Ledwell-Brown's study of genre users within the Heath Care Company, a Canadian arm of a large, multinational pharmaceuticals company. Brown studied 22 managers, directors, and employees, drawing on interview data, review of documents, and recorded observations. She found that organizational values—such as teamwork, commitment to quality services, and salesmanship—shape writer's expectations and rhetorical strategies but that these values often run counter to the values cultivated during the employees' university education. Ledwell-Brown notes that the genre expectations of the workplace—presenting cases in ways that will get desired results—are "a far cry from the demands placed on writers in school, where writing is hardly expected to change anything, desired outcomes other than grades are not in the balance, and the single reader does not expect to be informed or changed by the writing" (220). These differences in values for newcomers leads Ledwell-Brown to argue for more guidance from supervisors and a focus on both implicit and explicit methods of socializing novices into the workplace, a topic of research explored further in the next section.

RESEARCH INTO GENRE LEARNING IN THE WORKPLACE

The focus in academic genre research on the tacit acquisition of genre knowledge carries over to research on workplace genres, through various studies of how novices learn the genres of their profession. In her chapter, "Learning New Genres: The Convergence of Knowledge and Action" (*Writing in the Real World*), Anne Beaufort tests Freedman's hypothesis of acquisition versus explicit teaching. Drawing on her ethnographic study of four writers at a Job Resource Center, a non-profit organization, Beaufort analyzes the genre of the press release, letter of request, and grant proposal. Examining how adult writers at advanced levels of literacy acquire competence in new genres, Beaufort posits that "understanding the social action the genre represents within the discourse community is . . . crucial" (111). Among her findings

were the claims that content and procedural knowledge worked together, that depth of genre knowledge grew over time, and that genre
knowledge was based on participation in the community. Comparing
Freedman's findings in an academic context to those in a workplace
context, Beaufort found that genre knowledge is largely tacit, although
she acknowledges that in order to learn a new genre, both immersion
and "coaching" are needed.

Continuing this focus on explicit teaching versus tacit acquisition in
a workplace context, Lingard and Haber carried out a study that seeks
to explore how the medical apprenticeship complicates explicit/tacit
debates in genre instruction. Their data was drawn from a 160-hour
observational study at an urban teaching hospital in California, where
they observed and conducted discourse-based interviews with 12 medical students. They found that while the apprenticeship experiences of
the medical students appeared to offer contextualized, authentic genre
instruction, in reality—as students participated in medical teams and
interacted with residents and attending physicians—the explicit genre
instructions were often given without clarification of rhetorical or contextual origins, intentions, or situational significance. For example,
one medical student, John, was told by a resident to make his patient
presentation of symptoms more concise, but when later communicating with the attending physician, the physician demanded more detail.
There were specific reasons for this difference (the attending physician was not "on call" as frequently and was thus unfamiliar with the
patient background), but they were not articulated. In addition, as a
counterpart to the study by Giltrow and Valiquette cited in the previous chapter on academic genre research, this study found that experts
in the organization, like instructors, do not always communicate the
wealth of tacit, experiential knowledge they have. As a result, "students
may interpret a-contextually the cryptic feedback that they receive on
rounds" (167). What Lingard and Haber ultimately call for is "meta-
awareness," similar to what Devitt has described as "genre awareness"
—teaching genres in the context of situated practice and explicitly articulating the interrelation of rhetorical strategies and social actions.

It is just such genre awareness or meta-awareness of genre that Graham Smart and Nicole Brown sought to develop in their participatory
action research of 25 interns in a professional writing program. The
interns were placed in a variety of organizations—high-tech companies, media and PR firms, and non-profit organizations—and they

spent 10-20 hours per week in the organization for 15 weeks, practicing multiple genres. As part of the action research, students were assigned to investigate how writing functions in the organization and to
reflect on their own experience, drawing on research questions that
connect textual features of the genre to ideologies of the worksite, an
approach based in "genre awareness": "the notion of genre had provided the student interns with a powerful theoretical tool for seeing
how written discourse is situated within local organizational contexts
and for understanding how writing functions to accomplish different
kinds of work" (251). Smart's and Brown's context-sensitive qualitative approach to research into genre learning was paired with their
collaborative action-based research to assist students in "developing a
rhetorical vision both useful across different workplace cultures and
significant to the formation of the interns' professional identities"
(Artemeva and Freedman 5). Student interns learned how to use their
genre knowledge to navigate new workplace sites and for understanding how genres function to accomplish different kinds of work within these sites—"how the activity of planning, producing, and using
documents enables co-workers to discuss issues, negotiate positions,
make decisions and develop relationships" (267). Unlike the results of
the previous study by Lingard and Haber that point out the mismatch
in novices' and experts' genre expectations, this study posits genre as
a tool for aligning the attention and levels of expertise of co-workers,
thus coordinating their efforts and actions. Acquiring competence in
a genre, then, is necessary for producing, organizing, and disseminating knowledge, the focus of the research studies described in the next
section.

RESEARCH ON WORKPLACE GENRES: CONSTRUCTING, DISTRIBUTING, AND NEGOTIATING KNOWLEDGE

While the previous section examined research that focuses on how
writers new to a workplace learn the genres of their professional organization, this section examines research studies of how genres are
used to create, disseminate, and negotiate knowledge. Anthony Paré,
in "Discourse Regulations and the Production of Knowledge," examines how genres shape expectations and how genre constraints influence the production of knowledge. Paré carried out a qualitative study
of writing done by social workers, with a focus on the genre of the

predisposition report (PDR), which is written by a social worker as an advisory report on the sentencing of an adolescent. The PDR is a genre that includes narrative versions of the incident from police, the adolescent, the parents, and the victim—all of whom are interviewed by the social worker; a section detailing prior convictions; assessment of the adolescent and family; and a summary and recommendation for sentencing. After interviewing eight social workers and collecting protocols from four of the subjects as they wrote PDRs, along with discourse-based interviews, Paré discovered that the genre of the PDR both reflected and reinforced the knowledge, beliefs (that adolescents fit a particular profile), and expectations (of delinquency) of the social work community. The very nature of the document "predisposed" social workers to connect the narrative of the adolescent's offense with prior convictions in order to make a recommendation for sentencing. In the case of a social worker, Sophie, before even meeting the adolescent, the PDR worked to shape her view of the adolescent male as "a bad boy" (117), and despite the adolescent's lack of a prior history, she felt constrained to produce a report portraying the community's expectations of a progression of delinquency.

Similar to the PDR's role in shaping expectations, Berkenkotter and Ravotas study how a genre of classification—the APA's *Diagnostic and Statistical Manual of Mental Disorders* (DSM-IV)—shapes interpretation and diagnosis. These researchers studied both the local situated writing of clinicians and the circulation of therapists' reports through the mental health system, carrying out linguistic and rhetorical analysis of five therapists' written evaluations and conducting follow-up interviews and participant-observer research. They discovered that the client's descriptive narrative is "recontextualized" into the acceptable genre of the diagnosis and codified classifications of the DSM-IV. Similar to the shaping power of the PDR described in the previous study, the DSM-IV shapes interpretation by classifying patients into categories based on population and activity (i.e. "borderline personalities" or "survivors of sexual abuse"). When a client tells the therapist "I just seem to be falling apart lately," this gets recontextualized in DSM-IV categories as "A predominantly dysphoric mood" (268). The client's narrative and local knowledge are factored out as the condition is taken up and resituated into a universal classification system based on the field-specific knowledge of medical psychiatry.

Related studies have examined the genre of the psychiatric interview, such as a Brazilian qualitative study of a patient diagnosed with bipolar disorder. Through observation of the filmed doctor/patient interaction as well as interviews with the doctor and his team, researcher Tânia Conceição Pereira described four forms of interaction that define the kind of information elicited and activity carried out in the genre of the psychiatric interview: 1) the opening frame, which establishes information about the patient; 2) the exploratory frame, which draws the patient into more of a conversation with the doctor; 3) the co-constructive experience frame, in which the patient takes on the role of speaker while the doctor listens; and finally, 4) the closing frame, in which the doctor reflects on the patient's present condition and treatment (40). Each of these frames of interaction is structured by the genre and, in turn, structures the roles of the participants.

The role genre plays in the formation and shaping of communal knowledge is also the subject of inquiry in a participant-observation study done by Aviva Freedman and Graham Smart. Freedman and Smart studied the genres produced at Bank of Canada, a federal agency that conducts monetary policy, and spent six years observing the site, interviewing BOC employees, collecting texts representing typical genres, and collecting reading protocols from managers. The researchers found that the written genres (annual report, monetary policy report, white book, inter-projection information package, notes and briefings) are linked to organizational interactions or interactive genres, such as meetings. Thus, the interwoven genres coordinated much of the work and reflected the complexity of policy making: "The BOC thinks and distributes its cognition through sets of genres" (247). For instance, the staff prepared the "White Book" every quarter in order to recommend an interest rate profile for the next eight quarters and offered a number of alternative scenarios and Risk Analyses, reflecting the negotiation between management and staff projections. Genres, then, are sites for reflecting on information and negotiating knowledge and "function consequently as repositories of communal knowledge, devices for generating new knowledge" (244).

HISTORICAL STUDIES OF PROFESSIONAL GENRES

If, as noted above, genres are "repositories of communal knowledge," then studying an organization's corpus of genres can give us insight into that community's practices and knowledge production, as well as insight into how genres emerge in a community, how genres are used by participants, and how genres evolve and change within organizations. Historical investigations of professional genres—including genres of the "academic workplace," such as research articles—have illustrated how such genres evolve in relation to changes in social context and cultural ideology. In his extensive study of the historical development of the experimental report, reported on in *Shaping Written Knowledge: The Genre and Activity of the Experimental Article in Science,* Charles Bazerman collected a corpus of 1000 articles from the first scientific journal in English, *Philosophical Transactions.* Analyzing one hundred articles from this corpus, in addition to 40 articles from *Physical Review* and scientific writings by Newton and Compton, he explored how changes in the generic features and structure of scientific articles are tied to changes in the social structures of the discipline, shifts in the theoretical composition of arguments, and changes in material practices within the sciences.

Further tracking the historical evolution of the scientific article from its debut in the 17th century to the present, Alan Gross, Joseph Harmon, and Michael Reidy mapped the changes in the generic features as they occurred across three languages: English, French, and German. Examining scientific articles from a cross section of journals and in the context of national and disciplinary differences, they concluded the following: "The scientific article is a developing vehicle for communicating the conceptual system of science and, in the case of argument, a developing means for creating that system" (15). This historical study of the genre of the scientific article, following Bazerman's study, further demonstrates how genres emerge from and in turn influence the shared goals, assumptions, and practices within the profession.

Historical research on the academic article has taken place not just in the sciences but also in the field of economics. Donald McCloskey, in his study of economics journals from 1920 to 1990, found a rise in the scientific ethos of authors, with early articles in the 20's taking a philosophical perspective and later articles taking a more mathematical perspective, reflecting a push toward more "testable hypotheses" (141). Additional historical studies of economics and genre appear in a collection of essays entitled *Economics and Language* (Henderson, Dudley-Evans and Backhouse; see also McCloskey, *If You're So Smart;*

The Rhetoric of Economics), including Bazerman's study of 18th century economist Adam Smith's major works, essays, and lectures ("Money Talks"). While the corpus of Smith's work reflects a skeptical view of economics in his early work, his later work is didactic, reflecting a shared social purpose and common goals for economic action. Similar to his findings from his historical study of the scientific article, Bazerman discovered that economic genres function as "a socio-psychological category," with "the opportunity to create shared communal beliefs by asserting a scheme that speaks to the shared experiences and conditions of the audience community" ("Money Talks" 181).

This negotiation between social systems and experiences of audiences is further explored in John Swales' historical study of six economics textbooks spanning two decades. While the stylistic and rhetorical features of economics textbooks have been examined in earlier studies (McCloskey, *The Rhetoric of Economics*; Henderson and Hewings), Swales focused his analysis on textbook treatments of a sub-topic in mainstream economics texts, the "paradox of value" or the discussion of the economic principle of use value versus exchange value ("The Paradox of Value" 226). He discovered that the textbooks present a vision of progress with regard to economic theory and that "this historicist approach adds a further kind of authority to the introductory textbook genre": that economics is a "subject which has succeeded—over time—in providing technical solutions to economic puzzles and perplexities" (236).

Historical studies of legal genres have similarly examined the ways in which genres shape participants' experiences within professional contexts, in this case the social-legal system. In "The Sociohistorical Constitution of the Genre Legal booklet," Leonardo Mozdzenski traced the historical antecedents of the legal booklet as they existed in religious and school primers, illuminist political pamphlets, and early legal/educational booklets. He found that "legal booklets not only support but strengthen the primary objectives of law, defining patterns of social behavior, and therefore guaranteeing the sustenance of the structured and well-established social-legal system" (100).

But perhaps the historical study that has had the most impact on professional genre studies is JoAnne Yates' *Control through Communication,* which—via comparative case studies—examined in detail the history of three businesses (railroads and manufacturing firms) and the role of communication in business changes. Focusing on printed

and archival documents from 1880-1920, Yates examined the developing genres of internal communication and the shared characteristics of
form and function of documents like reports and memos. Observing
that "the genres of internal communication that emerged during the
late 19th and early 20th century evolved in response to new demands
put on them by growth and by changing management philosophy"
(100), Yates established the interrelationship between communicative
genres and managerial functions. As business philosophies and functions changed, new genres—such as letters, manuals, forms, in-house
magazines, and meetings—emerged in order to meet the changing
needs and roles of participants in the organization. Yates' research
on how new genres develop in response to new situation contexts has
made important contributions to the study of professional genres and
to research on the relationship among genres within communities or
organizational systems, the subject of the next section.

RESEARCH STUDIES OF GENRE SYSTEMS IN THE WORKPLACE

Researchers have examined the role of genre systems in the workplace
and are interested in how groups of connected genres or a range of
interrelated genres comprise the complex communicative interactions of organizations, from insurance companies, to banks, to social
work agencies, to engineering firms. In "Systems of Genre and the
Enactment of Social Intentions," Bazerman carried out a study of patents and the multiple participants (inventors, patent office) and corresponding legal documents to illustrate the complex nexus of system,
genre, and intention. Through his study, he presented "a system of a
complex societal machine in which genres form important levers" (79)
and identified systems of genres as "interrelated genres that interact
with each other in specific settings" (97).

Further providing a glimpse into a "genre system" or "set of genres
interacting to accomplish the work" of an organization ("Intertextuality in Tax Accounting" 340), Amy Devitt conducted research on a tax
accounting community's genres. Devitt interviewed accountants and
asked them to identify genres. Thirteen genres constituting what Devitt calls a "genre set" (a particular set of genres used by members to
accomplish particular tasks within a system of genres—see Chapter 6
for more discussion of genres sets, genre systems, and activity systems)
were identified, reflecting the professional activities and social rela-

tions of tax accountants. The interconnected genres defined organizational roles and reflected and reinforced expectations:

> Since a tax provision review has always been attached
> to an audit, for example, a review of the company's
> tax provisions is expected as part of the auditing ac-
> tivity; since a transmittal letter has always accompa-
> nied tax returns and literature, sending a return may
> require the establishment of some personal contact,
> whether or not any personal relationship exists. ("In-
> tertextuality in Tax Accounting" 341)

Furthering this research on how genre systems structure interaction, Carol Berkenkotter began her study, "Genre Systems at Work," by noting "a burgeoning interest in the intertextual and interdiscursive character" of professional genres (327). She examined the various genres produced in a rural mental health clinic and the ways in which these interconnected genres coordinated the complex activity in this setting and across professional and institutional settings. As a genre system, the various reports by mental health aides on their interactions with clients living in group homes were written up—whether reports on a social or medical visit—and circulated from writer to supervisor to psychiatrist: "The various paperwork genres produced in a medical or mental health clinic coordinate the many different kinds of activity occurring within that setting" (333). One type of activity, therapist notes, also reflected a system of genres consisting of an oral session, written evaluation, initial assessment, treatment plan, progress reports, and termination summary. Drawing on the previous study of the DSM-IV (which recontextualizes patient conditions in terms of scientific classifications), Berkenkotter expanded the study to explore how the DSM-IV functions to link the social worlds of therapist-practitioner, psychiatrist, physician, social worker, insurance company auditor, and lawyer with that of client (338). She argues that the concept of genre system is a useful tool for researching the complex, historically mediated text/context relationships.

Like Berkenkotter, Dorothy Winsor draws on the framework of genre system, applying this framework to her study of engineers on the job. She reported on four case studies from a nine-year study of entry-level engineers writing at work. She was interested in the genre of "documentation," defined as "the representation of past or future action used to build agreement about how that action is to be defined or perceived" ("Genre and Activity Systems" 207). The genre of documentation coordinates work and provides ways to deal with conflict and maintain consensus. As the entry-level engineers made the transition from students to employees, they documented actions to protect themselves (CYA) and to prompt action by putting decisions and instructions in writing. One engineer, Al, became a labor relations representative for his facility, thus acting as a "mediator" between the union and management. Whether interviewing workers accused of violating work rules, responding to a filed grievance, or taking minutes during contract negotiations, Al used documentation genres to "control understanding of both these past events and future ones" in order "to maintain the overall activity system in which all of his company's employees participated" (219).

Furthering this study of how text and context are mutually constitutive, Orlikowski and Yates propose using—in the place of "genre system"— "genre repertoire" (following Bakhtin's use of the term) as an analytic tool for investigating the structuring of communicative practices. They argue that "to understand a community's communicative practices, we must examine the set of genres that are routinely enacted by members of the community. We designate such a set of genres a community's 'genre repertoire'" (542). The researchers conducted a study of computer language designers located at universities and company sites dispersed geographically through the U.S. and for whom interactions were conducted mostly through electronic correspondence. Based on their collection of transcripts and interviews with subjects, the researchers identified a genre repertoire consisting of three genres: the memo (for general communicative purposes), proposal (for recommending courses of action), and dialogue (responses to previous interactions). Examining the group's genre repertoire revealed aspects of the organizing process:

> The presence of the memo genre and the absence of the report genre . . . reveal that the CL participants implicitly organized themselves as a temporary organization. . . . The rising use of the dialogue genre over the course of the project suggests that the CL participants came to rely increasingly on ongoing conversations as an effective means for conducting their deliberations about language design. (570)

Not only did the concept of genre repertoire act as an analytical tool for "operationalizing and investigating communicative practices in communities," but it was also useful for tracking change over time and for examining differences in structure, outcomes, and performance (571). Research studies employing a social framework focused renewed attention on how genres function as sites for enculturation into communities or systems of discourse, a subject of research studies described in the section that follows.

ETHNOGRAPHIC STUDIES OF WORKPLACE GENRES

In his book *Other Floors, Other Voices,* John Swales employs a method of research that he calls "textography," which he defines as "something more than a disembodied textual or discoursal analysis, but something less than a full ethnographic account" (1). Swales considers the local, institutional context of textual production, examining the system of texts embedded in the literate culture of the university, particularly on three floors of the North University Building, which are occupied by three different disciplines (computing, taxonomic botany, and ESL). While carrying out a complex analysis of texts that is context-sensitive, the text itself remains the primary tool of analysis. Joining in Bazerman's call for "a richer, more empirical" picture of how texts are used in organizations ("Speech Acts" 322), Anthony Paré and Graham Smart , in "Observing Genres in Action: Toward a Research Methodology," propose an alternative approach rooted in the social sciences, specifically, ethnomethodology. Such an approach, they argue, would allow those researching professional organizations and workplace settings insight into not just the textual practices and process of learning genres but also the social role of participants and initiation into a workplace community or organization. They propose a definition of genre and research methods "that can help researchers explore the full range of social action that constitutes an organization's repeated rhetorical strategies or genres" (153). In addition, they define a research tool and lens for examining the process of learning genres, how genres are learned through initiation and participation in a community, and how a genre constrains or enables participation in a community.

Exploring the socialization of participants in a workplace organization, Anne Beaufort ("Learning the Trade") draws on data from a larger ethnographic study of a non-profit organization, focusing on two writers new to the organization, Pam and Ursula, who are both experienced and effective writers. Via weekly interviews with the women, collection of their writing, and observation of the work site, Beaufort discovers how genres intersect with the communal goals of the workplace and thus play a significant role in the writer's goals and in the social apprentice model. For example, as Pam and Ursula learn the hierarchy of genres, they also learn about the hierarchy of social roles—for instance, that grant proposals are produced by the Executive Director and take precedence over form letters or press releases sent by lower-level employees. Genres, then, are important keys to socialization and identity within a workplace organization.

Moving from the research site of an NPO to a financial institution, Graham Smart conducts research that further seeks to describe the role of genre in carrying out social goals, research that "suggests a reinterpretation of genre as a broad rhetorical strategy enacted, collectively, by members of a community in order to create knowledge essential to their aims" ("Genre as Community Invention" 124). He studies a community of executives and research staff at the Bank of Canada, where he carries out participant/observer research as an in-house writing trainer. Through analysis of interviews with research staff, reading protocols by executive readers, field notes and collection of written texts, Smart discovers that the family of genres used at BOC is an important community resource that generates and structures the intellectual activity of the community:

> Genres contributing to discussion of monetary policy include, for example, the note to management, which describes and interprets current economic or financial trends in Canada or other countries; the research memorandum, which presents macroeconomic work of a theoretical, of econometric nature; and the staff economic projection, which provides forward-looking analyses of the Canadian, American, and global economies. (130)

Based on his understanding of genre as "a community-enacted, knowledge building rhetorical strategy," Smart argues that generic discourse responds to contextual influences and that, in turn, the interplay of contextual influences determines common (and distinct) genre features.

Further exploring the dynamic interaction of genre and context, Geoffrey Cross analyzes two genres produced by an insurance company, an executive letter and a planning report. In his ethnographic study of the group writing of two different genres within a particular organizational culture, Cross collected data while doing a 20-hour internship at the site and followed up with discourse-based interviews and collection of texts and drafts, including observation of brainstorming and editing sessions. Cross found that "Generic and contextual differences helped create two very differing collaborative processes" (146). In the letter-writing process, conflict emerged over how best to carry out the genre's purpose of recounting the year's progress, with one account more favorable to the company's success or operating profit and the other representing the company as "struggling within a troubled industry" (146). With regard to context and genre, the report writing was smoother and goals more shared, perhaps because the more "multivocal genre"—which includes descriptions of the previous year, plans for the new year, and plans to execute—allowed the report to emphasize success while reporting the operating loss, thus resolving the conflict. Overall, Cross found that genres cannot be considered apart from the social forces that shape and are shaped by them. He concludes by arguing that "we need to conduct more real-world studies of the group writing of different genres in different contexts" (152), and this focus on the conflict and multiplicity of genres is the subject of the next section.

Research on Conflict and Change in Professional/Workplace Contexts

As genre research moved from analysis of single genres to groups of connected genres and the relationships among genres within activity systems, researchers were able to uncover the complex communicative interactions that shape social actions and professional identities and define genre sets, genre systems, and genre repertoires. Drawing on the framework of "genre repertoire" and conducting an "interpretive ethnography" that allowed him to read the group's genres to learn something about the group and its activities, Graham Smart, in "Reinventing Expertise: Experienced Writers in the Workplace Encounter a New Genre," studied how experienced writers encounter an unfamiliar genre. He observed staff economists at the Bank of

Canada as they went about producing, for the first time, an article for the *Bank of Canada Review,* an internally produced publication for external readership. Smart was interested in the contrast between writers' habitual, skilled participation in the mainstream discourse practices of the Bank of Canada and their contrary experience with an unfamiliar, rhetorically dissimilar genre (224). Comparing the *Review* articles to internal research memos, Smart discovered that writers have difficulty with the external *Review* audience and difficulty in adopting an institutional persona and communicating the Bank views to the public. He found that "making a successful transition to the genre . . . involves adjusting to a complex array of new rhetorical constraints, textual forms, and social relations" (245), a complex mediation of genre conventions and negotiation between individual choice and generic constraints.

As a counterpart to studies examining how writers negotiate new or conflicting genre expectations, some studies examine how workplace writers challenge and resist existing genres. In "A Time to Speak, a Time to Act: A Rhetorical Genre Analysis of a Novice Engineer's Calculated Risk Taking," Natasha Artemeva reports on a case study (as part of a six-year longitudinal study of 10 engineers over the course of their academic and professional careers) of a novice engineer, Sami, who learns to successfully challenge a workplace genre. The study focused on two research questions: "1) What are the ingredients of rhetorical genre knowledge that allow a novice to be successful in challenging and changing rhetorical practices of the workplace? 2) Where and how does a novice accumulate rhetorical knowledge of professional genres?" (192). Disappointed by what he sees as "Time, money and other resources constantly being wasted due to bad or lack of documentation," Sami drew on a proposal for a new implementation plan and presented it to management, who accepted his proposal. Based on his previous personal experiences (a family of engineers), educational experiences (in particular, an engineering communication course he had taken), along with his workplace experiences, Sami was able to use his engineering genre knowledge to adapt to the exigencies of a particular situation (217). Even as a novice engineer and new employee, he understood the flexibility of genres, which "underlies the importance of the rhetor's understanding of the improvisational qualities of genre" (225).

Following genre studies like those above that explored the dynamic interaction of text and social structure and text and culture, recent genre studies have also examined how genres reflect and reinforce ideologies. In her study entitled "Ordering Work: Blue-collar Literacy and the Political Nature of Genre," Winsor explores the political aspect of genre as a form of social action, arguing that previous research has neglected this aspect (155). She observed the work of three engineers and three technicians at AgriCorp, a large manufacturer of agricultural equipment. Winsor was interested in exploring the tension between lab technicians and engineers and, as a result, chose to analyze the genre of the work order, which negotiates between these two groups and "is used to both bridge and maintain an existing social structure" at AgriCorp (158). Work orders are generic textual tools that contain instructions for conducting tests of replacing parts (engineers set the tasks for technicians). Through 36 hours of observation of engineers as they wrote work orders and technicians as they carried out work orders, in addition to interviews with engineers and analysis of work orders, Winsor found that work orders both triggered and concealed the work of technicians and worked to maintain the corporate hierarchy. A hierarchical divide existed as engineers envisioned technicians as little more than tools that they activated through the work order, instead of seeing them as agents and participants in the social action. In this way, "genre is a profoundly political force" (183).

The political force and very real material consequences of genre are clearly evident in a study of the closing argument in the Brazilian legal system. Cristiane Fuzer and Nina Célia Barros conducted a linguistic analysis of how "the public prosecutor and the defense attorney in the genre of final arguments create different characterizations of actors to enlist the court in various representations of truth" (80). They note, for example, how the defense closing argument is constructed as if created by the defendant in order to humanize the bureaucratic process. Because the basic function of the closing argument is to request the defendant's conviction or acquittal or to sentence the defendant, this genre plays a powerful role, with significant material consequences.

The powerful role that genre plays in professional settings is the subject of studies done by Anthony Paré that examine the complexities of power in the rhetorical activity of social work. Through his interviews with social workers and apprentices and analysis of social work genres (referral forms, initial assessments, progress reports, transfer reports), Paré ("Writing as a Way into Social Work") found that "Within the genre system of the hospital, social work texts are important insofar as they provide knowledge to the hospital's more prestigious communities of practice. Social work newcomers learn to collaborate in community knowledge-making activities, or genre sets, that are shaped by levels of power and status within the larger genre system" (160). In a later, related study more focused on a particular social work culture and genre (record keeping), Paré ("Genre and Identity") reported on his study of Inuit social workers, all women, from arctic Quebec, who were responsible for record keeping. What he found is that, due to their location between Inuit and Canadian cultures (63), there was a reluctance to keep detailed records to give to white authorities and a resulting tension between the workers' lived experience of daily life and their professional role. In this way, the genres of records demanded an erasure of self and transformation into professional identity.

Further exploring the genre of records and the relationship between genre and power, Catherine Schryer designed a study of records within a veterinary medical context. In "The Lab vs. the Clinic: Sites of Competing Genres," Schryer focused on two genres characteristic of research and practice in this context: the experimental article, expressed as IMRDS, and the medical record keeping system, the POVMR (106). According to Schryer, "These genres reflect and help to maintain a research-practice division characteristic of disciplines like medicine" (106). Schryer's ethnographic inquiry consisted of 80 interviews with students, faculty, and practitioners; 200 hours of participant-observation (in the classroom, lab, and clinic); 10 reader protocols of faculty evaluating student papers; and extensive document collection. Schryer found that IMRDS (reporting genres) and POVMR (recording genres) differed in purpose, addressivity, and epistemology. Through her participation in the community and examination of its genres, Schryer found that the new system of record keeping mirrored the way that practitioners solved complicated medical problems and coordinated social action as other staff members later added to the records. In addition, by comparing competing genres— comparing the new system of records to the former system—Schryer was able to discern varying social purposes and values implicit in these two genres, divergences that revealed tensions between researchers and practitioners in the college. These professional genres "deeply enact their ideology" (122) by expressing clear power relations. Because research on genre suggests that genres coordinate the work of groups and organizations. Schryer concludes with a call for more research on the inherent ideological and socializing forces at work within genres (122).

Responding to her own call for genre researchers to explore the interrelationship of genre and power, Schryer conducted a later study whose purpose is to "assist in the development of methodological and theoretical tools that genre researchers can use to explore the ways genres work to reproduce power relations within and between organizations and individuals" ("Genre and Power" 74). She applied this perspective to one representative genre—examples of 'bad news' letters produced by an insurance company, demonstrating how contextual approaches (participant accounts) can enrich textual approaches or close readings of texts that instantiate a genre. Schryer framed her critical methods for studying genres within two major approaches that "overlap and mutually influence each other"—rhetorical and linguistic approaches (76). Reporting on a case study of negative letters in an insurance company, which included critical discourse analysis of 26 letters and interviews with 3 writers, Schryer found that all writers followed the same structure of delaying bad news (the buffer, explanation, decision, closing structure), even though they believed readers did not follow that structure. Based on her analysis of linguistic resources and strategies, she discovered that the letters revealed "a world in which readers are kept waiting, a world in which their movements are restricted often to speech acts, a world in which they are not encouraged to respond, and a world in which they are often judged harshly" (94). She concluded, "At its heart, this genre attempts to freeze its readers in space and time and reduce them to passivity and nonresponse" (94). In conjunction with the textual analysis, the contextual information gathered through interviews with the writers revealed "a network of power relations" as writers felt constrained to enact and reproduce the set of discursive practices, even as they were uncomfortable making decisions that affect their readers' lives. Like the letter-writers, all writers are "genred all the time," that is, socialized through genres and their exposure to various genres, which are "profoundly ideological" (95), a finding that has implications for further research. Schryer calls for further examination of the genres negotiated within organizations and "in particular the ideologies they create and especially the subject positions they create and maintain" (95). The next chapter, which focuses on genre research in public and new media contexts, takes up Schryer's call to focus on genres as actions or verbs, as structures that are "strategy-produced and driven" and that "produce strategy" (95).

9 Genre Research in Public and New Media Contexts

As dynamic discursive formations used to carry out particular social activities, language practices, and interpersonal relations, genres function as sites of ideological action. As such, they are also tools for accessing, critiquing, and bringing about change within cultures and publics. While most genre studies have focused on professional and workplace genres or academic and disciplinary genres, more recent studies have turned our attention toward public genres. As with studies of workplace and academic genres, researchers who examine public genres are interested in how genre knowledge is produced and disseminated in publics, how genres are embedded in overlapping and shifting cultures, and how public genres evolve and change. In addition, as the communicative landscape changes, researchers are beginning to see the potential for studying social relations and actions as they are transformed by digital or electronic communicative forms and new media. In "Genre and Identity: Citizenship in the Age of the Internet and the Age of Global Capitalism," Charles Bazerman exhorts rhetoricians to take note of how "the changes facilitated by the internet and the social creativity released by the new medium facilitates rhetoric's responsiveness to changing politics" (34). This chapter will focus on public genres that contribute to "the protean shape of the several and evolving public spheres" as well as the "changing forms" of participation brought about by new media (34).

Research on Public Genres: Constructing and Maintaining Knowledge

A few studies to date have focused on public genres and their role in constructing and maintaining knowledge and disseminating information. Charles Bazerman has examined how tax forms demonstrate the interaction of information and genre, motivating citizens to produce appropriate information as they fill out forms. The Internal Revenue Service tax form "orients taxpayers to a land filled with requests for particular information to be reported in particular formats" (qtd. in Bazerman, Little, Chavkin 458). These forms compose a bureaucratic identity and create an informational landscape that is intergeneric and composed of past filings and current documents prepared by employers, clients, financial institutions, charitable organizations, and other financial entities. Tax forms demonstrate a salient interaction between information and genre:

> When the tax form annually arrives in the taxpayer's mailbox, the taxpayer knows that there will be consequences if he or she does not fill the blank spaces. The taxpayer must fill it, moreover, with information of the proper form and with proper pedigrees produced in related genres that are part of adjacent activity systems. (459)

These publicly genred sites enact participation as citizens produce information and seek to represent themselves and to construct a relationship with governmental agencies.

The ways that public genres create and maintain knowledge is also the focus of a study by Janet Giltrow, entitled "Genre and the Pragmatic Concept of Background Knowledge." Giltrow studies crime reports in a Canadian metro newspaper, comparing 1950 reports to 1990 reports. Drawing on discourse and genre analysis, Giltrow focuses on three features: types of events, use of reported direct and indirect speech, and forms of expression used to refer to the offender. Her findings reveal gaps in conceptual background knowledge, with 1950 reports, unlike 1990 reports, assuming background knowledge of the family as a support structure that wards off violent action while assuming no background knowledge of therapeutic responses to violence (such as mentions of counseling). Giltrow concludes that, because news report genres situate violent acts, background knowledge assumptions will change as situations change. This evidence of change "confirms the richness of genre as an archive of cultural imprints" (174).

Moving from a Canadian to a Brazilian journalistic context, Adair Bonini examines the border between two newspaper genres: news and reportage. From a corpus of 337 texts, including news and reportage from three editions of *Jornal do Brasil*, Bonini selects 84 texts to analyze. He finds that the boundaries between these journalistic genres are blurred, with overlap in rhetorical moves. The activity systems of newspapers revolve around obtaining information, but this shared activity system can result in multiple genres—genres that emerge from the data and information gathered. Drawing on the concept of genre ecologies (Spinuzzi 2003), Bonini argues that "genres exist in a complex ecology of gradual distinctions" and given cultural differences (such as the differences between Brazilian and American journalistic contexts), "we could affirm that there are different journalistic genre ecologies in the world" (222). Further confirming the richness of genres as "ecologies" or as cultural archives, the next section will focus on archival, historical research of public genres.

HISTORICAL RESEARCH ON PUBLIC GENRES

Historical research of public genres examines how genres evolve and change, reflecting cultural shifts and changes. One of the earliest genres, the letter, is the subject of study in David Barton and Nigel Hall's collection of essays, *Letter Writing as a Social Practice*. Researchers in this collection explore how letter writing is embedded in particular historical and cultural contexts and how letters have mediated, throughout history, a diverse range of human interactions. In his essay in this collection, "Letters and the Social Grounding of Differentiated Genres," Charles Bazerman examines the history of letter-writing as well as the history of genres that have emerged from letter-writing, arguing that letters have served as antecedent genres for some of the most powerful forms of text, from business genres (forms, invoices, reports) to the scientific article, to the patent, to the stockholder's report.

In addition to the letter's role in the formation of genres across various public and professional communities, letters also played more particular roles structuring human relations within specific social and institutional contexts, as chronicled by Les Perelman in "The Medieval Art of Letter Writing" (in Bazerman and Paradis). In his historical overview of letter writing in the Middle Ages, Perelman argues that the genre of the letter, particularly formal letter writing or ars dictaminis, stabilized secular transactions at a time when rapid change was taking place and ecclesiastical authority was increasing in medieval Europe.

The papal encyclical or didactic letter is one of three public genres (including state of the union addresses and congressional replies) examined by Kathleen M. Jamieson in "Antecedent Genre as Rhetorical Constraint." While Jamieson describes her method as "genre criticism," she carried out a systematic analysis of a corpus of historical texts. To illustrate the ways in which genres are culturally embedded and culturally evolve, Jamieson identified antecedent genres, such as Roman imperial documents that give rise to the papal encyclical or the King's Speech to the Parliament that gives rise to early presidential inaugural addresses in the United States. She concludes, "Without recourse to generic method, the early state of the union addresses and their replies as well as the contemporary papal encyclical would be in some important ways inexplicable" (415).

Extending this focus on public communication addressed to citizens or their representatives, Karlyn Kohrs Campbell and Kathleen M. Jamieson *(Deeds Done in Words)* carried out a study of presidential genres, including the inaugural address, state of the union, veto messages, farewell addresses and speeches on war, impeachment, and pardons. Drawing on linguistic, genre, and institutional analysis, they explored how these public genres mediate between contextual forces and individual choices and between stability and change. Noting that some genres have undergone change as institutional boundaries have been redefined, while others have remained fairly stable from the time of George Washington to the present, they reinforced the importance of a genre-based method of research: "A generic perspective applied to the major types of presidential discourse emphasizes continuity within change and treats recurrence as evidence that symbolic institutional needs are at least as powerful as the force of events in shaping the rhetoric of any historical period" (8).

The power of genre to shape events can be seen in a study of nineteenth century land deeds used to appropriate land from indigenous people in British Columbia, Canada. Focusing on deeds used in the 1850s, researcher Shurli Makmillen found that there are conflicting interpretations of the colonial treaty, with "widely divergent uptakes" by 1) European colonists who needed access to land sanctioned by colonial policies and laws and 2) aboriginal groups who needed control of their fate (99). Based on her research findings, she introduces a con-

cept of a "contact genre" whereby two or more groups participate in a
genred activity but have conflicting purposes and no shared sense of
the rhetorical situation to which the genre responds.

Continuing this focus on conflict within genred activities, Amy
Devitt ("Genre as Textual Variable") applies a generic perspective to
her quantitative study of stylistic variation and linguistic change, examining two complementary sets of data: results from a study of linguistic usage in Scots-English genres between 1520 and 1659 and of
usage in American English genres between 1640 and 1810. Exploring
the correlation between genre and language, she found that "genre
functions as a historical variable, as different genres are affected differently by language change over time" (293). Like Campbell and Jamieson, Devitt acknowledges the significant impact of a genre perspective
on methods of data collection and ultimately argues for making genre
a significant variable in linguistic research. The results of her research
raised the question of "why a text's genre should correlate so significantly with linguistic usage," which she explained by turning to the
relationship between situation and genre: "Each genre reflects its own
recurring situation, and those situations and those genres will be different in different times and different cultures" (301).

Further illustrating how public genres evolve and change, Bazerman conducted a study of the patent and examines the early antecedents of the patent in 17th and 18th century petitions to the Crown
and royal grant. His study of a corpus of texts composing the genre
of the patent illustrates the highly intertextual, intergeneric nature of
complex social systems. Bazerman describes the system the patent participates in as follows:

> The patent is a legal document that has been ap-
> proved by the patent office, under authorizing and
> regulating legislation from the US Congress in ful-
> fillment of constitutional provisions. The patent ap-
> plication is reviewed by a patent examiner who takes
> action to approve or disapprove the patent accord-
> ing to particular criteria, established by the enabling
> law and interpreted through the courts. The patent
> grants economic ownership to the invention claimed
> therein for a specified number of years (17 in the
> nineteenth century and today). Thus through legal
> means the patent realizes a policy of trading tempo-

> rary monopoly privileges for the encouragement of
> new arts and the public dissemination of these arts
> with the end of general improvement of the national
> economy. ("Systems of Genres and the Enactment of
> Social Intentions" 81)

Bazerman's study moves on to explore the historical evolution and
mutual development of the patent genre, patent intentions and the
social system of patent grant. Examining the genre's petitionary format and features, Bazerman discovered that inventor and examiner
collaborated in the creation of the patent, resulting in a "multivocal"
patent text. They also created "new value" or "a new property to be
owned—and that property was a license to attempt to make money
from a particular technology" (95). As a result, the patent is a genre
that also participates in legal systems, participating in a complex web
of interrelated genres and discourse circulation systems.

Research Studies of Genre Systems in Publics

Extending this research of knowledge production within a large social
system is A.D. Van Nostrand's study of the US government's sponsor-
ship of military research and development (R&D). Van Nostrand carried out a study of the public genres that formulate a record of how the
Department of Defense (DoD) procures Research and Development
and the labs that perform R&D. These public genres "constitute the
public record of a culture." The participants in this culture include
"customers" or agencies within DoD that fund research and "vendors"—the hundreds of university laboratories and other non-profits
that perform the research (134). As these participants interact over the
terms of a project, they may have differing objectives and conflicting priorities. However, six transactional pre-contract genres are used
to mediate between these roles, with three initiated by the customers and three initiated by the vendors. Drawing on Swales' five crite-
rial features of genre, Van Nostrand finds that all six genres share a
basic structural similarity and rhetorical mode of problem-solution.
However, while the genres carry out a shared communicative purpose
from a synchronic standpoint, diachronically, they test Swales' notion
of how the commonality of purpose links genre to discourse community: "Considered over a period of time, the discourse community is a
construct of separate audiences that form and dissolve and form again

in different alignments to serve the governing purpose of forming an R&D project" (144). In this culture, the roles of the participants illustrate rhetorical complexity, with purposes ranging from collaboration to competition. In addition, rhetorical purpose varies from one research project to another, resulting in a discourse community with shifting alliances and blurred boundaries.

The shifting and complex relationship of participants in a public genre system is also explored by Ryan Knighton in "(En)Compassing Situations: Sex Advice on the Rhetoric of Genre." Knighton carried out a case study of two syndicated sex-advice columns, one called "Ask Rhona," an internationally syndicated column appearing in the weekend edition of Vancouver's *The Province* newspaper, and the other Dan Savage's "Savage Love," an "alternative" column that appears weekly in Vancouver's *The Georgia Straight*. Based on his collection of a corpus of columns from 1997, Knighton examined the rhetorical strategies in the exchanges between solicitation and advice letters. He found that the solicitation letter encompasses the situation (defines a problem) in such a way as to constrain or enable possible responses or "uptakes." The advice letter then "re-encompasses" situation and generates different valuations and generates a course of action. While the generic encompassment preserves the community and goals of the participants, it also regenerates the genre, thus regenerating the community and mediating between "outlanders" and "inlanders."

RESEARCH ON THE MEDIATION OF
INDIVIDUAL AND PUBLIC ACTION

Following studies of public genres that play a mediating role, such as sex advice columns, a few studies have examined genres that mediate between public and personal, such as Judy Segal's study of breast cancer narratives. Studying personal narratives of breast cancer across a range of media—books, popular magazines, websites, blogs, and chat rooms—Segal argues that the personal narrative dominates public discourse on breast cancer, thus regulating the potential range of responses that might be useful to other cancer patients. This powerful genre of the personal narrative, with its standard conventions and storyline, works to "suppress or replace other genres in which breast cancer might be queried or explored" ("Breast Cancer Narratives as Public Rhetoric" 4).

Personal accounts appearing in the public media are also the subject of a study by Débora de Carvalho Figueiredo, who investigates three women's accounts of their cosmetic plastic surgery as they appear in Brazilian women's magazines. She concludes that this genre constructs hegemonic models of female identity, which is reflected by the structure of the personal accounts—all moving from the initial negative physical description of the narrators, to their decision to undergo cosmetic plastic surgery, to the final positive evaluation of results. According to Figueiredo, "certain genres of the media (such as media personal accounts) perform the social action of creating idealized identities that interpolate and imbricate individuals by and into gendered narratives" ("Narrative and Identity Formation" 261).

While the above studies share findings regarding how genres constrain action or change, other studies have demonstrated how genres can bring about changes in behavior or public policy. Bazerman explores the role of informational genres in mobilizing citizens and fostering public opposition to government policy on nuclear testing in the 1950s. He analyzes a corpus of citizen-produced texts, with a focus on three issues of a 1958 activist newsletter called *Information*, which establishes a "citizen science" for conveying information that serves the public interest ("Nuclear Information" 285). Once the citizens' information is established, the newsletter broadens its informational scope, moving from anti-nuclear testing issues to environmental issues, with the newsletter eventually evolving into the scientific journal called *Environment* and playing a significant role in the formation of the environmental movement.

Further exploring environmental genres, Bazerman, Joseph Little, and Teri Chavkin carried out a case study of the genre of the environmental impact statement (EIS), examining how the genre responds to a perceived social need for information about the effects of human activity on the environment. For instance, the 1972 Federal Insecticide, Fungicide, and Rodenticide Act "[set] in motion standard genres for the registration of pesticides, the reporting of data, regulatory judgment, and criminal prosecution, in the pattern of other regulatory agencies" (461). In addition, the National Environmental Protection Act carried out its regulatory goals via the genre of the EIS, which required the production and presentation of extensive information regarding the environmental impact of a proposed action (adverse environmental effects, alternatives to the proposed action, short-term uses of the environment versus long-term productivity, and irreversible commitments of resources). The EIS is a highly rhetorical genre that functions for multiple audiences and agencies and for which the informational landscape is shaped by the goals and needs of the agencies. Through their study of the genre system of the EIS, the researchers discovered that the EIS and related genres worked to change the social landscape of knowledge production and use: "Creating genres for the production, contemplation, and decision making of information is an essential part of the reflective monitoring of collective behavior and its impact on the world" (474).

While the previous studies carry out systematic research on public genres, further research on public genres is needed. In "Genre and Identity: Citizenship in the Age of the Internet and the Age of Global Capitalism," Bazerman sketches out a brief history of the genres of citizenship and political participation, beginning with classical genres of forensic, deliberative and epideictic rhetoric and moving to literate genres of written law and court records, polemics and manifestos, ballots and newspapers and, finally, his main interest—political websites. Bazerman's interest in publics as discursive sites points the way to possible avenues of research on public/private oppositions, the identity of citizenship, and the perceived decline in the quality of citizens' participation. Similarly, Bazerman is interested in how a public, through its genres, "speaks and inscribes itself into existence and by which individuals talk and write themselves into citizens" (34). Further research is needed on how public genres embody not just the rhetorical practices that construct and sustain but also challenge publics. Studies of public genres—genres whose social function is to bring about action/change—would enable rhetoricians to examine sites of intervention, analyzing how such genres enable participation in public processes while also limiting intervention and social action. Studying public genres might also challenge rhetorical genre studies to look beyond fairly stable, bounded, institutionalized contexts like workplaces or academics and to examine what happens when genres are much more diffused.

RESEARCH ON GENRES AND NEW MEDIA

Bazerman's interest, noted above, in electronic public genres—such as political websites—is another area of research gaining ground in

Rhetorical Genre Studies. Recent studies of genre and new media, while still very few in number, are beginning to examine how participation in genres and genre systems is not only shaped by activity systems, social groups, and organizations—whether academic, workplace, or public—but by medium, with researchers using genre as a tool to explore how communicative practices across contexts are influenced by new media. These studies seek to explore how established print genres are imported into a new medium or how genre variants or even new genres develop and emerge in electronic environments. The principle of genre re-mediation—how familiar genres are imported into new mediums—has been the subject of studies by researchers who have examined the email template as genre descendent of the memo heading or by researchers who have studied weblogs' genre antecedents in journals or written logs.

Bazerman's travel metaphor is particularly apt for describing this process of genre use in new media or new communicative domains: "When we travel to new communicative domains, we construct our perception of them beginning with the forms we know. Even our motives and desires to participate in what the new landscape appears to offer start from motives and desires framed in earlier landscapes" ("Life of Genre" 19). The "new communicative domains" of new media have changed the generic landscape, and in doing so, have brought about new research interests in how the medium that genres participate in shapes genre knowledge and genre action. For example, Jack Andersen describes new genre-based research in Library Information Sciences— studies on digital libraries—that have broadened understanding of how knowledge is organized and communicated. Noting that "genre-related research in LIS is closely linked to the growth of digital media," Anderson demonstrates how genre-oriented perspectives on digital document genres can inform research across a range of topics, from electronic document management to web structuring to information retrieval to organizational communication to e-democracy (345). A genre approach to new media sites can increase understanding of new communicative forms in the digital universe.

In "The Evolution of Internet Genres," Marcy Bauman argues that genre theory should "well equip us to understand the widespread changes now sweeping educational and institutional landscapes"— changes brought about by technology and new media literacies. Likewise, Gunther Kress, in *Literacy in the New Media Age*, has described how multimedia and multimodalities are leading to increasingly hybrid genres. Researchers are interested not only in how genres are "remediated" but in how digital contexts for communication alter access to genres, reconfigure constraints (including time constraints), and bring about new forms of collaboration—an "evolution" of genres that is of interest to those who study the functions of genres in both academic and workplace contexts.

Studies of New Media Genres in Academic Contexts

In "Academic Literacies in a Wired World: Redefining Genres for College Writing Courses," Alice Trupe argues that "the move into electronic environments rapidly began to revolutionize classroom practices and genres" (1). Her study has convincingly argued that texts produced electronically require a new set of literacy skills and challenge our teaching of single mode genres, moving us toward a model of multimodal or hybrid genres. Contributing to our understanding of multimodal genres, Chris Anson, Deanna Dannels, and Karen St. Clair conducted a study that focused, additionally, on oral and spoken contexts for communication and the effect on genre. Their "teacher-research" or classroom-based study forecasts challenges not only to teachers of writing but also students who find it difficult to participate in what they call "generic border-crossing." They argue that "students clearly need to be more fully supported in their acquisition of strategies and skills in an increasingly complex world of discourse" (190), and they conclude by calling for further research that might explore these complexities.

Responding to this call, a few recent studies have explored the integration of media genres in the classroom for teaching both oral and written genres. Marcos Baltar carried out action research on the production of radio genres in an elementary school in Brazil. For their school radio broadcast, students wrote and revised scripts and then recorded programs on school news and events and on topical issues like the environment, technology, and food and health. Through a mix of qualitative and quantitative methods—meetings, interviews, questionnaires, direct observation in the classroom—Baltar found that students' performance of radio genres does indeed develop the critical reading and production skills of oral and written genres, engages students in meaningful language activities, and strengthens students'

socio-discursive interactions with the school community. In addition
to "the systematic teaching/learning work of written and oral genres,"
school radio offers "the possibility of developing a series of skills, providing the subjects involved with a more stimulating educational dynamic" (68).

In addition to radio genres, web genres have also been the subject of pedagogically based research studies. Mike Edwards and Heidi
McKee conducted a classroom-based study of web-based writing assignments in their first-year composition courses and collected digital
copies of students' websites along with their writings about their websites. They also kept teaching journals and interviewed each other's
students about their experiences creating their websites. Both teachers
asked their students to develop a persuasive essay as a multipage Web
site incorporating links and graphics. While some student essays tended to follow a mode of argumentation much closer to print-based arguments—with a linear progression—others were more "multilinear"
and challenged the syllogistic reasoning and progression of thought
usually associated with argument. Both teachers discovered, however,
that students' success often depended on their familiarity with the variety of web genres and that this prior genre knowledge influenced
the rhetorical choices they made in their own web documents. When
students were asked during interviews if they had any types of sites in
mind as they were planning their own, they often pointed to various
commercial sites, such as couples sites or profile sites (personal web
pages) that emphasized the need to focus more on understanding and
analyzing genres. According to the researchers, "we discovered that we
had missed opportunities to engage with students in critical discussions of how Web genres get constructed, circulated, accepted, and
altered" (214) by failing to draw on the genre knowledge that students
brought with them to class. Edwards and McKee further discovered
that the web genres and web sites they were familiar with as teachers
did not always match the websites that students were reading and were
familiar with. As a result, the researchers discovered that "employing genre as an analytic tool requires that we not only recognize the
multigeneric nature of Web texts, but also develop strategies for helping students—and ourselves—identify and analyze the origins of our
frequently differing conceptions of Web genres" (214). Their research,
then, supports a genre approach in the classroom. By focusing class
time on genre analysis—cultural and rhetorical analysis of the Web

sites students frequently read—students will be better prepared to participate in these new media genres as knowledgeable, critically aware writers of digital texts.

This genre awareness was found lacking in students in a study that Mike Palmquist carried out on student web sites in writing and writing-intensive courses across the disciplines. Palmquist's case study approach involved interviews with six students writing for the web in different disciplines: two each from a speech communication course, an undergraduate Web development course, and a graduate Web writing course. He explains that he chose students from three courses "to increase the likelihood of obtaining findings that were not influenced by the genre conventions suggested by a particular faculty member" (226). In the interviews, Palmquist asked students to reflect on their experiences reading and writing Web documents and to reflect on genre features like document structure, navigation tools, digital illustrations, and page design. Although all six students had used the Web for personal and academic purposes, only two students had ever developed their own Web sites, making it a new genre for most of the students. Additionally, Palmquist found that the undergraduate students were less familiar with the genre and thought of Web sites as a more monolithic genre; however, graduate students had a more nuanced understanding of the multiple genres on the Web and the different functions among types of Web sites, such as search sites, news and information sites, educational sites, commercial sites, government sites, organizational sites, etc. Palmquist also discovered that when faced with a newly emerging and evolving genre, students tend to turn to other genres to search for recurrent patterns in structure and design and that they also borrow from print genres, such as structuring a site based on an academic essay or including a table of contents, a navigation tool familiar in print genres. As in the previous study by Edward and McKee, Palmquist's findings confirm that there is no stable genre definition of Web documents. As a result, he encourages instructors to emphasize the emergent nature of genres on the web and the range of choices that writers have: "If instructors inform their assignments with an understanding of the Web as a home to multiple genres, those assignments are more likely to attend to issues concerning organizational structure, page design, navigational tools, and the use of digital illustrations" (244). Following the implications from the previous study,

Palmquist's research supports a pedagogical approach informed by critical genre analysis, which we examine in more detail in Chapter 10.

GENRE-BASED STUDIES OF WEBLOGS IN ACADEMIC SETTINGS

While the above studies focus on students' creation of web genres or web sites, a few studies have examined "emergent" genres of weblogs. Just as the above studies argue for approaches to teaching digital genres that are informed by critical genre analysis, this section will begin with a genre analysis of the weblog, an analysis informed by empirical research.

In "Blogging as Social Action: A Genre Analysis of the Weblog," Carolyn Miller and Dawn Shepherd study the substance, form, and rhetorical actions of weblogs or "blogs." Drawing on ethnomethodology, they examine a corpus of blogs and collect and analyze bloggers' reflections on their blogs, noting that blogs carry out typified social actions of self-expression and community development. Through the function of self-disclosure, bloggers seek to develop relationships and build connections with others or manipulate their opinions through the features of linking and commentary. An important aspect of their study is examining the evolution of the genre; as a result, Miller and Shepherd also examine the history of blogs and their ancestral genres, claiming that the blog is a complex rhetorical hybrid with genetic imprints from prior genres, such as the diary, clipping services, broadsides, commonplace books, and even ship's logs. Ultimately, they argue that the blog is a distinctive genre that combines the personal and public in its rhetorical form and allows bloggers to cultivate the self in a public way, noting that "the blog-as-genre is a contemporary contribution to the art of the self" (11).

Testing Miller and Shepherd's finding that blogs contribute to "the art of the self," Kathryn Grafton and Elizabeth Maurer carry out a case study of two blogs that perform public actions, one focused on a community literary event (Canada Reads) and the other on the issue of homelessness. Through analysis of blog posts and the blogs' interactions with other public texts, such as news articles and broadcasts, the researchers find that bloggers construct "mediated selves" within publics and cultivate and validate self "by engaging directly with publics and arranging for their discourse to be recognized by these publics" (50).

Another finding by Miller and Shepherd is that "the blog is already evolving into multiple genres, meeting different exigencies for different rhetors" (6). Extending this discussion of multiple weblog genres as well as the interaction of public and private, a group of researchers—Kevin Brooks, Cindy Nichols, and Sybil Priebe—studied different types of weblogs (journal, community, or notecard/filter) and sought to discover which weblogs engage or motivate student writers. Drawing on survey data and responses to open-ended questions, the researchers investigated the relationship between these weblog genres and student motivation over two semesters in a variety of courses, from first-year to graduate courses. In these courses, students were asked to set up and maintain a personal blog and to contribute entries about controversial social issues discussed in class. While Miller and Shepherd found that blogs integrate public and private, these researchers found that first-year students were not interested in the public dimension of weblogs or their academic potential but instead preferred the personal and expressive dimensions. For that reason, the journal weblog was most preferred, while the graduate students appreciated and valued both the journal and the community weblog, where they could share observations about a reading or discuss issues relevant to class (for a study of collective blogs in K-12 education, see Sousa and Soares). The researchers concluded that journal weblogging is most popular because it remediates a familiar print genre (journals) with positive connotations. However, it can also cause generic interference for learning other types of weblog genres.

While Miller and Shepherd define blogs as a new genre and Brooks, Nichols, and Priebe argue that there are multiple weblog genres, a study by Susan Herring, Lois Ann Scheidt, Sabrina Bonus, and Elijah Wright suggests that weblogs are a "bridging genre"—a hybrid genre that is neither unique or new nor remediated or reproduced. In their quantitative analysis of 203 weblogs, the researchers seek to provide an empirical snapshot of weblogs and to contribute to a theoretical understanding of how technological changes trigger new genres and change the genre ecology of the Internet. Their research is based on the assumption that "recurrent electronic communication practices can meaningfully be characterized as genres" (144). Their results reinforce findings in the previously discussed studies, noting that blogs are very much an individual enterprise and are used primarily for a personal purpose. Blogs resemble another online genre—the online journal—a genre reproduced from diaries and share similarities to digital genres like homepages. Extending the list of ancestral genres noted by Miller and Shepherd, Herring et al. argue that blogs also have offline antecedents in genres of editorials and letters to the editor in print newspapers. Rather than having a single source as an anteced- ent genre, blogs are "a hybrid of existing genres, rendered unique by the particular features of the source genres they adapt, and by their particular technological affordances" (163). They conclude that "the flexible, hybrid nature of the blog format means that it can express a wide range of genres, in accordance with the communicative needs of its users" (164). This flexibility in composing in new media contexts and the ability to formulate a wide variety of genres or multi-genre responses to meet the communicative needs of users obviously has im- plications not just for research on academic genres but for research on genres in workplace or professional contexts, which is the focus of the next section.

Studies of Electronic Genres in Workplace Contexts

New electronic technologies and the demand for more efficient and effective forms of interaction are influencing organizational commu- nication as well as research on organizational communication. In an overview of communication media and organizational genres entitled "Genres of Organizational Communication: A Structural Approach", JoAnne Yates and Wanda Orlikowski identify two streams of research on new media: one focusing on the factors that influence use of me- dia in organizations and the other focused on how media influences communicative behavior. The limitation of this prior research, they argue, is that these approaches fail to acknowledge "the reciprocal and recursive relationships between media and communication over time" (310). Another concern is the conflation of the terms "genre" and "me- dia." While careful to differentiate between genres of communication and the communication media, Yates and Orlikowski posit that "me- dium may play a role in both the recurrent situation and the form of a genre" (310), making the combined lenses of genre and medium "a powerful alternative approach to studying communication in organi- zations" (311). Utilizing this research approach, Yates and Orlikowski trace the emergence and institutionalization of the memo genre over time, from its status as a business letter in the mid-1800s to the elaboration of the memo genre in email in the 1970s-1990s. Examining the reciprocal relationship between genre and medium, they study (via historical and contextual methods) the influence of the established memo genre on communication in email and the widespread use of email that sets the stage for the emergence of new computer mediated genres of organizational communication. They conclude with a look toward future research: "Empirical research is needed to investigate the various social, economic, and technological factors that occasion the production, reproduction, or modification of different genres in different sociohistorical contexts" (320), noting that new media may be triggering the modification of existing genres.

In a number of their articles, Orlikowski and Yates reiterate their argument that genre is a useful tool for investigating the effects of new media in professional organizations or workplace settings. In "Genre Systems: Structuring Intervention through Communicative Norms," they illustrate this claim empirically as they study the use of a collaborative electronic technology in a corporate setting. In order to illustrate how genre systems structure communicative interactions in organizations, their study focused on three teams of employees in a high-technology company in the northeastern US ("Mox Corporation") and their use of a collaborative application called "Team Room" technology. After tracking the posting of 492 messages over seven months of use, they carried out a genre analysis of the messages and conducted interviews with team members using a variation of the discourse-based interview. Their study identified three genre systems used by all three teams: meeting, collaborative authoring, and collaborative repository. The meeting genre system consisted of communicative activity surrounding face-to-face meetings, such as postings of logistics or agenda and distribution of minutes. Collaborative authoring referred to the circulation of drafts and responses, with interactions among all team members. Collaborative repository included communicative activities such as coordinating schedules, brainstorming, or initiating discussions—for example, using the Team Room as a "Place to Brainstorm on Communication Ideas" as one team invited members to "Compose comments whenever you get inspired" (22). Yates's and Orlikowski's findings indicate that the enactment of the three genre systems within the framework of the new media of Team Room both reinforced and, in some cases, changed the communicative interactions. In addition, as these genre systems structured interaction in Team Room, there was sometimes an explicit awareness of genre expectations and their coordinating role, and in other cases, it was more tacit and habitual. Yates and Orlikowski conclude by noting that "For users of such new media, we believe that making assumptions explicit that have previously been tacit may facilitate adjustment to the new medium, both to avoid misunderstandings and to encourage experimentation that may lead to change in genre systems" (33).

Further exploring the changes in a workplace community's genre repertoire within the context of electronically mediated communication is a study by Cristina Zuccchermaglio and Alessandra Talamo called "The Development of a Virtual Community of Practices Using Electronic Mail and Communicative Genres." This study is focused on three research questions related to the ways in which the e-mail system contributed to the construction of specific genres, the ways in which the community's genre repertoire changed over time, and the ways in which the changes in genre repertoire reflect and reinforce changes in the community members' relationships. Examining electronic-mail communication within an organization of software-developers, the researchers gathered a data corpus of 794 e-mail messages produced over a three-year period by an interorganizational group creating a software interface and categorized each of the messages according to its communicative goal and formal features. Results indicated that the community members identified five genres as part of their repertoire: the note, report, dialogue, proposal, and memo, with notes (brief, informal and often personal communications) comprising the most-used genre in the repertoire and constituting 66% of the messages exchanged (265). Other genres, such as memos and proposals, represented a much smaller percentage of the e-mail communication, perhaps reflecting, according to the researchers, "the prevalence of an informal communicative and work style" among these organizational members (281). Perhaps most interesting is that the e-mail system contributed to the construction of specific genres, such as the dialogue genre, which the researchers define as "a form of written interaction modeled on oral conversation and made possible by electronic mail's capacity to insert all or part of a preceding message (defined as embedded text) in the new text the writer is creating" (267). Dialogue genres share the communicative goal of responding to a preceding message and share unique formal features of embedded text from previous exchanges. For this single virtual community, then, the technologically mediated communicative practices resulted in changes to the genre repertoire and facilitated informal exchanges among co-workers.

While the above studies examine electronically mediated genres within community contexts, one recent study explores genres that are uprooted from their native contexts by new mobile technologies, such as personal digital assistants or PDAs. In "Coherent Fragments: The Problem of Mobility and Genred Information," Jason Swarts conducted an observational case study of a veterinary teaching hospital and fourth-year students with PDAs. Because PDAs make information mobile across space and time and beyond particular contexts of use, it is up to the user to adapt the information to context or "recontextualize" the information. Making it more difficult to recontextualize and translate information across contexts of use is the fact that, for PDAs, the genre's characteristic features are both semantically and physically reduced, thus obscuring the connections between fragments of information and a context in which they are used. The purpose of Swarts' case study was "to observe how students used PDA-accessible information, in conjunction with environmentally accessible information, to create information artifacts that supported cooperative medical activity" (176). The veterinary students that Swarts studied were each supplied a PDA by the school, and the PDAs were preloaded with medical calculators, tutorials, procedure videos, clinical references, and relevant databases. Based on observations of seven students on two rotations and interviews with students about their PDA use, Swarts examined how students connected the fragmented information on their PDAs (a virtual genre ecology) with environmentally available information. Most significant in terms of findings is Swarts' observation that understanding a genred context of use means understanding "the modality of information" that complicates an understanding of a genre's "embeddedness" in a culture.

The modality of information is also the subject of Helen Caple's study of a corpus of 900 news stories from the *Sydney Morning Herald*. Based on her analysis, she proposes that a new multimodal genre has emerged, which she calls the "image-nuclear news story." She is interested in the element of play between the textual and visual in the corpus she analyzes, particularly the interaction between the heading and image, which are often light and playful, thus putting them in start contrast to the hard news story. The headings and photos appeal to human interest, using idiomatic expressions and cultural allusions that create solidarity with readers and that encourage them to read the news story that follows. However, Caple concludes that this new genre "has demonstrated great awareness of the potential of the internet and other media platforms to threaten [the] future" of traditional news genres while also holding the promise of increasing readership and circulation (256).

As multimedia and multimodal texts interact within new genre ecologies and systems and genres mediate discourse activities across contexts and medium, the problems and possibilities of "recontextualization" will be ripe for further study. In addition, further studies, such as Orlikowski's and Yates's research on collaborative electronic technologies will facilitate understanding of changes in communicative interactions associated with the adoption of new electronic media:

> Understanding organizing processes mediated by new technologies becomes increasingly important, as more and more organizational work becomes a matter of electronic symbol manipulation and information exchange. The genres through which information is shaped and shared for particular purposes (reports, spreadsheets, meetings, or teleconferences) are no longer merely an aspect of organizational work; rather they are the organizational work. ("Genre Repertoire" 572)

As communities adopt and use new media, further studies will be needed to examine the process of importing existing genres and genre systems, improvising around them, and learning to take advantage of new and emergent genres.

Conclusion

In the 15 years since Aviva Freedman issued her call for more research on genre, genre scholars have conducted a wealth of studies in academic and workplace contexts, with some studies of genre in public and electronic contexts becoming more prevalent. In fact, in a recent book with Natasha Artemeva called *Rhetorical Genre Studies and Beyond*, Freedman has since acknowledged the "especially extensive empirical research" that "has provided composition researchers with a very rich body of highly textured, largely qualitative work that has explained and elaborated on the discursive practices of professionals in their workplace and students in universities" (1). Freedman is able to reflect on how the body of empirical research has revealed gaps or limitations in genre theory and to illustrate how scholars have addressed these gaps by turning to other complementary theories, such as activity theory, theories of situated learning, perspectives on distributed cognition, and linguistic approaches. In "Interaction Between Theory and Research," Freedman acknowledges the complex, reciprocal relationship between theory and empirical research, noting that "sometimes the data force researchers to reconsider the theory—to modify, revise, or possibly even reject aspects or the whole of a theory that had been in use" (102). While research has strengthened the powerful conceptual framework of rhetorical genre studies, it has also informed our "use" of theory, namely through approaches in the classroom. The next two chapters in Part 3 will focus on pedagogical applications informed by genre theory and research.

Part 3: Genre Approaches to Teaching Writing

10 From Research to Pedagogy: Multiple Pedagogical Approaches to Teaching Genres

Part 2's focus on empirical research—research into how genres are learned, how they function in particular contexts, and how they carry out communicative goals and reflect/reinforce ideologies—illustrates how research can inform our practices as writing teachers. Research into genre learning and acquisition has provided teachers with useful methods for situating learning and for fostering meta-cognition that connects new and already-acquired knowledge. In addition, research into genre knowledge and performance has motivated pedagogical applications that work to facilitate the transfer of genre knowledge and writing skills from one writing context to another, from first-year composition (FYC) courses to courses in the disciplines, and from academic writing to workplace writing. Finally, recent studies of how genres function socially and ideologically have led to increased attention to critical pedagogical methods and to approaches to genre grounded in critique and an awareness of genre difference and change. In order to examine the varied goals that drive differing agendas, this chapter will focus on a range of pedagogical approaches informed by genre research and scholarship, while the next chapter will focus on pedagogical approaches emerging from Rhetorical Genre Studies (RGS), as these have informed genre teaching in Rhetoric and Composition studies.

Multiple Pedagogical Approaches to Genre

Amy Devitt argues that while all genre pedagogies "share an understanding of genres as socially and culturally as well as linguistically embedded. . . . [d]ifferent genre pedagogies result . . . from emphasizing different theoretical concerns" ("Teaching" 346). This has led to attempts to conceptualize and create taxonomies of varied, but over-lapping, pedagogical approaches. Devitt, for example, uses Kenneth Pike's metaphor of particle, wave, and field to describe genre pedago-gies with different emphases on teaching particular genres (particle), building on prior genre knowledge for learning new genres (wave), and teaching students how to critique and change existing genres (field) (348-50; Aviva Freedman has likewise used the metaphor of particle and wave to distinguish between genre research traditions—see "Interaction"). Devitt's overview of pedagogical approaches cor-responds to Marilyn Chapman's conceptions of genre learning as they apply to K-12 instruction: learning genres, learning through genres, and learning about genres—that is, teaching genres as rhetorical strat-egies, as processes, and as cultural tools or resources.

Researchers interested in Second Language (L2) instruction have further explored the tensions and differences in approaches to genre instruction. Ann Johns, in *Genre in the Classroom: Multiple Perspec-tives,* identifies three different pedagogical approaches to genre, draw-ing on the theoretical traditions earlier identified by Sunny Hyon. These three main traditions of genre teaching (which we examine in detail in Chapters 3, 4, 5, and 6) are as follows:

1) *The Sydney School approach,* which is a carefully developed and sequential curriculum developed out of systemic functional lin-guistics. Educators begin by modeling genres and explicating the features of those genres using the Hallidayan socially based system of textual analysis. Students are then expected to repro-duce these genres and thus "acquire" them.

2) *English for Specific Purposes (ESP),* which informs an approach to teaching specific genres (often disciplinary genres) and train-ing in the formal and functional features of these texts. Swales' text-based theory of moves is central to an ESP approach, which includes "analyzing features of texts and relating those features to the values and rhetorical purposes of discourse communities" (Johns 7).

3) *The New Rhetoric,* or what we refer to as "Rhetorical Genre Studies" in Chapters 5 and 6, which is a contextualized ap-proach to genre that teaches students to critically consider genres and their rhetorical and social purposes and ideologies. New Rhetoric theorists see genre as dynamic and evolving and

"[prefer] to start (and sometimes end) with a discussion of the rhetorical situation rather than with a more specific analysis of lexico-grammatical elements within the text" (Johns 9).

To this taxonomy we might add a fourth approach—the Brazilian educational model or didactic approach. This pedagogical approach, informed by the Swiss genre tradition and theories of "socio-discursive interactionism" (see Chapter 5), has influenced curricular initiatives and genre pedagogy in Brazil. Drawing on Bakhtinian perspectives of communicative interaction and Vygotsky's learning and activity theory, this approach is marked by a) characterization of the sphere in which genre circulates; b) study of the social-history of genre development; c) characterization of the context of production; d) analysis of the thematic content; and e) analysis of the compositional construction of the genre, such as the genre's style and the author's style (Furlanetto 371). Whereas the Sydney School and ESP approaches might move from context to text, and the New Rhetoric from text analysis to context, the Brazilian model begins with early production of the genre based on writers' previous knowledge and experience, then moves to analysis of genre within rhetorical and social contexts, culminating with (re)production of the genre, thus bringing together a focus on genre awareness, analysis of linguistic conventions, and attention to social context.

While there is overlap in these perspectives in most genre pedagogies, the next sections will examine different models or applications that emphasize implicit approaches to genre awareness (such as Freedman's model), explicit or text-based approaches to genre acquisition (such as the teaching/learning cycle or Swales' model), and interactive models (models by RGS scholars like Devitt and Coe as well as Brazilian interactionist models) that bring into dynamic interaction the genre schemas of individual writers and the complex context in which the text is to be produced.

IMPLICIT GENRE PEDAGOGIES

While early research on genre focused on cognitive views of prior genre knowledge (especially in development of children's learning), this research was largely displaced in the late 1980s by studies that applied a social perspective and examined how genre knowledge was shaped communally and culturally. In his recent chapter, "Genre

and Cognitive Development: Beyond Writing to Learn," Charles
Bazerman renews our attention to genres as cognitive tools, providing
a comprehensive overview of Vygotskian theories and perspectives on
the "Writing to Learn" (WTL) movement. According to Bazerman,
research on WTL suggests "the possibility that the cognitive task and
practices associated with the production of genres may be related to
their potential for supporting various forms of learning" (287).

Aviva Freedman's body of research on genre acquisition is closely
connected to her interest in pedagogical implications for how students
learn new genres ("Learning to Write Again"). Her model of genre
learning, based on an understanding of genre knowledge as "tacit"
knowledge, begins with students' "dimly felt sense" of the new genre
they are attempting, which is modified and developed through the
composing process and in the course of the unfolding text. Student
writers begin with a broad schema for academic discourse based on
their previous school writings and assignments, and this schema is
modified when they face a new writing assignment or discipline-specific genre. This sense of genre that Freedman describes exists "below
the conscious" and draws on "creative powers that [are] neither verbal
nor rational" (104). There is no explicit teaching of features of the new
genre, no modeling of texts in the genre, and no attention to specific
strategies for acquiring the genre. Instead, writers "create the genre" in
the course of producing it, guided by a sense of genre that is modified
through the assignment, class lectures and discussion, and feedback
on writing. In "Learning to Write Again," Freedman describes what
she calls a "model for acquiring new genres"—an implicit pedagogical
model informed by her own research as well as the research of Sondra
Perl and Janet Emig. It is defined as follows:

Freedman's Model for Acquiring New Genres

1. The learners approach the task with a 'dimly felt sense' of the
   new genre they are attempting.

2. They begin composing by focusing on the specific content to be
   embodied in this genre.

3. In the course of the composing, this 'dimly felt sense' of the
   genre is both formulated and modified as (a) this 'sense,' (b)

the composing processes, and (c) the unfolding text interrelated and modify each other.

4. On the basis of external feedback (the grade assigned), the learners either confirm or modify their map of the genre. (102)

What, then, are the pedagogical implications of this implicit understanding of genre learning? If students acquire a new genre "in the course of writing—in the performance itself" and in "learning to write by writing" (107), a pedagogy that stresses composing processes, invention, and feedback is crucial. Freedman advocates teaching genre by immersing students in writing genres. Instead of having students read and explicate models, a successful genre pedagogy is based on "eliciting appropriate thinking strategies" (111) through indirect or implicit methods. Freedman argues that "full genre knowledge (in all of its subtlety and complexity) only becomes available *as a result of having written*. First comes the achievement or performance, with the tacit knowledge implied, and then, through that, the meta-awareness which can flower into conscious reflexive knowledge" ("'Do As I Say'" 205).

Explicit Genre Pedagogies

Freedman's immersion model stands in contrast to more text-based or linguistic models that focus on explicit teaching of genres, such as those advocated by specialists in Systemic Functional Linguistics (SFL), particularly the Sydney School approaches (see Chapter 3 for further discussion of this approach). The theories and pedagogical applications of the Sydney School approach to genre—aimed at primary and secondary school and adult education programs—are outlined in a recent book by J.R. Martin and David Rose, called *Genre Relations: Mapping Culture*, which examines a scaffolded curricula and attention to "staged" pedagogical genres (stories, histories, reports, procedural accounts). Mary Macken-Horarik describes the SFL approach as an "explicit pedagogy" in which "the teacher inducts learners into the linguistic demands of genres which are important to participation in school learning and in the wider community" (26). She also describes one of the most salient features of this pedagogy, the "teaching-learning cycle," which involves three stages:

1. *Modeling:* The teacher builds up the context relevant to the field of inquiry and provides learners with models of the genre in focus in this context, helping learners explore the social purpose of text, its prototypical elements of structure, and its distinctive language features.

2. *Joint Negotiation of Text:* The teacher prepares learners for joint production of a new text in the focus genre. Teachers and students compose a new text together drawing on shared knowledge of both the learning context itself and the structure and features of the genre.

3. *Independent Construction of Text:* The learners work on their own texts using processes such as drafting, conferencing, editing, and publishing. . . . (26)

Macken-Horarik goes on to focus on a case study of one teacher's application of the above model and her movement between teaching text and context and relating linguistic patterns to social, disciplinary patterns. She concludes that explicit approaches, such as SFL-based genre pedagogies, can provide students with meta-linguistic resources that assist them in producing genres while also developing long-term rhetorical competence that transfers to other writing situations.

While Macken-Horarik describes an SFL-oriented genre pedagogy that functions in Australian academic settings, Desiree Motta-Roth applies an SFL approach to Brazilian educational contexts, proposing a pedagogy that emphasizes the reciprocal relationship between text and context. With this in mind, she argues that it is important to teach students selected SFL principles, such as discourse analysis, a model of training students that has also been proposed by Ann Johns (*Text, Role, and Context*) and Ian Bruce. In "The Role of Context in Academic Text Production and Writing Pedagogy," Motta-Roth describes a pedagogical model she calls the "academic writing cycle," which consists of three activities:

1. Context Exploration: involves learning to interact with the environment in order to learn the language, observing research practices and understanding the role of language in knowledge production practices.

2. Text Exploration: involves experiencing analytically the relationship between text and context, how language appropriately

constructs the context and vice versa, by analyzing genre systems and genre sets;

3. Text Production, Revising and Editing: involves becoming a discourse analyst by writing, revising and editing one's text as well as others,' focusing on how linguistic resources are used for engagement and participation in social and discursive academic practices. ("The Role of Context" 329)

This cycle breaks down into specific tasks and exercises that involve analysis of a community and its genre system and sets; analysis of genre exemplars in the community and their linguistic and rhetorical patterns; and, finally, more focused analysis of the lexico-grammatical features of texts. Teaching novice academic writers how to become discourse analysts, according to Motta-Roth, increases their awareness of the social and discursive practices within communities they wish to join, which is the centerpiece of other text-based pedagogies, such as ESP approaches.

John Swales' groundbreaking work on analyzing genres as they carry out the communicative purposes of a discourse community has played a central role in English for Academic Purposes (EAP) and English for Specific Purposes (ESP) pedagogical approaches. In his chapter, "The Concept of Task" in *Genre Analysis*, Swales offers a pedagogical illustration of a task-based genre approach. This rhetorical approach begins with providing students with several samples of a genre (in this case three short request letters). Students then complete four tasks: 1) analyzing the similarities/ differences in the subject and purpose of the samples; 2) describing what changes they might make to increase rhetorical effectiveness; 3) examining the sentences and word choice and their appropriateness to the situation, followed by composing their own request letters; and finally, 4) gathering examples of correspondence they have received in the form of short letters (80-81). Swales defines the features of "task" in this task-oriented pedagogical approach as "one of a set of differentiated, sequenceable, goal-directed activities drawing upon a range of cognitive and communicative procedures relatable to the acquisition of pre-genre and genre skills appropriate to a foreseen or emerging sociorhetorical situation" (81). Swales' goal of moving students toward membership in a disciplinary community via study and use of genres within that community has formed the basis of his textbook for non-native graduate students, *Academic Writing for Graduate Students* (co-authored with Christine

B. Feak). In addition, his text-based theory of rhetorical moves (CARS model: Creating a Research Space), emerging from his genre analysis of research article introductions, has been very influential in genre and writing pedagogy at both the undergraduate and graduate levels. Swales' CARS model has been adapted and used widely, and provides an example of how genre analysis can be turned into a heuristic for writing instruction:

Move 1: Establishing a territory

Step 1: Claiming centrality, and/or

Step 2: Making topic generalization(s), and/or

Step 3: Reviewing items of previous research

Move 2: Establishing a niche

Step 1A: Counter-claiming, or

Step 1B: Indicating a gap, or

Step 1C: Question raising, or

Step 1D: Continuing a tradition

Move 3: Occupying the niche

Step 1A: Outlining purposes, or

Step 1B: Announcing present research

Step 2: Announcing principal findings

Step 3: Indicating research article structure (141)

Swales' "move analysis" of research articles, while designed for professional writers or advanced academic writers, has been adapted to teaching research papers to first-year writers as well. By connecting rhetorical actions to rhetorical structures, the model provides a useful heuristic for investigating rhetorical structures and the underlying

motives of writers' rhetorical choices. In addition, the moves can lead
students through a process of staking their claim and establishing the
significance of their topic, to contextualizing the topic and the conversations surrounding it, to, finally, joining the conversation by presenting their claim or "occupying the niche." Brian Sutton, in "Swales's
'Moves' and the Research Paper Assignment," describes a checklist he
developed, based on Swales' CARS model, for teaching the genre of
the research paper in FYC:

Checklist for Using Swales's Moves in a Research Paper Introduction

1. Do you begin by establishing the significance of your research
   area?

2. Do you summarize previous relevant research in the area?

3. Do you point out a "gap" in that previous research—perhaps
   an area the research has overlooked (such as whether or not its
   conclusions apply to the local situation), or possibly a question
   as to whether the research methods or interpretations of results
   in previous studies are completely reliable?

4. Do you make clear (whether or not you state it explicitly) that
   in the rest of your paper you will present your own original
   research to fill the "gap" pointed out in #3? (451)

Swales' genre-centered approach has had a significant impact on EAP
and ESP pedagogies (Hyon, "Genre and ESL Reading"; Hyland,
Genre and Second Language Writing; Paltridge, *Genre and the Language
Learning Classroom*); in addition, with its focus on linguistic and sociorhetorical dimensions of genres, Swales' work on genre analysis has
significantly influenced New Rhetoric or North American approaches, which we will discuss in the following sections.

INTERACTIVE GENRE PEDAGOGIES

Whether genre study is situated within text-based pedagogies, such as
SFL or ESP, or situated within implicit approaches that develop students' "felt sense" of genre, scholars seem to agree that "explicit teaching must always be done in the context of, or in very close proximity

to, authentic tasks involving the relevant discourse" (Freedman "Do as I say" 205). Anne Beaufort and John A. Williams, in their study of teaching history writing, noted the difficulty instructors faced with articulating tacit knowledge of conventions, thus creating a problem of clear expectations. They argue, "While genre theory is not a panacea, these problems of pedagogy and evaluation can . . . be ameliorated by clearer articulation of the genres students should learn and a well thought-out pedagogy to teach those genres" (63). Their pedagogical approach includes both immersion in a context in which students discuss and analyze the knowledge, assumptions, and values of a disciplinary community as well as receiving practical, explicit instruction for writing that community's genres. Based on similar findings from her case study research, Mary Soliday proposes a pedagogical approach that considers how "writers acquire genre knowledge both consciously and unconsciously" (66). As a result, she recommends making tacit knowledge explicit by designing rubrics prompting students to analyze the purposes of formal features and by providing maps of textual features while also emphasizing learning via modeling genres and discussing them in class, offering feedback, and sequencing assignments (80). Agreeing with this simultaneous focus on both implicit and explicit methods, Lingard and Haber, based on their study of medical student apprenticeships, conclude that "there is a role for rhetorically explicit genre instruction in the context of situated practice" (168).Devitt agrees with pedagogical models employing both explicit and implicit instructional methods, proposing an approach based in explicit teaching of genre awareness, which entails a "meta-awareness of genres, as learning strategies rather than static features" (*Writing Genres* 197). In "Teaching Critical Genre Awareness," Devitt shares her sequence of assignments for teaching critical genre awareness, building on her particle-wave-field approach to teaching particular genres, building on prior genre knowledge, and teaching students to critique and change existing genres:

- Project 1: analyzing a familiar, everyday genre, as a class, learning the techniques of rhetorical analysis
- Project 2: writing that familiar genre differently, with a major shift in treatment of purpose, audience, subject, or setting
- Project 3: analyzing a genre from another culture or time, working in groups to gather samples, analyze the genre, and learn about the historical or cultural context

- Project 4: analyzing an academic genre chosen as a potential antecedent genre, working as a class on a common genre
- Project 5: writing that academic genre within a specific writing task for this class
- Project 6: critiquing that genre and recommending specific changes that might better meet each student's needs
- Project 7: analyzing, critiquing, and writing flexibly another potential antecedent genre, chosen individually to serve the individuals' needs (depending on the group, either a public genre or a future [academic] major or workplace genre) (353)

Devitt describes a model of moving back and forth between familiar and unfamiliar genres—and between analysis and production of genres—in order to teach an awareness of how contexts shape generic responses.

Similarly, Richard Coe describes an approach that seeks to teach students "an understanding of genre as the motivated, functional relationship between text type and rhetorical situation" ("The New Rhetoric of Genre" 197) by developing assignments that ask writers to analyze and produce unfamiliar genres, such as brochures or political briefs. Coe describes a three to four-week unit in which students are exposed to three persuasive genres (traditional argument, Rogerian argument, and the political brief) and are asked to produce the one "that is most rhetorically complex" (207). For political briefs, which are designed to influence a public decision-making body (giving students experience with diverse audiences), students evaluate their rhetorical situation and, in the process of shaping their topic, purpose, and audience, "come to understand generic structures as rhetorical strategies and genres as social processes" (207).

Applying this analysis of unfamiliar genres to K-12 teaching in their book *Writing Outside Your Comfort Zone*, Cathy Fleischer and Sarah Andrew-Vaughan describe a sequence of assignments they call an Unfamiliar Genre Project (UGP) that draws on the potential for genre study to "truly [integrate] the English language arts" and to explore multiple kinds of writing for varied situations and the multiple processes that writers might use for various genres (2-3). Noting the limitations of text-based approaches that focus on the learning of particular genres (five paragraph essay, personal narrative, reports, etc.), Fleischer and Andrew-Vaughan argue that "learning writing from a genre-based stance will result in strategies that can help [students]

when they face multiple genres in the real world" (4). Briefly, the Unfamiliar Genre Project involves the following steps: 1) picking a challenging genre and explaining why it was chosen; 2) collecting samples
of and reading in the unfamiliar genre; 3) analyzing generic patterns
and composing a "how-to book" on writing the unfamiliar genre; 4)
creating an annotated bibliography of model samples of the genre; 5)
writing in the unfamiliar genre; 6) writing a reflective letter on the
experience of studying and producing the genre; and soliciting a letter
of response from an outside reader (67-68). This approach emphasizes implicit methods as students are immersed in reading and writing
genres, with opportunities for metacognitive reflection on the process as well as opportunities for feedback. But it also draws on explicit
teaching as students read model genres, analyze generic features and
move from description of these features to production of the genre.

Also synthesizing implicit and explicit pedagogies and cognitive,
textual, and social approaches is the Brazilian model. Based on socio-
discursive interaction theory (which we describe in Chapter 5), the
Brazilian didactic model emphasizes a "didactic sequence," which is
"a set of teaching-learning sequential activities which must necessarily include an initial and a final written production" (Guimarães 33).
One of the key steps of this sequence is the initial "early production"
of a text in the genre under study, based only on the student's previous
knowledge and/or experience; this is followed by analysis of the textual and rhetorical features of the genre, analysis of the communicative situation, and finally, the student's final production of the genre.
In "A Genre Teaching in Different Social Environments," Guimarães
provides an example of the didactic sequence as it was applied to the
teaching of detective stories in a fifth-grade classroom, which illustrates this interactive approach and which is summarized below (see
her article for a fuller discussion of workshop components):

Guimarães's Didactic Sequence for
Genre of the Detective Story

Students' early productions: The teacher briefly introduced the project,
mentioned its aims and asked the students if they knew terror, mys-
tery, crimes and detective stories. After that, students were asked to
write their early production of a detective story.

Workshop 1: Characterization of the detective story genre with the students through questions such as "Has anyone here already read detective stories, watched them on TV or at the movies?"; "Do you know a book, movie, story or even a famous detective?" Discussion of the main aspects of the detective story genre: vocabulary, structure, character analysis, analysis of the cover.

Workshop 2: Identification of the text that shows detective story characteristics, using as material three texts of different genres (fairy tale, detective story and terror story).

Workshops 3 to 7: Reading and analysis of samples in a "reading diary"; creation of a poster of the narrative sequence.

Workshop 8 to 10: Beginning the production stage of the detective stories; development of outline; final production of detective story.

Workshop 11 to 12: Proofreading and feedback. In groups, students selected 5 narratives to be "published" in a special book based on genre characteristics.

Workshop 13: Students received a book containing the 5 best detective stories they selected. They also received another book containing the 5 best detective stories from the 5th grade class from another school where the same didactic sequence was developed (37-38).

Based on various studies of the curricular implementation of the didactic model (Cristovão, "The Use of Didactic Sequences and the Teaching of L1"; Baltar et al, "School Radio: Socio-Discursive Interaction Tool in the School"; Furlanetto, "Curricular Proposal of Santa Catarina State"), researchers claim that students are more apt to internalize writing strategies by participating in learning approaches that develop cognitive capacities while encouraging participation in socio-communicative activities. For example, the activities of students reading and analyzing genres and then producing and sharing their detective stories with each other and with other fifth-grade classes can teach socio-discursive interaction by helping students situate and negotiate their socio-discursive actions in relation to various genres, while learning and practicing authentic texts-in-use. This socio-discursive approach shares similar goals with the socio-cognitive approach described by Bazerman in which "[s]tudents learn how to produce the kinds of thoughts appropriate to the assigned genres, using the concepts and discursive tools expected in the genres, and they learn how to locate their findings, analysis, and thought within the communal project of academic learnings" ("Genre and Cognitive Development" 295). While defining distinctive genre approaches for different audiences (K-12 versus college-level writers), RGS and Brazilian models promote multiple, overlapping methods that develop cognitive abilities related to genre awareness, that teach acquisition of linguistic or text-based strategies, and that demonstrate how cognitive and textual knowledge of genres are shaped by the sociocultural context. The next chapter will focus on interactive models from RGS.

11 Rhetorical Genre Studies Approaches to Teaching Writing

As we have discussed earlier, Rhetorical Genre Studies' sociological understanding of genre has revealed genre as a rich analytical tool for studying academic, workplace, and public environments, but it has also left RGS researchers with questions about the pedagogical possibilities of teaching genres explicitly in classroom environments, outside of the contexts of their use. The challenge for RGS has been how to develop genre-based approaches to teaching writing that attend to this dynamic—how, that is, we can teach genres in ways that maintain their complexity and their status as more than just typified rhetorical features. As we have described, RGS scholars have for the most part advocated an apprenticeship-based approach to teaching and learning genres, but the challenge, especially for scholars and teachers in composition studies, remains: How can we bring our knowledge of genre to bear on the teaching of writing? In what follows, we focus on RGS pedagogical approaches, with attention to various teaching issues: how to develop genre knowledge that transfers across writing situations; how to teach a critical awareness of genre; how to teach students to move from critique to production of alternative genres; and, finally, how to situate genres within the contexts of their use, whether public, professional, or disciplinary contexts.

RGS Pedagogies and the Transfer of Genre Knowledge

With the ongoing development of university-wide writing programs and the continued growth of Writing Across the Curriculum courses has come, from within the field of rhetoric and composition studies, renewed questions about the transfer value of writing courses—questions about whether skills, habits, strategies, and knowledge learned in First-Year Composition (FYC) courses transfer to and enable students to succeed in other disciplinary and workplace contexts that college students will need to negotiate. Research on writing transfer has begun to shed some light on the challenges students face as they negotiate disciplinary and professional writing contexts (see, for example, Bazerman, "What Written Knowledge Does"; Beaufort, *Writing in the Real World*; Berkenkotter and Huckin, *Genre Knowledge in Disciplinary Communication*; Carroll, *Rehearsing New Roles*; Dias et al, *Worlds Apart*; Dias and Paré, *Transitions*; McCarthy, "A Stranger in a Strange Land"; McDonald, *The Question of Transferability*; Sommers and Saltz, "The Novice as Expert"; Walvoord and McCarthy, *Thinking and Writing in College*), and while this research has generally ranged from mixed to pessimistic regarding the transfer value of FYC, this has only raised the stakes for the need to articulate what transfers from FYC courses and how we might re-imagine these courses in light of such research. As Elizabeth Wardle recently put it, we "would be irresponsible not to engage issues of transfer" ("Understanding 'Transfer' from FYC" 66), a charge that follows David Smit's identification of "transferability" as a primary consideration for writing instruction, in his book *The End of Composition Studies*.

Research in education and psychology identifies meta-cognition as an important component of knowledge transfer, especially across dissimilar contexts of the sort students will encounter between FYC courses, courses in different academic disciplines, and workplace settings. In their well-known research on knowledge transfer, D.N. Perkins and Gavriel Salomon distinguish between what they call "low road" and "high road" transfer. Low road transfer "reflects the automatic triggering of well-practiced routines in circumstances where there is considerable perceptual similarity to the original learning context," for example, how learning to drive a car prepares one to drive a truck (25). High road transfer, on the other hand, "depends on deliberate, mindful abstraction of skill or knowledge from one context for application to another" (25). Because knowledge and skills do not automatically transfer across dissimilar contexts, high road transfer requires "reflective thought in abstracting from one context and seeking connections with others" (26). As Perkins and Solomon suggest, the ability to seek and reflect on connections between contexts, to abstract from skills and knowledge, to know what prior resources to draw on, how to use these resources flexibly, and what new resources to seek are all preconditions for effective writing transfer across different contexts.

Some RGS scholars have argued that genre analysis and awareness enable such meta-cognition. In "Genre and Cognitive Development: Beyond Writing to Learn," Bazerman describes the process of learning new genres as a "cognitive apprenticeship" that can facilitate metacognitive activity:

> Genres identify a problem space for the developing writer to work in as well as provide the form of the solution the writer seeks and particular tools useful in the solution. Taking up the challenge of a genre casts you into the problem space and the typified structures and practices of the genre and provide the means of solution. The greater the challenge of the solution, the greater the possibilities of cognitive growth occurring in the wake of the process of solution. (295)

This interest in teaching genres as learning strategies or tools for accessing unfamiliar writing situations (or for solving "problem spaces") is taken up by Anne Beaufort in her recent longitudinal study, *College Writing and Beyond: A New Framework for University Writing Instruction.* Throughout the course of her study, Beaufort explores how genre knowledge can serve as a "mental gripper" for students negotiating new writing situations and how teaching genres as learning strategies can provide students with tools that transfer to multiple contexts. As she tracks one student's (Tim's) writing experiences across first-year composition, history courses, engineering courses, and post-college jobs, Beaufort acknowledges the centrality of genre knowledge, which plays a prominent role in her discussion of how students apply abstract concepts in different social contexts and writing situations. In her study she found that Tim, despite no explicit instruction in genre, did deepen his genre knowledge, leading her to the question: "What opportunities might there have been for deepening Tim's genre knowledge if this knowledge domain had been discussed more explicitly in the curriculum? Could it have enabled a more efficient and effective transition to understanding the shifts in genre expectations in the new discourse communities he would encounter?" (53). Her answer is that novice writers would more readily gain access to writing situations and genres if explicitly taught genres in relation to the social contexts in which they function.

To support these claims, Beaufort proposes an approach to writing instruction geared toward positive transfer of learning, a pedagogical approach very much situated in genre theory, as evidenced by the genre-centered teaching apparatus she includes at the end of the book. Providing a pedagogical illustration of teaching students to write an abstract for a journal article or a book, Beaufort begins with the first step—an analysis of genre—and what it tells writers about the participants in a community and the rhetorical occasion, including the subject matter. Writers might discover that an abstract is a genre read by members of several communities—researchers in the field, librarians, and editors—but with a common rhetorical purpose, which is to interest others in the new work. The writer also uses his/her genre knowledge to make decisions about writing process and rhetorical choices: what the required content of the genre is, how best to sequence the content, and what stylistic level of formality to adopt. An approach to teaching writing via genre analysis, then, functions to simultaneously bring multiple knowledge domains—subject matter, rhetorical knowledge, discourse community knowledge, and writing process knowledge—into dynamic interaction. In response to a final question posed by her research—"How can we set students on a life-long course of becoming expert writers?"—Beaufort responds, "Let them practice learning new genres and the ways of new discourse communities . . . and challenge them to apply the same tools in every new writing situation" (158).

RGS Approaches to Teaching Genre Analysis

RGS scholars—taking up this challenge to develop students' genre knowledge in ways that can better prepare them to access, understand, and write in various situations and contexts—have developed fruitful methods for cultivating meta-genre awareness. In the RGS approach to teaching genre analysis, students learn how to recognize genres as rhetorical responses to and reflections of the situations in which they are used; furthermore, students learn how to use genre analysis to participate and intervene in situations they encounter. To illustrate this genre-based pedagogy, we have included below a genre analysis heuristic from our textbook (with Amy Devitt) entitled *Scenes of Writing: Strategies for Composing with Genres,* a text that features prominently in Beaufort's proposed "new framework for university writing instruction":

Guidelines for Analyzing Genres

1. **Collect Samples of the Genre.** If you are studying a genre that is fairly public, such as the wedding announcement, you can look at samples from various newspapers. You can also locate samples of a genre in textbooks and manuals about the genre, as we did with the complaint letters. If you are studying a less public genre, such as the Patient Medical History Form, you might have to visit different doctors' offices to collect samples. Try to gather samples from more than one place (for example, wedding announcements from different newspapers, medical history forms from different doctors' offices) so that you get a more accurate picture of the complexity of the genre. The more samples of the genre you collect, the more you will be able to notice patterns within the genre.

2. **Identify the Scene and Describe the Situation in which the Genre is Used**. Try to identify the larger scene in which the genre is used. Seek answers to questions about the genre's situation such as the ones below:

   Setting: Where does the genre appear? How and when is it transmitted and used? With what other genres does this genre interact?

   Subject: What topics, issues, ideas, questions, etc. does the genre address? When people use this genre, what is it that they are they interacting about?

   Participants: Who uses the genre? *Writers:* Who writes the texts in this genre? Are multiple writers possible? What roles do they perform? What characteristics must writers of this genre possess? Under what circumstances do writers write the genre (e.g., in teams, on a computer, in a rush)? *Readers:* Who reads the texts in this genre? Is there more than one type of reader for this genre? What roles do they perform? What characteristics must readers of this genre possess? Under what circumstances do readers read the genre (e.g., at their leisure, on the run, in waiting rooms)?

   Purposes: Why do writers write this genre and why do readers read it? What purposes does the genre fulfill for the people who use it?

3. **Identify and Describe Patterns in the Genre's Features.** What recurrent features do the samples share? For example: What *content* is typically included? What excluded? How is the content treated? What sorts of examples are used? What counts as evidence (personal testimony, facts, etc.)? What *rhetorical appeals* are used? What appeals to logos, pathos, and ethos appear? How are texts in the genres *structured?* What are their parts, and how are they organized? In what *format* are texts of this genre presented? What layout or appearance is common? How long is a typical text in this genre? What types of *sentences* do texts in the genre typically use? How long are they? Are they simple or complex, passive or active? Are the sentences varied? Do they share a certain style? What *diction* (types of words) is most common? Is a type of jargon used? Is slang used? How would you describe the writer's voice?

4. **Analyze What These Patterns Reveal about the Situation and Scene.** What do these rhetorical patterns reveal about the genre, its situation, and the scene in which it is used? Why are these patterns significant? What can you learn about the actions being performed through the genre by observing its language patterns? What arguments can you make about these patterns? As you consider these questions, focus on the following:

   What do participants have to know or believe to understand or appreciate the genre? Who is invited into the genre, and who is excluded? What roles for writers and readers does it encourage or discourage? What values, beliefs, goals, and assumptions are revealed through the genre's patterns? How is the subject of the genre treated? What content is considered most important? What content (topics or details) is ignored? What actions does the genre help make possible? What actions does the genre make difficult? What attitude toward readers is implied in the genre? What attitude toward the world is implied in it? (93-94)

The questions above stress the interaction between genre and context, guiding the students from analysis of the situation to the genre and then from genre back to the situation, in a trajectory that reflects RGS approaches to genre analysis. Students start by identifying the situation from which the genre emerges. Students might explore context through interviews and observations, trying to identify where and when the genre is used, by whom, and why. After that, students ana-

lyze the genre for what it tells them about that situation. Such analysis involves describing the genre's rhetorical patterns, from its content
down to its diction, and then making an argument about what these
patterns reveal about the attitudes, values, and actions embedded in
the genre. In so doing, students revisit the situation through the genre
that reflects and maintains it. The idea here is to create a temporary
analytical space between the genre and its situation, a space in which
students can inquire into and connect rhetorical and social actions.
The goal is not so much for students to master a particular genre, but
to develop transferable genre-learning skills.

Other RGS textbooks aimed at first-year composition writers effectively use genre as a frame for formulating rhetorical strategies and responding to various communicative situations, reinforcing the transfer
value of genre knowledge. John Trimbur's *The Call to Write* integrates
a genre approach and begins each unit with a section entitled "Thinking about Genre." This section is focused on explaining the rhetorical and textual features of various genres—such as letters, proposals,
memoirs, and reviews—as well as their social functions. Following
their reflection on their experience with and the social relationships
constructed in the genre in the "Thinking about Genre" exercise, students read sample texts in the genre, analyze the features of the genre
and its context, and then produce their own example of the genre.

A similar approach is taken in the *Norton Field Guide to Writing*
(Richard Bullock), which also integrates genre considerations, noting
how genres frame reading and writing assignments. Students are ad-
vised to begin each assignment by identifying the genre they are asked
to write. Like *The Call to Write,* the *Norton Field Guide* includes a section on "Thinking about Genre" and integrates the following genre
heuristic, which encourages students to consider how the rhetorical
features of genres (content, tone, language, medium, design) are linked
to the rhetorical actions they perform—the purposes they carry out
and the audiences they address:

- What is your genre, and does it affect what content you can
  or should include? Objective information? Researched source
  material? Your own opinions? Personal experience?
- Does your genre call for any specific strategies? Profiles, for
  example, usually include some narration; lab reports often explain a process.

- Does your genre require a certain organization? Most proposals, for instance, first identify a problem and then offer a solution. Some genres leave room for choice. Business letters delivering good news might be organized differently than those making sales pitches.
- Does your genre affect your tone? An abstract of a scholarly paper calls for a different tone than a memoir. Should your words sound serious and scholarly? brisk and to the point? objective? opinionated? Sometimes your genre affects the way you communicate your stance.
- Does the genre require formal (or informal) language? A letter to the mother of a friend asking for a summer job in her bookstore calls for more formal language than does an email to the friend thanking him for the lead.
- Do you have a choice of medium? Some genres call for print; others for an electronic medium. Sometimes you have a choice: a résumé, for instance, can be mailed (in which case it must be printed), or it may be emailed. Some teachers want reports turned in on paper; others prefer that they be emailed or posted to a class Web site. If you're not sure what medium you can use, ask.
- Does your genre have any design requirements? Some genres call for paragraphs; others require lists. Some require certain kinds of typefaces—you wouldn't use Impact for a personal narrative, nor would you likely use Dr Seuss for an invitation to Grandma's sixty-fifth birthday party. Different genres call for different design elements. (10-11)

As illustrated by the above examples, a rhetorical genre approach teaches students how to recognize and perform genres as rhetorical responses to and reflections of the situations in which they are used. As Aviva Freedman and Peter Medway point out in *Learning and Teaching Genre,* "To analyze school writing in light of the recent reconception of genre is a *demystifying* move, in that it affords explanations of conventional forms that previously appeared arcane and arbitrary" (12). In other words, students can access and participate effectively in academic situations by identifying the assumptions and expectations regarding subject matter, their roles as writers, the roles of readers, and purposes for writing that are embedded in the genres. Again, such approaches to genre analysis do not focus so much on the acquisition of a particular genre as they do on the development of a rhetorical awareness that can transfer and be applied to various genres and their contexts of use.

Teaching Critical Awareness of Genre

Just as Freedman and Medway point out that a genre approach can "demystify" writing situations, they also warn that "the slide is easy from the discovery that conventions are not arbitrary or unmotivated to the assumption that they are right and should be acquired" (*Learning and Teaching Genre* 14) by students, which is also a danger. In response, RGS pedagogical approaches have also focused on the need for instructors to be critical in their uses of genre and to teach this critical awareness to students.

To recognize genres as socially situated and culturally embedded is to recognize that genres carry with them the beliefs, values and ideologies of particular communities and cultures. This extends to the genres that instructors assign, emphasizing the importance of teaching a critical consciousness of genres. In their collection of articles exploring the ideological nature and power of genres, *The Rhetoric and Ideology of Genre,* Richard Coe et al. include in their introduction a heuristic for critical analysis of genre that was earlier developed by Coe and Aviva Freedman. While the heuristic above, "Guidelines for Analyzing Genres," describes strategies for using genre to make sense of and function effectively within communicative environments, the following heuristic asks writers to critique genres for how they both enable and limit access and may privilege certain users:

- What sorts of communication does the genre encourage, what sorts does it constrain against?
- Who can—and who cannot—use this genre? Does it empower some people while silencing others?
- Are its effects dysfunctional beyond their immediate context?
- What values and beliefs are instantiated within this set of practices?
- What are the political and ethical implications of the rhetorical situation constructed, persona embodied [cf., subject positioning], audience invoked and context of situation assumed by a particular genre? (Coe et al. 6-7)

Ideologies are embedded not only in the genres we assign students to write but in the genres we use as instructors, such as assignment prompts, syllabi, and comments on papers. As a result, it is important for teachers to teach critical awareness of classroom genres. Charles Bazerman uses an apt travel metaphor to describe the culture of the classroom and students' knowledge of genres as passports into the academic culture:

> In our role as teachers we constantly welcome strangers into the discursive landscapes we value. But places that are familiar and important to us may not appear intelligible or hospitable to students we try to bring into our worlds. Students, bringing their own road maps of familiar communicative places and desires, would benefit from signs posted by those familiar with the new academic landscape. However, guideposts are only there when we construct them, are only useful if others know how to read them. . . . ("Where is the Classroom" 19)

One way to construct useful guideposts for navigating academic culture is through demystifying classroom genres, like the teacher's end comments on student papers, the student-teacher conference, writing assignment prompt, and the syllabus. In "The Genre of the End Comment: Conventions in Teacher Responses to Student Writing," Summer Smith reveals typified moves teachers make within their end comments, arguing that these moves become so habitual that teachers and students inhabit them unconsciously, in ways that render the genre of end comment less effective. Laurel Black has also analyzed the genre of teacher-student conferences in order to show how conferences exist somewhere between talk and teaching. Black calls for more explicit discussion of student-teacher conferences (their purposes, the social roles they invite, and the conventions that carry out these purposes and social relations) so that students can inhabit such a genre more critically and effectively. Likewise, in our textbook, *Scenes of Writing,* students are asked to analyze their course syllabus to uncover the underlying assumptions and expectations of the course. After sharing sample syllabi in groups and analyzing what the rhetorical patterns reveal about the academic scene and its participants, students critique the syllabus using the following questions as a guide:

> What is expected of students in college courses? How
> are they expected to behave, according to the syllabi's
> assumptions? What kinds of roles are teachers expect-
> ed to take, as reflected in the syllabus genre? What
> kinds of things do the syllabi seem to stress, and what
> does that say about the expectations within the aca-
> demic scene? (197)

Students then follow this analysis with a critique of the genre of the
syllabus, responding to the following questions:

> What does the genre enable its users (both teachers
> and students) to do, and what does it not allow them
> to do? Whose needs are most and least served by the
> genre? What limitations does the genre place on par-
> ticipation in the writing course scene and larger aca-
> demic scene? (197)

The above exercises ask students to analyze the assumptions embedded in the genres participants use within these academic scenes, thus
using genres as maps for gaining access to these academic scenes.

Another way students can learn to access and participate effectively
in academic scenes is by identifying expectations embedded in writing assignments or prompts. Irene Clark, in "A Genre Approach to
Writing Assignments," argues that a genre-based approach to writing
prompts can help (both teachers and students) uncover implicit genre
expectations or assumptions that might not be explicitly spelled out.
Students can discover rhetorical strategies, clues about their roles as
writers and the roles of their readers, and the social goals of the assignment. Drawing a comparison to stage directions, Clark points out that
"a writing assignment constitutes an invitation, not a set of specific instructions. Helping students understand what is involved in responding to that invitation appropriately will enable them to participate in
the performance more successfully."

As Bazerman and others have noted, classrooms are complex spaces that are "always invented, always constructed, always a matter of
genre" ("Where is the Classroom?" 26). Students bring with them
their own genre histories and, based on the intellectual and institutional context of the writing class, teachers build into the classroom
certain generic expectations. As a result, classroom genres are inescapable from power, social difference, and cultural factors. As Devitt has

argued, "The first and most important genre pedagogy, then, is the teacher's genre awareness: the teacher being conscious of the genre decisions he or she makes and what those decisions will teach students" ("Teaching Critical Genre Awareness" 343).

TEACHING THE PRODUCTION OF ALTERNATIVE GENRES

A teaching approach that develops a critical awareness of genre should, in addition to teaching students to critique a genre's ideologies, teach them an awareness of how to produce alternatives. One criticism that has been leveled against a RGS approach to literacy teaching is that it focuses on analysis and critique of genres, stopping short of having writers produce alternative genres or practice using genres to enact change. Susan Miller, for instance, draws a distinction between what she calls "a smart awareness of generic power" and "practice in manipulating genres" and argues that "guided hermeneutic tours have not shown students how to make writing result in motivated action" (483). How, then, do teachers work to develop students' critical awareness to counter potential ideological effects of genres and to produce alternative genres that mediate between constraint and choice? Brad Peters, in "Genre, Antigenre, and Reinventing the Forms of Conceptualization," describes a college composition course in which students read about the U.S. invasion of Panama from a book that takes a Panamanian perspective. The students were then told to write an essay exam that followed a particular format moving from a summary of the argument, to the three most compelling points for a Latin American reader, to the three most fallacious points for a Latin American reader, and finally the student's reaction compared to the Latin American reader's. One student, Brenda—an African American student—opened her essay with an analogy between the racism in Panama and that in the U.S. Peters contends that Brenda had remained silent during class discussions and not until she had a format for framing and expressing her dissent did she do so. Another student, Rita, wrote the essay exam from the fictional perspective of her close friend Maria, a native Latin American and after completing the rhetorical analysis part of the exam, dropped the persona and took up her own in the form of a letter to Maria. Peters identifies this as an "antigenre" but points out that Rita's response satisfies the social purpose of the genre while reconstituting voice and varying the format of the genre. This demonstrates that even when the writing assignment is fairly prescriptive and students are asked to write a fairly traditional genre, there is room for them to maneuver within (and because of) the constraints of the genre.

Another approach to teaching genres as both constraining and enabling is to have students write critical analyses of genres but also participate in the production of new generic responses. For example, Richard Coe asks students to choose a specific type of writing—storybooks for young children, feature articles for ski magazines, feminist critical articles on Shakespeare—and has students create a mini-manual for people who want to learn to write those particular genres. In this way, students not only gain experience writing a specific genre (the manual) but they also analyze a variety of sample genres and, in their manual, make explicit the features and constraints of these genres ("Teaching Genre as a Process" 164). Students could even investigate and do a critical study of genres before writing these genres themselves. Bruce McComiskey, for example, pairs assignments—having students write a critical analysis of education followed by a brochure for high school students or pairing an analysis of the cultural values of advertisements with letters to advertisers arguing the negative effect on consumers. While students conduct genre analysis in order to identify linguistic and rhetorical patterns and to critique the cultural and social values encoded in the genre (what the genre allows users to do and what it does not allow them to do, whose needs are most/least served, how it enables or limits the way its users do their work), the final step asks students to produce new genres or genres that encode alternative values for the purpose of intervening.

A related approach is to have students read multiple examples of the same genre to discover that there's more than one way to respond to a situation. In the study cited above, Peters assigns autobiographies in his FYC classes and has students read samples of this genre as well as some "antigenres"—such as an autobiography by a Japanese woman that was composed of a series of testimonies by people who had influenced her, rather than a traditional first person point of view. One of Peters' students used features of this "antigenre" in his own autobiography. In the same vein, another student—assigned a biography—wrote the biography in the form of a play, which fit with her desire to explore her subject's life as a dramatic presentation. If we provide students with multiple situations and let them decide how to respond most appropriately, we might encourage them to see genres not as "forms dictated" but as a "matter of forms to be found," a genre approach that Ruth Mirtz describes as "part of the form-finding process of meaning-making" (192). In this way, genre analysis can move beyond teaching academic forms to teaching purposeful rhetorical uptakes for social action and can enable students to engage more critically in situated action, the focus of the next section.

TEACHING GENRES IN THEIR CONTEXTS OF USE

The previously discussed pedagogical approaches to teaching genre analysis—including teaching variation and production of alternatives—have been challenged by critics who argue that genre learning cannot take place outside the complex, dynamic sociocultural contexts and set of uptakes that give rise to them (see Chapter 6, for example, where we discuss genre and uptake knowledge). In the well-known and previously cited debate in *RTE* regarding explicit teaching of genres, Aviva Freedman poses the question, "Can the complex web of social, cultural and rhetorical features to which genres respond be explicated at all, or in such a way that can be useful to learners?" ("Show and Tell?" 225). Freedman's concern is with studying genres outside the contexts that they function for—with abstracting genres from the complex and dynamic social and cultural contexts that shape and are shaped by them. Genre-based pedagogical approaches have been criticized for locating the study of genres outside of the "living situations" of their use (Bleich) and for limiting the understanding of genres to features that writers already recognize (Bazerman, "Speech Acts"). In response to this criticism, RGS scholars have recommended teaching genres within their contexts of use by employing field research or ethnographic methods, following approaches already used in English for Academic Purposes (EAP).

For example, in his genre-based approach to an EAP program, Brian Paltridge includes ethnographic components as students carry out a study of fellow students' attitudes toward English. In "Genre, Text Type, and the English for Academic Purposes (EAP) Classroom," Paltridge highlights a task that asks students to interview fellow students to find out "their reasons for studying English, and their opinions regarding different varieties of English" (85). He then assigns the following case study: "Observe a fellow student in this course over a period of several weeks and identify the communication strategies s/he uses when speaking English. Discuss your observations with the student" (85). Similarly, in her book *Text, Role, and Context: Developing Academic Literacies*, Ann Johns casts students in the role of researchers with the objective of getting students to interview professors and investigate the academic and disciplinary settings in which they are writing and to interrogate the values and expectations of the genres they are being asked to produce. Applying a similar approach to more advanced students or teacher-researchers, Bazerman highlights assignments that draw on ethnographic methods in order to situate classroom genres (for example, by examining a set of papers from all students in class and by interviewing students and instructors to discover their understanding of the genre of the assignment). One activity asks students to analyze the genre set of a professional:

> Interview a professor or other professional to determine what kinds of texts [they] receive and write in the course of a typical day. If possible, collect samples. You may wish to shadow them for a day to notice what kinds of texts they receive and produce. Write a paper analyzing the genre set you have found. ("Speech Acts" 337)

A genre approach that incorporates field or ethnographic approaches—observations of a group's interactions, participation in the group, interviews with individuals who read or write in a genre—can situate genre analysis and give students access to authentic contexts for language use.

RGS practitioners have begun to integrate participant/observation research of communities in order to enable students to examine and to see first-hand how communities use genres to carry out social actions and agendas. The following heuristic, "Guidelines for Observing and Describing Scenes," from the textbook *Scenes of Writing: Strategies for Composing with Genres*, seeks to provide students with tools for analyzing genres within their contexts of use:

Guidelines for Observing and Describing Scenes

1. **Select and Gain Access to a Scene**. Once you have selected a scene, determine how you will gain entry into it. Whenever possible, ask for permission from somebody in that scene with the authority to grant it. Tell him or her what you are doing and why you are doing it. Ask also if you could get permission to interview participants in the scene.

2. **Observe the Scene in General**. With a notebook in hand, you are now ready to begin your observations. Begin by describing the scene in general terms. Ask yourself and, whenever possible, ask the participants in the scene: What sort of place is this scene? What activities take place within the scene? Who participates in these activities? What is it that brings people together in this scene? What are the participants' shared objectives?

3. **Identify the Situations of the Scene**. To identify the situations within a scene, use the following questions: What sorts of interactions do you see happening in this scene? Are different interactions occurring in different settings? Do different people participate within these different interactions? Are different subjects discussed within these different interactions?

4. **Observe and Describe the Situations of a Scene**. Once you have identified some of the situations within a scene, you can begin observing some of these situations more closely in order to describe them more fully. In your observation notes, try to describe the participants, setting, subject, and purposes of the interaction for each situation. Keep these questions in mind: Who is participating in this situation? How do the participants seem to be relating to each other? Where exactly is their interaction taking place within the scene? When does this interaction typically take place? What are they interacting about? And what is the nature of their interaction? What sort of language are they using? What sort of tone do they use? Why do they need or want to interact? What is the purpose of their interaction?

5. **Identify the Genres in the Scene**. To identify the genres of a scene, look for patterns or habits in the interaction within a situation. Ask yourself: What patterns of speaking do you notice in those

situations? What written documents typically appear in and are used repeatedly? Because you might not be able to observe all of the genres in action, interview participants in the situation about their genres, and, if possible, collect samples. Try to get responses to the following questions: What "kinds of texts" do the participants typically write in that situation? What are these texts called? What do these texts look like? Who uses these texts, when, where, and why? (44-45)

These questions guide students through the process of gaining access to a scene, to carrying out ethnographic observations of the scenes' participants and activities, to exploring and analyzing the genres used within that scene. In addition to collecting samples of the community's genres, students are urged to interview participants about their uses of the genre as well as take observational notes on the patterns or habits of interaction within a situation. Through their simultaneous participation in ethnographic inquiry and genre analysis—their observation of "meaningful discourse in authentic contexts"—students may come closer to accomplishing what Freedman defines as the two necessary criteria for effective writing instruction: the "exposure to written discourse" combined with "immersion in the relevant contexts" ("Show and Tell?" 247).

Teaching Genres in Public Contexts

In *Genres Across the Curriculum,* Herrington and Moran argue that students can learn ways of thinking and problem solving by writing in authentic contexts, via participation in public genres (9). This view is backed up by research on the socio-discursive model used in Brazilian pedagogy, which teaches literacy skills through genres such as radio genres (see Baltar et al., "School Radio") that have a broader reach to audiences beyond academic audiences. In addition, with the recent proliferation of writing courses focused on public or civic rhetoric, a spectrum of pedagogical approaches for public writing have evolved, ranging from rhetorical analysis of public discourse to direct experience and intervention in public spaces—approaches that can promote genre critique, the production of alternative genres, a situated approach to teaching genres in authentic contexts, as well as the transfer of genre knowledge to public writing situations. Public genres allow teachers to focus on academic objectives of analysis and critique while bring-

ing into the classroom genres that function as sites of intervention
in public spheres. Richard Coe, for example, has focused on having
students write political briefs designed to influence a public decision-
making body ("The New Rhetoric of Genre"); Christian Weisser describes a class where students enter into public discourse by generating
their own genre on environmental issues; and John Trimbur describes
a course in which students write news articles on public health policy and then work in groups to produce an appropriate genre of their
choosing—brochure, pamphlet, flyer, poster, video, radio announcement, web site, etc. ("Composition and the Circulation of Writing").
Trimbur's textbook, *The Call to Write,* also focuses on a range of public
genres—from speeches, Web sites, op ed pieces, and letters to listservs,
ads, fliers, and newletters. Teaching these public genres provides students with "the opportunity to inform and influence readers on issues
they truly care about" (15), thus potentially creating more authentic
contexts for writing or authentic engagement of writers.

The textbook *Scenes of Writing* includes a chapter on public genres
(highlighting opinion editorials and letters to the editor) that gives
students opportunities to analyze and critique public genres—particularly the ways in which they intervene in publics—while also choosing
a public organization and selecting and writing a genre appropriate to
the organization's goals. For example, one of our students researched
the living wage campaign on his campus and produced a flier for the
United Campus Workers, allowing him to imagine and respond to
exigencies different from those of academic genres and to intervene
in sites where discourse can have significant effects. Teaching public
writing through genre analysis of public discourse includes, as Susan
Wells describes it, "an orientation to performance . . . inside and outside of texts" (339). It can teach students that texts do things in the
world and that rhetorical features are tied to social practices. Moving
from public contexts to professional contexts, the next section focuses
on genre approaches that connect rhetorical features to disciplinary
practices.

TEACHING GENRE IN DISCIPLINARY CONTEXTS: A GENRE APPROACH TO WAC/WID

Writing across the Curriculum (WAC) programs, since their inception
in the 1970s and growth in the 1980s, have focused on two strands:

writing to learn (writing as a tool for discovering and shaping knowledge) and learning to write in the disciplines (learning the specific genres and conventions of a discourse community). Since genres function both as cognitive tools and cultural resources, genre analysis is a useful method to employ in writing courses across the curriculum (for an historical and theoretical overview of WAC, including genre and discipline specific applications, see Bazerman et al, *Reference Guide to Writing Across the Curriculum*). Early on in RGS, scholars recognized genre's pedagogical potential for teaching writing across the curriculum (see for example Bazerman's *The Informed Writer* and *The Informed Reader*). As Elaine Maimon noted, "The configurations that form our surface definition of genre have a heuristic potential. Through a study of genre in all disciplines in the arts and sciences, we can learn more about the varieties of thinking in the academy and in the larger world of professional and public activity" (112).

If genres are ways of knowing and acting within differentiated learning domains, can a genre approach help us re-envision the relationship between writing to learn and learning to write? In "Clearing the Air: WAC Myths and Realities," Susan McLeod and Maimon seek to dispel the myth that writing to learn and learning to write are two competing approaches, arguing that learning to write in the disciplines "is not just an exercise in formalism and technical correctness; to the contrary, it is an exercise in epistemology" (580). If learning disciplinary genres functions both as a process of socialization into the disciplinary community as well a "cognitive apprenticeship" (Bazerman, "Genre and Cognitive Development" 294), an approach to WAC or WID (Writing in the Disciplines) that integrates genre analysis can bridge the gap between writing to learn and writing in the disciplines and can focus on the importance of metacognitive awareness that facilitates the transfer of knowledge from one writing context to another.

In their book *Genre across the Curriculum,* Anne Herrington and Charles Moran identify the complementary nature of these two strands of WAC scholarship and pedagogy, noting the potential for genres to serve as "flexible guides for the invention and social action within a given discourse community" (10). Their book features a number of research studies and pedagogical approaches that apply genre approaches to teaching writing in the disciplines, from an examination of how genres are negotiated in comparative literature, history, and biology to analysis of discipline specific genres such as spiritual autobiographies, mini-review essays, and resumes (see our discussion of disciplinary genre research in Chapter 7). In addition, Bazerman et al's *Genre in a Changing World*—the volume drawing from the Fourth International Symposium on Genre—broadens the scope of genre-based WAC approaches by including international perspectives, such as a study (by David Russell et al, "Exploring Notions of Genre") that compares the U.S. WAC movement to the British higher education Academic Literacies movement as well as studies of disciplinary-focused writing courses in an Argentinian and Brazilian University context (see our description of Aranha's study of Brazilian graduate courses in the disciplines, Chapter 7).

Ann Johns ("Genre Awareness for the Novice Academic Student: An On-going Quest") has also recently proposed two promising genre pedagogies that engage with WAC/WID approaches. One approach entails the formation of interdisciplinary learning communities and would cast students in roles as researchers in their content classes, with a focus on discourse community analysis and interviews of faculty in the disciplines. Such an approach promotes genre awareness and situates genre learning (thus teaching rhetorical flexibility), encouraging students to consider the complexity of genres and their varied realizations in real world contexts. The second interdisciplinary approach, drawing on work by WAC specialist Michael Carter, organizes disciplinary writing into four "macro genres" of response: Problem-Solving, Empirical Inquiry, Research from Written Sources, and Performance. Rather than simply training students to learn specific text types, this taxonomy, argues Johns, "educates for a broad knowledge of academic disciplines" (Johns, "Genre Awareness" 21), teaching students varied genres of response that illustrate different ways of knowing. In a similar approach in the textbook *Scenes of Writing*, students are asked to compare how two genres from two different disciplines make use of analysis, argument, and/or research and to analyze what these similarities and differences reveal about each of these disciplinary domains (see *Scenes of Writing*, Chapter 8: Writing in Unfamiliar Academic Scenes and Genres). Finally, in her book *Academic Writing: Writing and Reading in the Disciplines,* Janet Giltrow provides a number of exercises that ask students to consider stylistic differences across various domains of academic writing.

WAC pedagogies that integrate genre approaches envision genres as situated actions that function both pragmatically and epistemologically—both as sites of material interaction within social environments and as tools for understanding and interpreting these interactions. As sites and strategies that locate writers and guide their rhetorical moves, genres are valuable tools for writers entering and navigating disciplinary cultures. A writer's engagement in a disciplinary genre provides access to that community and promotes particular ways of knowing and acting within the disciplinary community.

CONCLUSION

As we have seen in the last two chapters, genre-based pedagogies are adaptable to multiple and varied institutional contexts, as evident by their use within ESL programs, graduate-level writing programs for international students, primary and secondary school writing curricula, first-year composition programs, and writing in the disciplines/ writing across the curriculum programs. Genre's range as a pedagogical tool reflects the range of traditions and intellectual resources that have informed its study over the past thirty years. It also reflects the pedagogical goals and conditions from which it has emerged and to which it has responded. How we utilize genre approaches, then, needs to be grounded in the context of this deeper understanding.

We hope this book—with its overview of genre within historical, theoretical, empirical, and pedagogical contexts—has provided readers the kind of breadth and depth of understanding of genre that will inform their work in multiple contexts: as scholars, researchers, writing teachers, and writing program administrators.

Glossary

Melanie Kill

Activity system—A system of mediated, interactive, shared, motivated, and sometimes competing activities. Within an activity system, the subjects or agents, the objectives, and the mediational means function inseparably from one another (Engeström, "Developmental Studies" 67). Context, when viewed with a focus on activity systems, is "an ongoing, dynamic accomplishment of people acting together with shared tools, including—most powerfully—writing" (Russell, "Rethinking Genre" 508-9). The discursive interactions of an activity system are mediated by genre systems, which maintain stabilized-for-now, normalized ways of acting and interacting that subjects can use to produce consequential, recognizable outcomes.

Brazilian educational model—A pedagogical approach informed by theories of socio-discursive interactionism and the Swiss genre tradition. The Brazilian model brings together a focus on genre awareness, analysis of linguistic conventions, and attention to social context. Its pedagogical sequence generally begins with writing activities that draw on writers' previous genre knowledge and experience, moves to analysis of genre within rhetorical and social contexts, and culminates with (re)production of the genre. See also GENRE AWARENESS and SOCIO-DISCURSIVE INTERACTIONISM.

Communicative purpose—Purpose as defined in relation to a discourse community's shared communicative goals. Communicative purpose often serves as a starting point for ENGLISH FOR SPECIFIC PURPOSES (ESP) genre analyses.

Context—A broad label for the conditions in which discourse occurs. Contexts exist not merely as backdrops or frames within which genres and actions take place, but form in a dynamic, inter-dependent, mutually-constructing relationship with the genre systems they situate. Through the use of genres and other mediational means, communicants perform context as they function within it. See also MEDIATIONAL MEANS.

Corpus linguistics—A linguistic research methodology that draws on large scale electronic text databases (or *corpora*) to allow researchers to conduct systematic searches for linguistic features, patterns, and variations in spoken and written texts.

Cultural Studies approaches to genre—A literary approach to genre that seeks to examine the dynamic relationship between genres, literary texts, and socio-culture. A Cultural Studies approach emphasizes the ways genres organize, generate, normalize, and help reproduce literary as well as non-literary social actions in dynamic, ongoing, culturally defined and defining ways.

Discourse—Language in use and understood as participating in social systems and so having determining effects in social life.

Discourse community—A way of conceptualizing context as defined by and emerging from a particular community. Discourse communities are characterized by common goals, specific genres, shared terminology, material mechanisms (*e.g.,* meeting rooms and newsletters) for communication, and a critical mass of members to pass along community goals and communicative purposes to new members (Swales, *Genre Analysis* 24-27). Genre, when defined in relation to discourse community, is understood as a relatively stable class of linguistic and rhetorical events that members of a discourse community have typified in order to respond to and achieve shared communicative goals. See also ENGLISH FOR SPECIFIC PURPOSES.

Distributed cognition—The ability to think "in conjunction or partnership with others" (Salomon xiii) made possible by the mediation of genre systems and genre sets within activity systems. Cognition is distributed among participants across time and space by the coordinating effects of genre systems and sets. See also ACTIVITY SYSTEM, GENRE SET, GENRE SYSTEM, and SITUATED COGNITION.

English for Specific Purposes (ESP)—A linguistic approach to genre characterized by analysis of the features of texts in relation to the values and rhetorical purposes of discourse communities. Within an ESP framework, a genre is seen as a relatively stable class of linguistic and rhetorical events that members of a discourse community have typified in order to respond to and achieve shared communicative goals. Research in ESP commonly focuses on the use of genre analysis for applied ends. ESP genre pedagogies target advanced, often graduate-level international students in British and U.S. universities and attend to community-identified genres used within specific disciplinary settings. See also DISCOURSE COMMUNITY.

Ethnography—A research methodology that aims for a holistic understanding of human activities in social context. Ethnographic approaches to genre research foreground how patterns of linguistic and rhetorical behavior are related to patterns of social behavior. Ethnography-informed genre pedagogies emphasize the importance of enabling students to encounter, analyze, and practice writing genres with attention to the contexts of their use.

Exigence—The element of a rhetorical situation characterized by urgency brought about by a need, obligation, or stimulus that calls for a response. While exigence is traditionally understood to be objectively perceivable on the basis of inherent characteristics (Bitzer), Carolyn Miller reconceptualizes exigence as "a form of social knowledge—a mutual construing of objects, events, interests and purposes that not only links them but makes them what they are: an objectified social need" ("Genre as Social Action" 30). How we define and act within a situation depends on how we recognize the exigence it presents, and this process of recognition is socially learned and maintained.

Explicit teaching of genre—A pedagogical approach focusing on the explicit teaching of prototypical features of genres, including syntactic, lexical, discursive, and rhetorical features. Both English for Specific Purposes (ESP) and Systemic Functional Linguistics (SFL) genre-based pedagogies are committed to the idea that the explicit teaching of relevant genres provides access to disadvantaged learners. There is ongoing debate about the roles and relative importance of explicit teaching and tacit acquisition in the teaching and learning of genre. See also ENGLISH FOR SPECIFIC PURPOSES, IMPLICIT TEACHING OF GENRE, and SYSTEMIC FUNCTIONAL LINGUISTICS.

Genre—A typified rhetorical way of recognizing, responding to, acting meaningfully and consequentially within, and thus participating in the reproduction of, recurring situations. Genres both organize and generate kinds of texts and social actions, in complex, dynamic relation to one another. While traditional views of genre emphasize its application as a tool of classification, contemporary rhetorical, linguistic, and literary views of genre understand it to be an ideologically active and historically changing force in the production and reception of texts, meanings, and social actions. This dynamic view of genre calls for the study and teaching of how formal features are connected to social purposes, why a genre's formal features come to exist the way they do, and how and why those features make possible certain social actions/relations and not others.

Genre awareness—A genre-based pedagogical approach that recognizes the tacit elements of genre knowledge and so teaches genres both in the context of situated practice and with explicit articulation of the interrelation of rhetorical strategies and social actions. The goal of teaching genre awareness is that students acquire "a critical consciousness of both rhetorical purposes and ideological effects of generic forms" (Devitt, *Writing Genres* 192). See also GENRE KNOWLEDGE.

Genre knowledge—A knowledge not only of a genre's formal features but also of what and whose purposes the genre serves, how to negotiate one's intentions in relation to the genre's social expectations and motives, what reader/writer relationships the genre maintains, and how the genre relates to other genres in the coordination of social life.

Genre set—A set of genres used by a particular community to perform their work. Genres in a set are "associated through the activities and functions of a collective but defining only a limited range of actions" (Devitt, *Writing Genres* 57). See also GENRE SYSTEM.

Genre system—A constellation of genre sets that coordinates and enacts the work of multiple groups within larger systems of activity. A genre system can involve the interaction of users with different types of expertise and levels of authority, yet the relationship of the genres as coordinated through a series of appropriately-timed and expected uptakes enables their users to enact complex social actions over time. See also GENRE SET and UPTAKE.

Ideology—An abstract system of beliefs, values, and ideas that directs goals, expectations, and actions. Ideology and genre are related in that to recognize genres as socially situated and culturally embedded is to recognize that genres carry with them the ideologies of particular communities and cultures. Genre provides the ideological context in which a text and its users function, relate to other genres and texts, and attain cultural value.

Implicit teaching of genre—A genre-based pedagogical approach emphasizing immersion in writing situations to elicit appropriate cognitive strategies without modeling or explication of genre features. In this model, indirect or implicit methods of instruction in genre are seen as the only way for students to achieve complex genre knowledge including the tacit knowledge beyond recognition of prototypical features. See also EXPLICIT TEACHING OF GENRE.

Linguistic traditions of genre study—See CORPUS LINGUISTICS, ENGLISH FOR SPECIFIC PURPOSES, and SYSTEMIC FUNCTIONAL LINGUISTICS

Literary genre theory—The tradition of genre study that has most informed popular beliefs about genre as either an exclusively aesthetic object or as a constraint on the artistic spirit. Recent literary genre scholarship challenges this bipolar attitude and offers a larger landscape for genre action. See CULTURAL STUDIES APPROACHES TO GENRE, NEOCLASSICAL APPROACHES TO GENRE, ROMANTIC AND POST-ROMANTIC APPROACHES TO GENRE, and STRUCTURALIST APPROACHES TO GENRE.

Mediational means—The social, cultural, and historical forms and objects available as means by which to take social action. Mediational means include both semiotic systems of representation (linguistic, visual, etc.) and material objects in the world that carry affordances and constraints.

Metacognition—Awareness and understanding of one's own thought processes, specifically the selection and application of particular cognitive strategies of problem-solving. Metacognition is an important component of genre knowledge transfer across dissimilar contexts.

Meta-genre—A genre that provides shared background knowledge and guidance in how to produce and negotiate genres within genre sets and systems. Meta-genres can take the form of guidelines or manuals for how to produce and use genres or simply shared discourse about genres. Some communities have defined, explicit meta-genres that guide their genre systems while other communities will have tacitly agreed upon meta-genres. Janet Giltrow defines meta-genres as "atmospheres surrounding genres" ("Meta-genre" 195) that function on the boundaries between activity systems to smooth over tensions individuals experience within and between activity systems by rationalizing the contradictions and conflicts.

Neoclassical approaches to genre—A literary approach to genre that utilizes a theoretical, transhistorical set of categories in order to classify literary texts according to internal thematic and formal relations. The main critique of such taxonomies has been the way they universalize the ideological character of genre rather than seeing genres as emerging from and responding to socio-historically situated exigencies.

New Rhetoric—A twentieth century shift in the rhetorical tradition from a classical emphasis on the centrality of persuasion in rhetorical discourse to an emphasis on the role of identification. A new rhetorical approach examines how people use rhetoric not only to persuade but also to relate to one another, to create shared experiences and versions of social reality. According to Kenneth Burke, the new rhetoric recognizes rhetoric as a dimension of all discourse and a form of symbolic action.

North American Genre Theory—See RHETORICAL GENRE THEORY.

Occluded genre—A genre that operates behind the scenes of more dominant genres and to which access is limited within the participating discourse community. Examples of occluded genres include submission letters, review letters, abstracts, etc. (Swales, "Occluded Genres" 46).

Pedagogy—The principles and methods of teaching and learning that guide instruction. Genre-based pedagogies inform classroom strategies for teaching both the production and analysis of discourse.

Phenomenology—A philosophical tradition established at the beginning of the twentieth century with the work of Edmund Husserl and later expanded by Martin Heidegger. Phenomenology emerged as a challenge to the Cartesian split between mind and world. It rejects the idea that consciousness is self-contained and privately held and, instead, seeks to account for how objects in the world manifest themselves and become available to human consciousness. At the heart of phenomenology's outer-directed view of consciousness and experience is the notion of intentionality understood as a cognitive, sense-making act. Phenomenology relates to genre theory in that in the same way intentions bring objects to our consciousness, genres bring texts and situations to our consciousness and so inform our intentions.

Primary and secondary genres—Levels of genre complexity and relationship to context as outlined by Mikhail Bakhtin. Primary genres form in the course of everyday communication. Secondary genres, such as the novel, re-contextualize these primary genres by placing them in relationship to other primary genres within its symbolic world.

Prototype theory—A theory of graded categorization based on Eleanor Rosch's theory of prototypes. Prototype theory identifies membership within genre not on the basis of shared, essential properties of texts but on the basis of more or less similarity to a prototypical text. This notion of more or less similarity has played an important role in historical and corpus linguistic approaches to genre categorization.

Rhetorical Genre Studies (RGS)—Also known as North American Genre Theory. A rhetorical approach to genre that emphasizes the study of genres as forms of situated cognition, social action, and social reproduction. RGS has contributed to the work of new rhetoric by examining how genres, understood as typified rhetorical ways of acting within and enacting recurring situations, function as symbolic means of establishing social identification and cooperation. Within RGS the focus of genre analysis is directed toward an understanding of social practices and events: the ideologies, power relations, epistemologies, and activities that animate them, and the role that genres play in how individuals experience and enact these practices in various sites of activity. An RGS approach raises questions about the pedagogical possibilities of teaching genres explicitly in classroom environments, outside of the contexts of their use. Work to develop RGS genre-based pedagogies face the challenge of teaching genres in ways that maintain their complexity and status as more than just typified rhetorical features. RGS scholars have for the most part advocated an apprenticeship-based approach to teaching and learning genres with attention to the following issues: how to develop genre knowledge that transfers across writing situations; how to teach a critical awareness of genre; how to teach students to move from critique to production of alternative genres; and, finally, how to situate genres within the contexts of their use, whether public, professional, or disciplinary contexts.

Rhetorical situation—The context of rhetorical action. Lloyd Bitzer defines a rhetorical situation as "a complex of persons, events, objects, and relations presenting an actual or potential exigence which can be completely or partially removed if discourse, introduced into the situation, can so constrain human decision or action as to bring about the significant modification of the exigence" ("The Rhetorical Situation" 304). Bitzer acknowledges that all discourse takes place in some context, but proposes that the distinguishing characteristic of a rhetorical situation is that it calls forth rhetorical discourse (which produces action). By positing rhetorical situation as generative of rhetorical action, Bitzer recognized the "power of situation to constrain a fitting response" (Bitzer 307). Carolyn Miller further observes that our recognition of a situation as calling for a certain response is based on our having defined it as a situation that calls for a certain response and so argues that "situations . . . are the result, not of 'perception,' but of 'definition'" ("Genre as Social Action" 29). Rhetorical situations, then, are social constructs, and genres are how we mutually construe or define situations as calling for certain actions. See also Exigence.

Romantic and post-Romantic approaches to genre—Literary approaches to genre that reject genre's constitutive power, arguing instead that literary texts achieve their status by exceeding genre conventions, which are perceived as prescriptive taxonomies and constraints on textual energy.

Socio-Discursive Interactionism (SDI)—A theoretical approach to discourse that "postulates that human actions should be treated in their social and discursive dimensions, considering language as the main characteristic of human social activity" (Baltar *et al.* 53). Within SDI, genres are considered both "as products of social activities . . . and as tools that allow people to realize language actions and participate in different social activities" (Araújo 46). Bakhtin's influence on SDI is evident in its focus on language-in-use and genres as typified utterances. Vygotsky's influence appears in SDI's key distinctions between *acting, activity,* and *action,* with 'acting' describing "any form of directed intervention," 'activity' referring to the shared, socially-defined notion of acting in particular situations, and 'action' indicating the interpretation of "acting" on an individual level (Baltar *et al.* 53). Genres play a mediating role between the social and behavioral dimensions of language (the activity and action). Within this framework, SDI pays attention to actors' *motivational plans* (their reasons for acting), *intentional plans* (their purposes for acting), *and available resources and instruments* (habitual strategies, familiar tools).

Structuralist approaches to genre—A literary approach to genre that understands genres as both organizing and shaping literary texts and activities within a literary reality. Structuralist (or literary-historical) approaches acknowledge the power of genre to shape textual interpretation and production. They examine how socio-historically localized genres shape specific literary actions, identifications, and representations. However, by focusing on genres as literary artifacts that structure literary realities, structuralist genre approaches overlook how all genres, not just literary, help organize and generate social practices and realities.

Sydney School approach—A pedagogical approach to genre that emerged in response to an Australian national curriculum aimed at K-12 students. Based largely in Systemic Functional Linguistics, the trajectory of teaching and learning begins with educators modeling genres and explicating genre features using the Hallidayan socially-based system of textual analysis. Students then work to reproduce these genres and thus acquire them. See also SYSTEMIC FUNCTIONAL LINGUISTICS.

Systemic Functional Linguistics (SFL)—A linguistic approach to genre, based on the work of M.A.K. Halliday, that operates from the premise that language structure is integrally related to social function and context. SFL holds that language is organized in particular ways in a culture because such an organization serves a social purpose within that culture. "Functional" refers to the work that language does within particular contexts. "Systemic" refers to the structure or organization of language that provides the "systems of choices" available to language users for the realization of meaning (Christie, "Genre Theory" 759). The concept of *realization* is especially important within SFL, for it describes the dynamic way that language *realizes* social purposes and contexts as specific linguistic interactions, at the same time as social purposes and contexts *realize* language as specific social actions and meanings. Systemic functional approaches to genre arose in part in response to concerns over the efficacy of student-centered, process-based literacy teaching, with their emphasis on "learning through doing."

Typifications—Socially defined and shared recognitions of similarities. Typifications are part of our habitual knowledge (Schutz 108); they are the routinized, socially-available categorizations of strategies and forms for recognizing and acting within familiar situations and thus they are central to a view of genre as social action.

Uptake—A concept originally established in J.L. Austin's speech act theory to refer to how an illocutionary act (saying, for example, "it is hot in here" with the intention of getting someone to cool the room) gets taken up as a perlocutionary effect (someone subsequently opening a window) under certain conditions. Anne Freadman applies uptake to genre theory, arguing that genres are defined in part by the uptakes they condition and secure. Uptake helps us understand how systematic, normalized relations between genres coordinate complex forms of social action. As Freadman is careful to note, uptake does not depend on causation but on selection. What we *choose* to take up and how we do so is the result of learned recognitions of significance that over time and in particular contexts becomes habitual. Knowledge of uptake is knowledge of what to take up, how, and when, including how to execute uptakes strategically and when to resist expected uptakes.

Writing Across the Curriculum (WAC)—A pedagogical movement to incorporate writing in courses across college curriculums. Since their inception in the 1970s and growth in the 1980s, WAC programs have focused on two strands: writing to learn (writing as a tool for discovering and shaping knowledge) and learning to write in the disciplines (learning the specific genres and conventions of a discourse community). WAC pedagogies that integrate genre approaches envision genres as situated actions that function both pragmatically and epistemologically—both as sites of material interaction within social environments and as tools for understanding and interpreting these interactions.

Writing In the Disciplines (WID)—A pedagogical movement emphasizing writing instruction in specific disciplinary contexts. See also WRITING ACROSS THE CURRICULUM.

Annotated Bibliography

Melanie Kill

Bakhtin, Mikhail M. "The Problem of Speech Genres." *Speech Genres and Other Late Essays.* Trans. Vern W. McGee. Eds. Caryl Emerson and Michael Holquist. Austin: U of Texas P, 1986. 60-102.

Written in 1952-53, the essay offers an early move toward an understanding of genre as socially-situated and relevant to discourse in all spheres of activity. Bakhtin describes genres as "relatively stable thematic, compositional, and stylistic types of utterances" (64) that emerge from particular functions and conditions of communication. He distinguishes between primary (simple) genres, which form in the course of everyday communication, and secondary (complex) genres, such as the novel, which form from an assemblage of primary genres re-contextualized in relationship to one another within the symbolic world of the secondary genre. Emphasis throughout is on the responsive and dialogic nature of discourse.

Bazerman, Charles. *Shaping Written Knowledge: The Genre and Activity of the Experimental Article in Science.* Madison: U of Wisconsin P, 1988.

A historical study of the evolution of the experimental article in science from its beginnings in correspondence reports read at Royal Society of London meetings. Bazerman collected a corpus of 1,000 articles from the first scientific journal in English, *Philosophical Transactions.* Analyzing one hundred articles from this corpus, in addition to 40 articles from *Physical Review* and scientific writings by Newton and Compton, he explores how changes in the generic features and structure of scientific articles from 1665 to 1800 are tied to changes in the social structures of the discipline, shifts in the theoretical composition of arguments, and changes in material practices within the sciences.

Bazerman, Charles, Adair Bonini, and Débora Figueiredo, eds. *Genre in a Changing World*. Fort Collins, CO: The WAC Clearinghouse and Parlor Press, 2009.

A collection of essays selected from presentations at the 2007 SIGET IV (the Fourth International Symposium on Genre Studies) in Tubarão, Santa Catarina, Brazil. The book includes international perspective synthesizing multiple genre traditions (North American genre theory, English for Specific Purposes, Systemic Functional Linguistics, Socio-Discursive Interactionism) and covering advances in genre theories, genre and the professions, genre and media, genre in teaching and learning, and genre in writing across the curriculum.

Beebee, Thomas O. *The Ideology of Genre: A Comparative Study of Generic Instability*. University Park: Pennsylvania State UP, 1994.

Beebee argues that literary genres can reveal cultural ideologies by denaturalizing and reconfiguring relations between everyday genres and their use values. Because genre provides the ideological context in which a text and its users function, relate to other genres and texts, and attain cultural value: "Genre gives us not understanding in the abstract and passive sense but use in the pragmatic and active sense" (14). It is within this social and rhetorical economy that a genre attains its use-value, making genre one of the bearers, articulators, and repro-ducers of culture—in short, ideological. In turn, genres are what make texts ideological, endowing them with a social use-value.

Berkenkotter, Carol, and Thomas N. Huckin. "Rethinking Genre from a Sociocognitive Perspective." *Written Communication* 10. 4 (1993): 475-509.

An examination of the socio-cognitive work that genres perform within academic disciplinary contexts. Berkenkotter and Huckin take as their starting point the notion that genres dynamically embody a community's ways of knowing, being, and acting and are "best con-ceptualized as a form of situated cognition" (477). Genres normalize activities and practices, enabling community members to participate in these activities and practices in fairly predictable, familiar ways in order to get things done. At the same time, though, genres are dynamic because they change as their conditions of use change. For genres to function effectively over time, Berkenkotter and Huckin surmise, they "must accommodate both stability and change" (481).

Bhatia, Vijay. *Analysing Genre: Language Use in Professional Settings.* London: Longman, 1993.

Bhatia presents genre analysis in relation to other methods of text and discourse analysis and offers a seven-step process for analyzing genres that follows a trajectory common to ESP genre approaches, moving from attention to context to textual analysis. There is a strong emphasis on examining a given genre-text in its professional context by attending to discourse community, communicative purpose, material conditions, and institutional context, in addition to lexico-grammatical features, language patterns, and larger structural patterns. In the final section of the book, Bhatia explores applications of this model to the teaching of languages and English for Specific Purposes.

Bitzer, Lloyd F. "The Rhetorical Situation." *Philosophy & Rhetoric* 1.1 (1968): 1-14.

Bitzer identifies "the nature of those contexts in which speakers or writers create rhetorical discourse" as an explicit concern of rhetorical theory (1). The essay marks a move to attend to the ways that discourse responds recursively to the exigence of a rhetorical situation rather than being determined by speaker, audience, or subject matter. Bitzer concludes by acknowledging that the discourse formations that develop in response to recurring situations join the set of constraints for that situation, and he thus raises questions about the social conditions of recurrence and typification that are foundational to rhetorical genre theory.

Campbell, Karlyn Kohrs, and Kathleen Hall Jamieson, eds. *Form and Genre: Shaping Rhetorical Action.* Falls Church, VA: Speech Communication Association, 1978.

Describing genres as "stylistic and substantive responses to perceived situational demands" (19), Campbell and Jamieson argue that situational demands (not theoretical, apriori categories) should serve as the basis for how we identify and define genres. What gives a genre its character is the "fusion" or "constellation" of substantive and stylistic forms that emerge in response to a recurring situation. It is this "dynamic constellation of forms" (24) within a genre that functions to produce a particular rhetorical effect in a recurrent situation.

Coe, Richard, Lorelei Lingard, and Tatiana Teslenko, eds. *The Rhetoric and Ideology of Genre: Strategies for Stability and Change.* New Jersey: Hampton Press, 2002.

A collection of essays exploring the ideological nature and power of genres through discussion of genre theory, professional discourses, educational discourses, and social and political discourses. Contributors include: Charles Bazerman, Anne Freadman, Anthony Paré, Catherine Schryer, JoAnne Yates and Wanda Orlikowski, Peter Medway, Lorelei Lingard, Janet Giltrow, David Russell, and Ryan Knighton.

Devitt, Amy J. *Writing Genres.* Carbondale: Southern Illinois UP, 2004.

Devitt reviews and extends a rhetorical theory of genre that "sees genres as types of rhetorical actions that people perform in their everyday interactions with their worlds" (2). Moving easily between genre theory, pedagogy, and research, Devitt offers a range of perspectives on genre and power, genre change, genre and linguistic standardization, literary genre, and the teaching of genre awareness. The book concludes with a call for further research on genre, including cognitive studies, historical studies, and collaborative research between sociologists and genre theorists (218).

Freedman, Aviva and Peter Medway, eds. *Genre and the New Rhetoric.* Bristol: Taylor and Francis, 1994.

A collection of essays from genre scholars working in North America and Australia addressing issues in genre theory, research on public and professional genres, and applications of genre in education. The introduction (Freedman and Medway) offers a historical overview of major theories and theorists to situate rhetorical genre studies. Reprints Carolyn Miller's "Genre as Social Action" and Anne Freadman's

"Anyone for Tennis?" and includes chapters by Charles Bazerman, Catherine Schryer, A.D. Van Nostrand, Anthony Paré and Graham Smart, Janet Giltrow, Richard Coe, and Aviva Freedman.

Frye, Northrop. *Anatomy of Criticism: Four Essays*. Princeton: Princeton UP, 1957.

Frye proposes a transhistorical system of categories (modes, archetypes, and genres) to describe literary texts and their relations. Frye offers a total of four distinct genres—epos, fiction, drama and lyric—defined neither by subject matter nor form but on the basis of the relation between author and audience. As Frye explains of Neoclassical approaches, "the purpose of criticism by genre is not so much to classify as to clarify such traditions and affinities, thereby bringing out a larger number of literary relationships that would not be noticed as long as there were no context established for them" (247-48).

Genette, Gérard. *The Architext: An Introduction*. Berkeley: U of California P, 1992.

Genette describes how Neoclassical literary taxonomies, which take as their basis the familiar literary triad of lyric, epic, and dramatic, mistakenly attribute to Aristotle what is actually the product of Romantic and post-Romantic poetics. He argues that this "all too seductive" triad has distorted and impeded the development of coherent classifications of literature and theories of genre.

Halliday, Michael. *Language as Social Semiotic: The Social Interpretation of Language and Meaning*. London: Edward Arnold, 1978.

Describes how the "social semiotic" of a culture is encoded in and maintained by its discourse-semantic system, which represents the culture's "meaning potential" (100, 13). Halliday argues that language is a form of socialization. He introduces the term *register* to refer to the "clustering of semantic features according to situation types" (68). By linking a situation type with particular semantic and lexicogrammatic patterns, register describes what actually takes place (the "field"), how participants relate to one another (the "tenor"), and what role language is playing (the "mode"). What happens at the level of context of situation in terms of field, tenor, and mode corresponds to what happens at the linguistic level in terms of what Halliday refers to as the three language "metafunctions": ideational, interpersonal, and textual. Halliday's work has served as a foundation for systemic functional approaches to genre.

Miller, Carolyn R. "Genre as Social Action." *Genre and the New Rhetoric.* Ed. Aviva Freedman and Peter Medway. Bristol: Taylor and Francis, 1994. 23-42.

Argues that genre is most usefully defined in terms of typified rhetorical action rather than conventional features of form or content. Miller proposes a conception of rhetorical genre based on social motives mediated by genre in recurrent situations, observing that "situations . . . are the result, not of 'perception,' but of 'definition'" (156). Rhetorical situations are thus socially constructed and exigence is reconceptualized as a form of social knowledge. It is our shared interpretation of a situation, through available typifications such as genres, that makes it recognizable as recurrent and that gives it meaning and value.

Russell, David. "Rethinking Genre in School and Society: An Activity Theory Analysis." *Written Communication* 14.4 (1997): 504-54.

Turns to activity systems as a way to account for dynamic, ecological interactions between genres and their contexts of use. Russell draws on Engestrom's systems version of Vygotskian activity theory and Bazerman's theory of genre systems to understand the relationship between classroom writing and wider social practices. He defines an activity system as "any ongoing, object-directed, historically conditioned, dialectically structured, tool-mediated human interaction" (510) with rules/norms, community, and division of labor supporting and informing the interaction between subjects, meditational means, and objects/motives.

Swales, John M. *Genre Analysis: English in Academic and Research Settings.* Cambridge: Cambridge UP, 1990.

Identifies two key characteristics of English for Specific Purposes genre approaches: a focus on academic and research English and the use of genre analysis toward applied ends. Swales presents detailed explanations of three key, inter-related concepts—*discourse community, genre,* and *language-learning task.* Proposing that "a genre is a class of communicative events" joined by "some shared set of communicative purposes" (45-46), Swales defines genres first and foremost as linguistic and rhetorical actions belonging to communities rather than individuals. The book offers an ESP analysis of the research paper and ideas for genre-based teaching.

Todorov, Tzvetan. "The Origin of Genres." *Modern Genre Theory.* Ed.
    David Duff. London: Longman, 2000. 193-209.

Todorov addresses issues of the relationship between text and genre, the formation of new genres out of older genres, and the relationship of literary genres and other speech acts. He defines genre as "nothing other than the codification of discursive properties" (18), distinguishing the descriptions of genre that can be given from perspectives of abstract analysis and empirical observation. Todorov proposes the word 'genre' designate only those genres that have a historical basis as evidenced by discourse on the genre.

Notes

¹ Responding to Plato in the *Poetics,* Aristotle offers a defense of artistic representations on the grounds that such representations are not imitations of appearances, mere copies, but rather contain their own organic integrity and principles of order. He begins the *Poetics* by explaining: "I propose to treat of poetry in itself and its various kinds, noting the essential quality of each" (50). Operating from this premise, Aristotle then proceeds to categorize epic, tragedy, and comedy as "modes of imitation" on the basis of their structure and function, particularly in terms of their medium, object, and manner of imitation (50). The *medium* of imitation can be rhythm, melody, or verse; the *object* of imitation involves human action, particularly high or low character; and *manner* of imitation can be presented either through narration or drama. On the basis of these distinctions, Aristotle describes epic, tragedy, and comedy as representing different kinds of poetic actions, classified according to how each configures particular relations between medium, object, and manner of imitation.

² Spatially, within the lyric, the writer is said to exist in spatial proximity to his or her text, being in the text, so to speak, whereas in the dramatic, the action takes place in its own spatial context that determines the interaction between two or more independent actors. Temporally, lyric is often associated with the present, dramatic with the future, and epic with the past (Genette 47-49), so that each represents a particular way of conceiving of literary temporality that affects literary actions. So the lyric, dramatic, and epic orient the way that time, space, and the activities that occur within them are configured and enacted in different literary texts. John Frow describes how, in Hegel's formulation, the triad also becomes connected with human development, so that, for instance, epic is an "objective disclosure of the exterior universe" that "corresponds to the childhood of the human race," while lyric is a "subjective disclosure of the inner world of particularized individuals, and it has to do with the separation of the personal self from the community," and drama is "the synthesis of the two, the objectification of subjectivities in dialogue and action" (Frow 60).

³ For example, both Genett and Todorov have argued that what Neoclassical approaches refer to as "genres" are actually not genres but rather "types" (Todorov, "Origin" 208) or "modes" (Genette 64)—abstract theo-

retical/analytical categories that classify genres, which are themselves more historically and culturally contingent, literary phenomena (Genette 74).

[4] As Beebee explains, "It is only in the deformations and contradictions of writing and thinking that we can recognize ideology; genre is one of those observable deformations, a pattern in the iron filing of cultural products that reveals the force of ideology" (18).

[5] Halliday's work did not specifically focus on genre. When he briefly refers to genre, Halliday locates genre as a mode or conduit of communication, one of the textual and linguistic means available within register that helps communicants realize the situation type. Functioning at the level of *mode*, within the field, tenor and mode complex, genre represents the vehicle through which communicants interact within a situation type. In Halliday's model, genres are thus relegated to typified tools communicants use within registers to enact and interact within a particular type of situation. It is this situation, Halliday explains, "that generates the semiotic tensions and the rhetorical styles and genres that express them" (113).

[6] For a helpful example of analysis based in generic structure potential, see Brian Paltridge's *Genre, Frames and Writing in Research Settings* (66-71). As Paltridge explains, an analysis based on generic structure potential should "demonstrate what elements *must* occur; what elements *can* occur; where elements *must* occur; where elements *can* occur; and *how often* elements can occur" (66).

[7] In his later work, Biber substitutes the term "register" for "genre," using register "as a general cover term for all language varieties associated with different situations and purposes" ("An Analytical Framework" 32).

[8] As Tardy and Swales note in their recent review of genre in writing research, while the twentieth century will be known as the era of large corpora, there are signs that "the first decade of the new century will turn out to be the decade of fairly small, genre-specific or multi-genre-specific corpora, such as a collection of 50 medical research articles" (574). Such smaller, genre-defined corpora can help make genre a significant variable in corpus linguistics, but while they will allow researchers to determine how often certain linguistic patterns appear in genres, they will still not be able to account for *why* these patterns appear, a subject that requires deeper rhetorical analysis.

[9] J.R. Martin has referred to such pre-genres as "instructional genres" ("A Contextual Theory") while William Grabe has called them "macro-genres" ("Narrative and Expository Macro-genres"). As Tardy and Swales explain, "what these schemes share is a relative independence from context, so that a macro-genre like exposition might encompass text types as diverse as research papers, textbooks, and pamphlets. Nevertheless, proponents of such classification schemes argue that their value lies in differentiating the functions and purposes of text forms on a broad level. . . . [Grabe] and others argue that these higher level structures have great value for raising writers'

awareness of discourse structure and for enhancing metalinguistic reflection" (566).

[10] An Cheng describes the range of existing ESP genre-based writing courses: from those targeting a specific audience, such as advanced Asian doctoral students in social psychology, to more general courses for advanced nonnative-speaking "junior scholars" learning to write literature reviews. The most typical "ESP genre-based writing class for international graduate students often involves guiding students from various disciplinary fields to explore the generic features and the disciplinary practices in research articles (RAs) that they themselves have collected. It also involves learners engaging in discipline-specific writing tasks" (Cheng 85).

[11] For a discussion of other recent trends in ESP genre approaches, including the use of community partnership models that enable students to analyze, write, and intervene in genres within contexts of their use, as well as the use of video technology to enable access to on-site genre analysis, see Diane Belcher's "Trends in Teaching English for Specific Purposes."

[12] Such calls for a critical approach to genre within ESP are presaged to some extent by Swales (1990), who warns:

> At the end of the day, we may come to see that genres as in-
> struments of rhetorical action can have generative power . . . ;
> they not only provide maps of new territories but also provide the
> means for their exploration. Yet the empowerment they provide
> needs to be accompanied by critical reflection in order to ensure
> that our students, as they journey forward, are not blind to the
> social consequences of their own actions and of those who have
> been there before them. (*Genre Analysis* 92)

Yet earlier in the same book, Swales explains why he has chosen to avoid ideological discussions of genre: "A specific reason for this exclusion is that the proposed approach is not activated by a wish to make a contribution to intellectual history or to construct a schematic version of disciplinary cultures, but rests on a pragmatic concern to help people, both non-native and native speakers, to develop their academic communicative competence" (9).

[13] For example, in a recent article in the *Journal of English for Academic Purposes,* Bronia P.C. So reinforces the "necessity of a genre-based pedagogy that helps learners realize how schematic structure and linguistic features are related to social context and purpose" (68). Yet for So, social context and purpose are used to inform/explicate/understand schematic structure and linguistic features, not the other way around. In this case, the attention given in So's analysis to "context of situation" is much briefer compared to the analysis of schematic structure and linguistic features (see So 71-73).

[14] The literary critic Tzvetan Todorov makes a similar argument, distinguishing between theoretically-based and historically-based genre categorizations. The former begin with apriori categories and proceed deductively,

while the latter begin with actual, historically-situated texts and proceed inductively. See Chapter 2 for a more detailed discussion of Todorov and other approaches to literary genre studies.

[15] As Sokolowski explains, our intentions are not only of physical objects, present or absent; we can also intend perceptions, memories, imagination, anticipation, judgment, etc. (191-92).

[16] As Miller explains, "this approach insists that the '*de facto*' genres, the types we have names for in everyday language, tell us something theoretically important about discourse. To consider as potential genres such homely discourse as the letter of recommendation, the user manual, the progress report, the ransom note . . . as well as the eulogy, the apologia, the inaugural, the public proceeding, and the sermon, is not to trivialize the study of genres; it is to take seriously the rhetoric in which we are immersed and the situations in which we find ourselves" (27).

[17] In her 1994 chapter "Rhetorical Community: The Cultural Basis of Genre," Carolyn Miller likewise turns to Giddens' theory of structuration. Prior to Berkenkotter and Huckin, Yates and Orlikowski had also used Giddens' work to study organizational genres in their 1992 "Genres of Organizational Communication: A Structurational Approach."

[18] Amy Devitt was one of the first scholars to consider the implications of a RGS-based approach to genre teaching. In "Generalizing about Genre: New Conceptions of an Old Concept," Devitt advocates an approach to genre teaching that is based not in textual explication but in an understanding of how genres work within situations and how genres orient textual production. She describes, for instance, how genres can help students learn about the communities that construct and use them (581), thereby developing in students a more complex understanding of situations and their relationship to texts. Also, a genre approach to teaching can help student writers "understand generic goals: what they are . . . how writers learn them, and how writers use them" (581). Such an understanding of generic goals can then enable students to make more effective, situated decisions during prewriting and revision processes (584). Finally, a genre approach can help teachers more effectively diagnose students' difficulties with writing for different situations. Devitt's approach to genre-based teaching represents more of an orientation towards how and why texts are made, as opposed to an approach based in explicating textual features. In Chapter 10, we will describe in more detail RGS approaches to genre teaching, including Devitt's later work, as well as her work with Reiff and Bawarshi, that promotes teaching genre awareness.

[19] At the heart of Bakhtin's dialogic view of genres, outlined in "The Problem of Speech Genres," is the distinction he makes between a sentence and an utterance. Bakhtin defines a *sentence* as "a unit of language" that is bounded grammatically and exists in isolation, outside of a sphere of communication. A sentence is a grammatical unit that does not evoke a responsive

reaction (74). An *utterance,* on the other hand, is "a unit of speech communication" (73) that is inherently responsive and that is bounded by a change in speaking subjects: "its beginning is preceded by the utterances of others, and its end is followed by the responsive utterances of others (or, although it may be silent, others' active responsive understanding, or, finally, a responsive action based on this understanding" (71). The key point for Bakhtin is that utterances are dialogically related to other utterances. And because genres are typified utterances, they are likewise dialogically related to other genres.

[20] Freadman's characterization of strategies and tactics here resembles Derrida's understanding of texts as participating in (not belonging to) genres. In Chapter 2, we describe in more detail Derrida's theory that every textual performance repeats, mixes, stretches, and potentially reconstitutes the genres it participates in.

[21] While the concept of genre systems has appeared in prior scholarship—Todorov ("Origin"), Fairclough (*Discourse and Social Change*)—and been anticipated by Latour and Woolgar in *Laboratory Life* (see Berkenkotter, "Genre Systems" for a brief history), Bazerman was the first to elaborate on it within RGS, and to connect it to typified actions, social intentions, and consequential relations.

[22] In "Genre and Identity," Paré describes the cultural tensions (what Russell refers to as the "double bind" ["Rethinking Genre in School and Society 519]) Inuit social workers experience when using social work genres in their native communities: "The Inuit workers were being forced to employ rhetorical strategies developed in the urban south, where workers and clients live apart and have no relationship outside the interview, the office, the courtroom. Transporting textual practices to the north meant transporting as well the elements of context and culture that had created and sustained them: the impersonal, detached persona of professional life, the anticipated narratives of southern social worker clients, the categories, lifestyles, values, beliefs, and power relations of the urban welfare state. As a result, the Inuit workers were forced into a position between cultures and into the role of professional representatives of the colonial power" (Paré, "Genre and Identity" 63). Working within this double bind, Inuit social workers "have created alternative methods of practice—methods developed within their own cultural and rhetorical traditions," although there are limits to their ability to resist or subvert the dominant genres (68-69).

Works Cited

Altman, Rick. *Film/Genre*. London: BFI, 1999. Print.

Andersen, Jack. "The Concept of Genre in Information Studies." *Annual Review of Information Science and Technology* 42 (2008): 339-67. Print.

Anson, Chris, Deanna P. Dannels, and Karen St. Clair. "Teaching and Learning a Multimodal Genre in a Psychology Course." *Genre across the Curriculum*. Ed. Anne Herrington and Charles Moran. Logan: Utah State UP, 2005. 171-95. Print.

Aranha, Solange. "The Development of a Genre-Based Writing Course for Graduate Students in Two Fields." *Genre in a Changing World*. Ed. Charles Bazerman, Adair Bonini, and Débora Figueiredo. Fort Collins, CO: The WAC Clearinghouse and Parlor Press, 2009. 473-90. Print.

Araújo, Antonia Dilamar. "Mapping Genre Research in Brazil: An Exploratory Study." *Traditions of Writing Research*. Ed. Charles Bazerman et al. New York: Routledge, 2010. 44-57. Print.

Aristotle. *Poetics*. *Critical Theory Since Plato*. Ed. Hazard Adams. Rev. ed. Fort Worth: Harcourt Brace Jovanovich, 1994. 50-66. Print.

Artemeva, Natasha. "A Time to Speak, a Time to Act: A Rhetorical Genre Analysis of a Novice Engineer's Calculated Risk Taking." *Rhetorical Genre Studies and Beyond*. Ed. Natasha Artemeva and Aviva Freedman. Winnipeg: Inkshed, 2006. 188-239. Print.

Artemeva, Natasha, and Aviva Freedman, eds. *Rhetorical Genre Studies and Beyond*. Winnipeg: Inkshed, 2006. Print.

Askehave, Inger, and John M. Swales. "Genre Identification and Communicative Purpose: A Problem and a Possible Solution." *Applied Linguistics* 22 (2001): 195-212. Print.

Bakhtin, Mikhail M. *The Dialogic Imagination*. Trans. Caryl Emerson and Michael Holquist. Austin: U of Texas P, 1981. Print.

—. "The Problem of Speech Genres." In *Speech Genres and Other Late Essays*. Trans. Vern W. McGee. Ed. Caryl Emerson and Michael Holquist. Austin: U of Texas P, 1986. 60-102. Print.

Baltar, Marcos, Maria Eugênia T. Gastaldello, and Marina A. Camelo. "School Radio: Socio-Discursive Interaction Tool in the School." *L1—Educational Studies in Language and Literature* 9.2 (2009): 49-70. Print.

Barton, David, and Nigel Hall. *Letter Writing as a Social Practice.* Amsterdam: John Benjamins Publishing, 1999. Print.

Bauman, Marcy L. "The Evolution of Internet Genres." *Computers and Composition* 16.2 (1999): 269-82. Print.

Bawarshi, Anis. *Genre and the Invention of the Writer: Reconsidering the Place of Invention in Composition.* Logan: Utah State UP, 2003. Print.

—. "Genres as Forms of In[ter]vention." *Originality, Imitation, Plagiarism: Teaching Writing in the Digital Age.* Ed. Caroline Eisner and Martha Vicinus. Ann Arbor, MI: U of Michigan P, 2008. 79-89. Print.

Bazerman, Charles. *Constructing Experience.* Carbondale: Southern Illinois UP, 1994. Print.

—. "Genre and Cognitive Development: Beyond Writing to Learn." *Genre in a Changing World.* Ed. Charles Bazerman, A. Bonini, and Débora Figueiredo. Fort Collins, CO: The WAC Clearinghouse and Parlor Press, 2009. 283-98. Print.

—. "Genre and Identity: Citizenship in the Age of the Internet and the Age of Global Capitalism." *The Rhetoric and Ideology of Genre: Strategies for Stability and Change.* Ed. Richard Coe, Lorelei Lingard, and Tatiana Teslenko. Creskill, NJ: Hampton, 2002. 13-37. Print.

—. "How Natural Philosophers Can Cooperate." *Textual Dynamics of the Professions.* Ed. Charles Bazerman and James Paradis. Madison, WI: U of Wisconsin P, 1991. 13-44. Print.

—. *The Informed Reader: Contemporary Issues in the Disciplines.* New York: Houghton Mifflin Harcourt, 1989. Print.

—. *The Informed Writer: Using Sources in the Disciplines.* 5th edition. New York: Houghton Mifflin, 1994. Print.

—. *The Languages of Edison's Light.* Cambridge: MIT Press, 1999. Print.

—. "Letters and the Social Grounding of Differentiated Genres." *Letter Writing as a Social Practice.* Ed. David Barton and Nigel Hall. Amsterdam: John Benjamins Publishing, 1999. 15-30. Print.

—. "The Life of Genre, the Life in the Classroom." *Genre and Writing: Issues, Arguments, Alternatives.* Ed. Wendy Bishop and Hans Ostrom. Portsmouth: Boynton/Cook, 1997. 19-26. Print.

—. "Money Talks: The Rhetorical Project of Adam Smith's Wealth of Nations." *Economics and Language.* Ed. Willie Henderson et al. New York: Routledge, 1993: 173-99. Print.

—. "Nuclear Information: One Rhetorical Moment in the Construction of the Information Age." *Written Communication* 18.3 (2001): 259-95. Print.

—. *Shaping Written Knowledge: The Genre and Activity of the Experimental Article in Science.* Madison: U of Wisconsin P, 1988. Print.

—. "Singular Utterances: Realizing Local Activities through Typified Forms in Typified Circumstances." *Analysing Professional Genres*. Ed. Anna Trosborg. Philadelphia: John Benjamins, 2000. 25-40. Print.

—. "Speech Acts, Genres, and Activity Systems: How Texts Organize Activity and People." *What Writing Does and How It Does It*. Ed. Charles Bazerman and Paul Prior. Mahwah, NJ: Lawrence Erlbaum, 2004. 309-39. Print.

—. "Systems of Genres and the Enactment of Social Intentions." *Genre and the New Rhetoric*. Ed. Aviva Freedman and Peter Medway. Bristol: Taylor and Francis, 1994. 79-101. Print.

—. "Textual Performance: Where the Action at a Distance Is." *JAC: Journal of Advanced Composition* 23.2 (2003): 379-96. Print.

—. "Theories of the Middle Range in Historical Studies of Writing Practice." *Written Communication* 25.3 (2008): 298-318. Print.

—. "What Written Knowledge Does: Three Examples of Academic Discourse." *Philosophy of the Social Sciences* 2 (1981): 361-87. Print.

—. "Where is the Classroom?" *Learning and Teaching Genre*. Ed. Aviva Freedman and Peter Medway. Portsmouth: Boynton/Cook, 1994. 25-30. Print.

—. "The Writing of Social Organization and the Literate Situating of Cognition: Extending Goody's Social Implications of Writing." *Technology, Literacy, and the Evolution of Society: Implications of the Work of Jack Goody*. Ed. David R. Olson and Michael Cole. Hillsdale, NJ: Lawrence Erlbaum and Associates, 2006. 215-40. Print.

Bazerman, Charles, Adair Bonini, and Débora Figueiredo. "Editor's Introduction." *Genre in a Changing World*. Ed. Charles Bazerman, Adair Bonini, and Débora Figueiredo. Fort Collins, CO: The WAC Clearinghouse and Parlor Press, 2009. ix-xiv. Print.

—, eds. *Genre in a Changing World*. Fort Collins, CO: The WAC Clearinghouse and Parlor Press, 2009. Print.

Bazerman, Charles, and James Paradis. *Textual Dynamics of the Professions: Historical and Contemporary Studies of Writing in Professional Communities*. Madison: U of Wisconsin P, 1991. Print.

Bazerman, Charles, Joseph Little, and Teri Chavkin. "The Production of Information for Genred Activity Spaces: Informational Motives and Consequences of the Environmental Impact Statement." *Written Communication* 20.4 (2003): 455-77. Print.

Bazerman, Charles, Joseph Little, Lisa Bethel et al. *Reference Guide to Writing Across the Curriculum*. Fort Collins, CO: The WAC Clearinghouse and Parlor Press, 2005. Print.

Beaufort, Anne. *College Writing and Beyond: A New Framework for University Writing Instruction*. Logan, UT: Utah State UP, 2007. Print.

—. "Learning the Trade: A Social Apprenticeship Model for Gaining Writing Expertise." *Written Communication* 17.2 (2000): 185-223. Print.

—. *Writing in the Real World: Making the Transition from School to Work.* New York: Teachers College Press, 1999. Print.

Beaufort, Anne, and John A. Williams. "Writing History: Informed or Not by Genre Theory?" *Genre across the Curriculum.* Ed. Anne Herrington and Charles Moran. Logan, UT: Utah State UP, 2005. 44-64. Print.

Beebee, Thomas O. *The Ideology of Genre: A Comparative Study of Generic Instability.* University Park: Pennsylvania State UP, 1994. Print.

Beer, Ann. "Diplomats in the Basement: Graduate Engineering Students and Intercultural Communication." *Transitions: Writing in Academic and Workplace Settings.* Ed. Patrick Dias and Anthony Paré. Creskill, NJ: Hampton, 2000. 61-88. Print.

Belcher, Diane D. "Trends in Teaching English for Specific Purposes." *Annual Review of Applied Linguistics* 24 (2004): 165-86. Print.

Benesch, Sarah. *Critical English for Academic Purposes: Theory, Politics, and Practice.* Mahwah, NJ: Lawrence Erlbaum, 2001. Print.

—. "ESL, Ideology, and the Politics of Pragmatism." *TESOL Quarterly* 27.4 (1993): 705-17. Print.

Bereiter, Carl and Marlene Scardamalia. *The Psychology of Written Composition.* Hillsdale, NJ: Lawrence Erlbaum, 1987. Print.

Berkenkotter, Carol. "Genre Systems at Work: DSM-IV and Rhetorical Recontextualization in Psychotherapy Paperwork." *Written Communication* 18.3 (2001): 326-49. Print.

Berkenkotter, Carol, and Thomas Huckin. *Genre Knowledge in Disciplinary Communication.* Hillsdale, NJ: Lawrence Erlbaum, 1995. Print.

—. "Rethinking Genre from a Sociocognitive Perspective." *Written Communication* 10.4 (1993): 475-509. Print.

Berkenkotter, Carol, and Doris Ravotas. "Genre as Tool in the Transmission of Practice Over Time and Across Professional Boundaries." *Mind, Culture, and Activity* 4 (1997): 256-74. Print.

Bhatia, Vijay. *Analysing Genre: Language Use in Professional Settings.* London: Longman, 1993. Print.

Biber, Douglas. "An Analytical Framework for Register Studies." *Sociolinguistic Perspectives on Register.* Ed. Douglas Biber and Edward Finegan. Oxford: Oxford UP, 1994. 31-56. Print.

—. *Dimensions of Register Variation: A Cross-Linguistic Comparison.* Cambridge: Cambridge UP, 1995. Print.

—. *Discourse on the Move: Using Corpus Analysis to Describe Discourse Structure.* Philadelphia: John Benjamins, 2007. Print.

—. *Variation Across Speech and Writing.* Cambridge: Cambridge UP, 1988. Print.

— and Edward Finegan, eds. *Sociolinguistic Perspectives on Register.* Oxford: Oxford UP, 1994. Print.

Bishop, Wendy, and Hans Ostrom, eds. *Genre and Writing: Issues, Arguments, Alternatives.* Portsmouth, NH: Boynton/Cook, 1997. Print.

Bitzer, Lloyd F. "The Rhetorical Situation." *Philosophy and Rhetoric* 1.1 (1968): 1-14. Print.

Black, Edwin. *Rhetorical Criticism: A Study in Method.* New York: Macmillan, 1965. Print.

Black, Laurel. *Between Talk and Teaching.* Logan: Utah State UP, 1998. Print.

Bleich, David. "The Materiality of Language and the Pedagogy of Exchange." *Pedagogy: Critical Approaches to Teaching Literature, Language, Composition, and Culture* 1.1 (Winter 2001): 117-41. Print.

Bonini, Adair. "The Distinction Between News and Reportage in the Brazilian Journalistic Context: A Matter of Degree." *Genre in a Changing World.* Ed. Charles Bazerman, Adair Bonini, and Débora Figueiredo. Fort Collins, CO: The WAC Clearinghouse and Parlor Press, 2009. 199-225. Print.

Bourdieu, Pierre. *The Logic of Practice.* Trans. Richard Nice. Stanford: Stanford UP, 1990. Print.

Bronckart, J.P. *Activité langagière, textes et discours: Pour um interactionisme socio-discursif. [Language activity, texts and discourse : Toward a socio-dicoursive interactionism].* Paris: Delachaux et Niestlé, 1997. Print.

Bronckart, J.P., Bain, D., Schneuwly, B., Davaud, C., & Pasquier, A. *Le fonctionnement des discours: Un modèle psychologique et une méthode d'analyse. [The functioning of discourses: A psychological model and an analytical method].* Paris: Delachaux et Niestlé, 1985. Print.

Brooks, Kevin, Cindy Nichols, and Sybil Priebe. "Remediation, Genre, and Motivation: Key Concepts for Teaching with Weblogs." *Into the Blogosphere: Rhetoric, Community and Culture of Weblogs.* Ed. Laura J. Gurak, Smiljana Antonijevic, Laurie Johnson, Clancy Ratliff, and Jessica Reyman. June 2004. Web. 10 April 2007.

Bruce, Ian. *Academic Writing and Genre: A Systematic Analysis.* London: Continuum, 2008. Print.

Bullock, Richard. *The Norton Field Guide to Writing.* Ed. Maureen Daly Goggin. New York: W.W. Norton & Co., 2005. Print.

Burke, Kenneth. "Rhetoric—Old and New." *The Journal of General Education* 5 (April 1951): 202-09. Print.

—. *Rhetoric of Motives.* Berkeley: U of California P, 1951. Print.

Campbell, Karlyn Kohrs, and Kathleen Hall Jamieson. *Deeds Done in Words: Presidential Rhetoric and the Genres of Governance.* Chicago: U of Chicago P, 1990. Print.

—, eds. *Form and Genre: Shaping Rhetorical Action.* Falls Church, VA: Speech Communication Association, 1978.

Caple, Helen. "Multi-semiotic Communication in an Australian Broadsheet: A New News Story Genre." *Genre in a Changing World.* Ed. Charles Bazerman, Adair Bonini, and Débora Figueiredo. Fort Collins, CO: The WAC Clearinghouse and Parlor Press, 2009. 247-58. Print.

Carroll, Lee Ann. *Rehearsing New Roles: How College Students Develop as Writers.* Carbondale: Southern Illinois UP, 2002. Print.

Carter, Michael. "Ways of Knowing, Doing, and Writing in the Disciplines." *College Composition and Communication* 58 (2007): 385-418. Print.

Casanave, Christine. *Controversies in L2 Writing: Dilemmas and Decisions in Research and Instruction.* Ann Arbor: U of Michigan P, 2003. Print.

Chapman, Marilyn. "The Emergence of Genres: Some Findings from an Examination of First Grade Writing." *Written Communication* 11 (1994): 348-80. Print.

—. "Situated, Social, Active: Rewriting Genre in the Elementary Classroom." *Written Communication* 16.4 (1999): 469-90. Print.

Cheng, An. "Understanding Learners and Learning in ESP Genre-Based Writing Instruction." *English for Specific Purposes* 25 (2006): 76-89. Print.

Christie, Frances. "Genres as Choice." *The Place of Genre in Learning: Current Debates.* Ed. Ian Reid. Geelong, Victoria: Deakin University, 1987. 22-34. Print.

—. "Genre Theory and ESL Teaching: A Systemic Functional Perspective." *TESOL Quarterly* 33.4 (1999): 759-63. Print.

Christie, Frances, and J.R. Martin, eds. *Genres and Institutions: Social Processes in the Workplace and School.* London: Cassell, 1997. Print.

Clark, Irene. "A Genre Approach to Writing Assignments." *Composition Forum* 14.2 (2005): n. pag. Web. 15 June 2008.

Coe, Richard. "The New Rhetoric of Genre: Writing Political Briefs." *Genre in the Classroom: Multiple Perspectives.* Ed. Ann Johns. New Jersey: Lawrence Erlbaum, 2002. 197-210. Print.

—. "Teaching Genre as a Process." *Learning and Teaching Genre.* Ed. Aviva Freedman and Peter Medway. Portsmouth, NH: Boynton/Cook, 1994. 157-69. Print.

Coe, Richard, Lorelei Lingard, and Tatiana Teslenko, eds. *The Rhetoric and Ideology of Genre: Strategies for Stability and Change.* New Jersey: Hampton, 2002. Print.

Cole, Michael, and Yrjo Engeström. "A Cultural-Historical Approach to Distributed Cognition." *Distributed Cognitions: Psychological and Educational Considerations.* Ed. Gavriel Salomon. Cambridge: Cambridge UP, 1993. 1-46. Print.

Cope, Bill, and Mary Kalantzis. *The Powers of Literacy: A Genre Approach to Teaching Writing.* Pittsburgh: U of Pittsburgh P, 1993. Print.

Cristovão, Vera Lucia Lopes. "The Use of Didactic Sequences and the Teaching of L1: An Analysis of an Institutional Program of Teaching Writing at

School." *L1—Educational Studies in Language and Literature* 9.2 (2009): 5-25. Print.

Croce, Benedetto. *Aesthetic.* Trans. Douglas Ainslie. New York: Noonday, 1968. Print.

Cross, Geoffrey. "The Interrelation of Genre, Context, and Process in the Collaborative Writing of Two Corporate Documents." *Writing in the Workplace: New Research Perspectives.* Ed. Rachel Spilka. Carbondale: Southern Illinois UP, 1993. 141-52. Print.

Culler, Jonathan. *Structuralist Poetics.* Ithaca: Cornell UP, 1975. Print.

Currie, Pat. "What Counts as Good Writing? Enculturation and Writing Assessment." *Learning and Teaching Genre.* Ed. Aviva Freedman and Peter Medway. Portsmouth, NH: Boynton/Cook, 1994. 63-80. Print.

Dean, Deborah. *Genre Theory: Teaching, Writing, and Being.* Urbana, IL: NCTE, 2008. Print.

Derrida, Jacques. "The Law of Genre." *Modern Genre Theory.* Ed. David Duff. London: Longman, 2000. 219-31. Print.

Devitt, Amy J. "First-Year Composition and Antecedent Genres." Conference on College Composition and Communication. Chicago, 24 March 2006. Conference Presentation.

—. "Generalizing about Genre: New Conceptions of an Old Concept." *College Composition and Communication* 44.4 (1993): 573-86. Print.

—. "Genre as Textual Variable: Some Historical Evidence from Scots and American English." *American Speech* 64 (1989): 291-303. Print.

—. "Integrating Rhetorical and Literary Theories of Genre." *College English* 62 (2000): 696-718. Print.

—. "Intertextuality in Tax Accounting: Generic, Referential, and Functional." *Textual Dynamics of the Professions: Historical and Contemporary Studies of Writing in Professional Communities.* Ed. Charles Bazerman and James Paradis. Madison: U of Wisconsin P, 1991. 335-57. Print.

—. "Teaching Critical Genre Awareness." *Genre in a Changing World.* Ed. Charles Bazerman, Adair Bonini, and Débora Figueiredo. Fort Collins, CO: The WAC Clearinghouse and Parlor Press, 2009. 342-55. Print.

—. "Transferability and Genres." *The Locations of Composition.* Ed. Christopher J. Keller and Christian R. Weisser. New York: State U of New York P, 2007. 215-28. Print.

—. *Writing Genres.* Carbondale: Southern Illinois UP, 2004. Print.

Devitt, Amy, Mary Jo Reiff, and Anis Bawarshi. *Scenes of Writing: Strategies for Composing with Genres.* New York: Longman, 2004. Print.

Dias, Patrick, Aviva Freedman, Peter Medway, and Anthony Paré. *Worlds Apart: Acting and Writing in Academic and Workplace Contexts.* Mahwah, NJ: Lawrence Erlbaum Associates, 1999. Print.

Dias, Patrick, and Anthony Paré, eds. *Transitions: Writing in Academic and Workplace Settings.* Creskill, NJ: Hampton, 2000. Print.

Diller, Hans-Jürgen. "Genre in Linguistics and Related Discourses." *Towards a History of English as a History of Genres.* Ed. Hans-Jürgen Diller and Manfred Görlach. Heidelberg: Universitätsverlag, 2001. 3-43. Print.

Dolz, J., M. Noverraz, and B. Schneuwly. "Seqüências didáticas para o oral e a escrita: Apresentação de um procedimento [Didactic sequences for speech and writing: Presenting a procedure]." *Gêneros orais e escritos na escola [Oral and written genres in the school].* Ed. B. Schneuwly & J. Dolz. Campinas, S.P.: Mercado de Letras, 2004. 95-128. Print.

Dolz, J., and B. Schneuwly. *Pour un enseignement de l'oral. Initiation aux genres formels à l'école.* Paris: ESF, 1998. Print.

Donovan, Carol A. "Children's Development and Control of Written Story and Informational Genres: Insights from One Elementary School." *Research in the Teaching of English* 35 (2001): 394-447. Print.

—. "Children's Story Writing, Information Writing and Genre Knowledge across the Elementary Grades." National Reading Conference. Scottsdale, AZ, 3-6 December 1997. Conference Presentation.

Donovan, Carol A., and Laura B. Smolkin. "Children's Understanding of Genre and Writing Development." *Handbook of Writing Research.* Ed. Charles A. MacArthur et al. New York: Guilford, 2008. 131-43. Print.

Dubrow, Heather. *Genre.* London: Methune, 1982. Print.

Duke, Nell K., and J. Kays. "Can I Say 'Once Upon a Time'?: Kindergarten Children Developing Knowledge of Information Book Language." *Early Childhood Research Quarterly* 13 (1998): 295-318. Print.

Edwards, Mike, and Heidi McKee. "The Teaching and Learning of Web Genres in First-Year Composition." *Genre across the Curriculum.* Ed. Anne Herrington and Charles Moran. Logan: Utah State UP, 2005. 196-218. Print.

Eggins, Suzanne, and J.R. Martin. "Genres and Registers of Discourse." *Discourse as Structure and Process.* Ed. Teun Van Dijk. London: Sage, 1997. 230-56. Print.

Engeström, Yrjo. "Activity Theory and Individual Social Transformation." *Perspectives on Activity Theory.* Ed. Y. Engeström, R. Miettinen, and R-L Punamaki. Cambridge: Cambridge University Press, 1999. 19-38. Print.

—. "Developmental Studies of Work as a Testbench of Activity Theory: The Case of Primary Care Medical Practice." *Understanding Practice: Perspectives on Activity and Practice.* Ed. S. Chaiklin and Jean Lave. New York: Cambridge UP. 1993. 64-103. Print.

—. *Learning by Expanding: An Activity Theoretical Approach to Developmental Research.* Helsinki: Orienta-Konsultit Oy, 1987. Print.

Fairclough, Norman. *Discourse and Social Change.* Cambridge: Polity Press, 1992. Print.

Feez, Susan, "Heritage and Innovation in Second Language Education." *Genre in the Classroom: Multiple Perspectives.* Ed. Ann Johns. Mahwah, NJ: Lawrence Erlbaum, 2002. 43-69. Print.

Feez, Susan, and H. Joyce. *Text-Based Syllabus Design.* Sydney: National Center for English Language Teaching and Research, 1998. Print.

Figueiredo, Débora de Carvalho. "Narrative and Identity Formation: An Analysis of Media Personal Accounts from Patients of Cosmetic Plastic Surgery." *Genre in a Changing World.* Ed. Charles Bazerman, Adair Bonini, and Débora Figueiredo. Fort Collins, CO: The WAC Clearinghouse and Parlor Press, 2009. 259-80. Print.

Fishelov, David. *Metaphors of Genre: The Role of Analogies in Genre Theory.* University Park, PA: Pennsylvania State UP, 1993. Print.

Fitzgerald, Jill, and Alan Teasley. "Effects of Instruction in Narrative Structure on Children's Writing." *Journal of Educational Psychology* 78 (1986): 424-32. Print.

Fleischer, Cathy, and Sarah Andrew-Vaughan. *Writing Outside Your Comfort Zone: Helping Students Navigate Unfamiliar Genres.* Portsmouth, NH: Heinemann, 2009. Print.

Fleming, David. "Rhetoric as a Course of Study." *College English* 61.2 (1998): 169-91. Print.

Flowerdew, John. "Genre in the Classroom: A Linguistic Approach." *Genre in the Classroom: Multiple Perspectives.* Ed. Ann Johns. Mahwah: Lawrence Erlbaum Associates, 2002. 91-102. Print.

Fraser, B. J., et al. "Synthesis of Educational Productivity Research." *International Journal of Educational Research* 11 (1987): 73-145. Print.

Freadman, Anne. "Anyone for Tennis?" *Genre and the New Rhetoric.* Ed. Aviva Freedman and Peter Medway. Bristol: Taylor and Francis, 1994. 43-66. Print.

—. "Uptake." *The Rhetoric and Ideology of Genre: Strategies for Stability and Change.* Ed. Richard Coe, Lorelei Lingard, and Tatiana Teslenko. Cresskill, NJ: Hampton UP, 2002. 39–53. Print.

Freedman, Aviva. "Development in Story Writing." *Applied Psycholinguistics* 8 (1987): 153-65. Print.

—. "'Do as I Say': The Relationship between Teaching and Learning New Genres." *Genre and the New Rhetoric.* Ed. Aviva Freedman and Peter Medway. Bristol: Taylor and Francis, 1994. 191–210. Print.

—. "Interaction between Theory and Research: RGS and a Study of Students and Professionals Working 'in Computers.'" *Rhetorical Genre Studies and Beyond.* Ed. Natasha Artemeva and Aviva Freedman. Winnipeg: Inkshed, 2006. 101-20. Print.

—. "Learning to Write Again: Discipline-Specific Writing at University." *Carleton Papers in Applied Language Studies* 4 (1987): 95–116. Print.

—. "Show and Tell? The Role of Explicit Teaching in the Learning of New Genres." *Research in the Teaching of English* 27.3 (Oct. 1993): 222-51. Print.

—. "Situating Genre: A Rejoinder." *Research in the Teaching of English* 27.3 (Oct. 1993): 272-81. Print.

Freedman, Aviva, and Christine Adam. "Write Where You Are: Situating Learning to Write in the University and Workplace Settings." *Transitions: Writing in Academic and Workplace Settings*. Ed. Patrick Dias and Anthony Paré. Creskill, NJ: Hampton, 2000. 31-60. Print.

Freedman, Aviva, and Peter Medway, eds. *Genre and the New Rhetoric*. Bristol: Taylor and Francis, 1994. Print.

—, eds. *Learning and Teaching Genre*. Portsmouth, NH: Boynton/Cook, 1994. Print.

Freedman, Aviva, and Graham Smart. "Navigating the Current of Economic Policy: Written Genres and the Distribution of Cognitive Work at a Financial Institution." *Mind, Culture, and Activity* 4.4 (1997): 238-55. Print.

Frow, John. *Genre*. London: Routledge, 2006. Print.

Frye, Northrop. *Anatomy of Criticism: Four Essays*. Princeton: Princeton UP, 1957. Print.

Fulkerson, Richard. "Composition at the Turn of the Twenty-First Century." *College Composition and Communication* 56.4 (2005): 654-87. Print.

Furlanetto, Maria Marta. "Curricular Proposal of Santa Catarina State: Assessing the Route, Opening Paths." *Genre in a Changing World*. Ed. Charles Bazerman, Adair Bonini, and Débora Figueiredo. Fort Collins, CO: The WAC Clearinghouse and Parlor Press, 2009. 357-79. Print.

Fuzer, Cristiane, and Nina Célia Barros. "Accusation and Defense: The Ideational Metafunction of Language in the Genre Closing Argument." *Genre in a Changing World*. Ed. Charles Bazerman, Adair Bonini, and Débora Figueiredo. Fort Collins, CO: The WAC Clearinghouse and Parlor Press, 2009. 79-97. Print.

Genette, Gérard. *The Architext: An Introduction*. Berkeley: U of California P, 1992. Print.

Giddens, Anthony. *The Constitution of Society: Outline of the Theory of Structuration*. Berkeley: U of California P, 1984. Print.

Giltrow, Janet. *Academic Writing: Writing and Reading in the Disciplines*. Ontario, Canada: Broadview, 1995. Print.

—. "Genre and the Pragmatic Concept of Background Knowledge." *Genre and the New Rhetoric*. Ed. Aviva Freedman and Peter Medway. Bristol: Taylor and Francis, 1994. 155-78. Print.

—. "Meta-Genre." *The Rhetoric and Ideology of Genre: Strategies for Stability and Change*. Ed. Richard Coe, Lorelei Lingard, and Tatiana Teslenko. Cresskill, NJ: Hampton, 2002. 187-205. Print.

Giltrow, Janet, and Michele Valiquette. "Genres and Knowledge: Students Writing in the Disciplines." *Learning and Teaching Genre.* Ed. Aviva Freedman and Peter Medway. Portsmouth, NH: Boynton/Cook, 1994. 47-62. Print.

Grabe, William. "Narrative and Expository Macro-Genres." *Genre in the Classroom: Multiple Perspectives.* Ed. Ann M Johns. Mahwah, NJ: Lawrence Erlbaum, 2002. 249-67. Print.

Grafton, Kathryn, and Elizabeth Mauer. "Engaging With and Arranging for Publics in Blog Genres." *Linguistics and the Human Sciences* 3.1 (2007): 47-66. Print.

Green, Bill, and Alison Lee. "Writing Geography: Literacy, Identity, and Schooling." *Learning and Teaching Genre.* Ed. Aviva Freedman and Peter Medway. Portsmouth, NH: Boynton/Cook, 1994. 207-26. Print.

Gross, Alan G., Joseph E. Harmon, and Michael Reidy. *Communicating Science: The Scientific Article from the 17th Century to the Present.* New York: Oxford UP, 2002. Print.

Guimarães, Ana Maria de Mattos. "Genre Teaching in Different Social Environments: An Experiment with the Genre Detective Story." *L1—Educational Studies in Language and Literature* 9.2 (2009): 27-47. Print.

Gurwitsch, Aron. "Problems of the Life-World." *Phenomenology and Social Reality: Essays in Memory of Alfred Schutz.* Ed. Maurice Natanson. The Hague: Martinus Nijhoff, 1970. 35-61. Print.

Halliday, M.A.K. *Language as Social Semiotic: The Social Interpretation of Language and Meaning.* London: Edward Arnold, 1978. Print.

Halliday, M.A.K., and Ruqaiya Hasan. *Cohesion in English.* London: Longman, 1976. Print.

Hammond, J., et al. *English for Social Purposes: A Handbook for Teachers of Adult Literacy.* Sydney: National Centre for English Language Teaching and Research, 1992. Print.

Henderson, Willie, and Ann Hewings. "Language and Model Building?" *The Language of Economics: The Analysis of Economics Discourse.* Ed. Anthony Dudley-Evans and Willie Henderson. London: Modern English Publications, 1990. 43-54. Print.

Henderson, Willie, Tony Dudley-Evans, and Roger Backhouse. *Economics and Language.* London: Routledge, 1993. Print.

Herring, Susan. C., Lois Ann Scheidt, Sabrina Bonus, and Elijah Wright. "Weblogs as a Bridging Genre." *Information, Technology & People* 18.2 (2005): 142-71. Print.

Herrington, Anne, and Charles Moran, eds. *Genre across the Curriculum.* Logan: Utah State UP, 2005. Print.

Hillocks, George, Jr. *Research on Written Composition: New Directions for Teaching.* Urbana, IL: NCTE, 1986. Print.

Hirsch, E.D. *Validity in Interpretation.* New Haven: Yale UP, 1967. Print.

Hitchcock, Peter. "The Genre of Postcoloniality." *New Literary History* 34.2 (2003): 299-330. Print.

Hyland, Ken. "Genre-Based Pedagogies: A Social Response to Process." *Journal of Second Language Writing* 12 (2003): 17-29. Print.

—. *Genre and Second Language Writing.* Ann Arbor: U of Michigan P, 2004. Print.

—. "Stance and Engagement: A Model of Interaction in Academic Discourse." *Discourse Studies* 7 (2005): 173-19. Print.

Hyon, Sunny. "Convention and Inventiveness in an Occluded Academic Genre: A Case Study of Retention-Promotion-Tenure Reports." *English for Specific Purposes* 27.2 (2008): 175-92. Print.

—. "Genre and ESL Reading: A Classroom Study." *Genre in the Classroom: Multiple Perspectives.* Ed. Ann M. Johns. Mahwah, NJ: Lawrence Erlbaum, 2002. 121-41. Print.

—. "Genre in Three Traditions: Implications for ESL." *TESOL Quarterly* 30 (1996): 693-722. Print.

Jameson, Fredric. *The Political Unconscious: Narrative as a Socially Symbolic Act.* Ithaca: Cornell UP, 1981. Print.

Jamieson, Kathleen M. "Antecedent Genre as Rhetorical Constraint." *Quarterly Journal of Speech* 61 (Dec. 1975): 406-15. Print.

Johns, Ann M. "Destabilizing and Enriching Novice Students' Genre Theories." *Genre in the Classroom: Multiple Perspectives.* Ed. Ann M. Johns. Mahwah, NJ: Lawrence Erlbaum, 2002. 237-48. Print.

—. "Genre and ESL/EFL Composition Instruction." *Exploring the Dynamics of Second Language Writing.* Ed. Barbara Kroll. Cambridge: Cambridge UP, 2003. 195-217. Print.

—. "Genre Awareness for the Novice Academic Student: An On-going Quest." Plenary Address. American Association of Applied Linguistics Conference. Costa Mesa, CA. 25 April, 2007.

—, ed. *Genre in the Classroom: Multiple Perspectives.* Mahwah, NJ: Lawrence Erlbaum, 2002. Print.

—. "Teaching Classroom and Authentic Genres: Initiating Students into Academic Cultures and Discourses." *Academic Writing in a Second Language.* Ed. Diane Belcher and G. Braine. Norwood, NJ: Ablex, 1995. 277-92. Print.

—. *Text, Role, and Context: Developing Academic Literacies.* New York: Cambridge UP, 1997. Print.

Johns, Ann M., Anis Bawarshi, Richard M. Coe, Ken Hyland, Brian Paltridge, Mary Jo Reiff, and Christine Tardy. "Crossing the Boundaries of Genre Studies: Commentaries by Experts." *Journal of Second Language Writing* 15 (2006): 234-49. Print.

Kamberelis, G., and T. Bovino. "Cultural Artifacts as Scaffolds for Genre Development. *Reading Research Quarterly* 34 (1999): 138–70. Print.

Kapp, Rochelle, and Bongi Bangeni. "'I Was Just Never Exposed to This Argument Thing': Using a Genre Approach to Teach Academic Writing to ESL Students in the Humanities." *Genre across the Curriculum.* Ed. Anne Herrington and Charles Moran. Logan: Utah State UP, 2005. 109-27. Print.

Kay, H., and Tony Dudley-Evans. "Genre: What Teachers Think?" *ELT Journal* 52 (1998): 308-14. Print.

Knighton, Ryan. "(En)Compassing Situations: Sex Advice on the Rhetoric of Genre." *The Rhetoric and Ideology of Genre: Strategies for Stability and Change.* Ed. Richard Coe, Lorelei Lingard, and Tatiana Teslenko. Creskill, NJ: Hampton, 2002. 355-71. Print.

Kohnen, Thomas. "Text Types as Catalysts for Language Change: The Example of the Adverbial First Participle Construction." *Towards a History of English as a History of Genres.* Ed. Hans-Jürgen Diller and Manfred Görlach. Heidelberg: Universitätsverlag, 2001. 111-24. Print.

Koustouli, Triantafillia, ed. *Writing in Context(s): Textual Practices and Learning Processes in Sociocultural Settings.* New York: Springer, 2005.

Kress, Gunther. *Literacy in the New Media Age.* London: Routledge, 2003. Print.

Langer, Judith. *Children Reading and Writing: Structures and Strategies.* Norwood, NJ: Ablex, 1986. Print.

—. "Reading, Writing, and Genre Development: Making Connections." *Reading/Writing Connections: Learning from Research.* Ed. Mary Anne Doyle and Judith Irwin. Newark, DE: International Reading Association, 1992. Print.

Latour, Bruno, and Steve Woolgar. *Laboratory Life: The Social Construction of Scientific Facts.* Princeton: Princeton UP, 1986. Print.

Lattimer, Heather. *Thinking Through Genre: Units of Study in Reading and Writing Workshops 4-12.* Portland, ME: Stenhouse, 2003. Print.

Lave, Jean, and Etienne Wenger. *Situated Learning: Legitimate Peripheral Participation.* New York: Cambridge UP, 1991. Print.

Ledwell-Brown, Jane. "Organizational Cultures as Contexts for Learning to Write." *Transitions: Writing in Academic and Workplace Settings.* Ed. Patrick Dias and Anthony Paré. Creskill, NJ: Hampton, 2000. 199-222. Print.

Lemke, Jay. *Textual Politics: Discourse and Social Dynamics.* London: Taylor and Francis, 1995. Print.

Lingard, Lorelei, and Richard Haber. "Learning Medical Talk: How the Apprenticeship Complicates Current Explicit/Tacit Debates in Genre Instruction." *The Rhetoric and Ideology of Genre: Strategies for Stability and Change.* Ed. Richard Coe, Lorelei Lingard, and Tatiana Teslenko. New Jersey: Hampton, 2002. 155-70. Print.

Liu, Barbara Little. "More than the Latest PC Buzzword for Modes: What Genre Theory Means to Composition." *The Outcomes Book: Debates and Consensus after the WPA Outcomes Statement.* Ed. Susanmarie Harrington et al. Logan: Utah State UP, 2005. 72-84. Print.

Longacre, Robert. *The Grammar of Discourse.* 2nd ed. New York: Plenum Press, 1996. Print.

Luke, Alan. "Genres of Power? Literacy Education and the Production of Capital." *Literacy in Society.* Ed. R. Hasan and A.G. Williams. London: Longman, 1996. 308-38. Print.

Macken-Horarik, Mary. "'Something to Shoot For': A Systemic Functional Approach to Teaching Genre in Secondary School Science." *Genre in the Classroom: Multiple Perspectives.* Ed. Ann Johns. New Jersey: Lawrence Erlbaum, 2002. 17-42. Print.

Macken, M.R. et al. *An Approach to Writing K-12: The Theory and Practice of Genre-based Writing, Years 3-6.* Sydney: Literacy and Education Research Network in Conjunction with NSW Department of Education, Directorate of Studies, 1989. Print.

Maimon, Elaine. "Maps and Genres: Exploring Connections in the Arts and Sciences." *Composition and Literature: Bridging the Gap.* Ed. W. Bryan Horner. Illinois: U. of Chicago P, 1983. 110-25. Print.

Makmillen, Shurli. "Colonial Texts in Postcolonial Contexts: A Genre in the Contact Zone." *Linguistics and the Human Sciences* 3.1 (2007): 87-103. Print.

Martin, J.R. "Analysing Genre: Functional Parameters." *Genre and Institutions: Social Processes in the Workplace and School.* Ed. Frances Christie and J.R. Martin. London: Cassell, 1997. 3-39. Print.

—. "A Contextual Theory of Language." *The Powers of Literacy: A Genre Approach to Teaching Writing.* Ed. Bill Cope and Mary Kalantzis. Pittsburgh: U of Pittsburgh P, 1993. 116-36. Print.

Martin, J.R., and David Rose. *Genre Relations: Mapping Culture.* London: Equinox, 2008. Print.

Martin, J.R., Frances Christie, and Joan Rothery. "Social Processes in Education: A Reply to Sawyer and Watson." *The Place of Genre in Learning: Current Debates.* Ed. Ian Reid. Geelong, Victoria: Deakin University, 1987. 58-82. Print.

Master, Peter. "Positive and Negative Aspects of the Dominance of English." *TESOL Quarterly* 32 (1998): 716-25. Print.

McCarthy, Lucille. "A Stranger in a Strange Land: A College Student Writing Across the Curriculum." *Research in the Teaching of English* 21.3 (1987): 233-65.

McCloskey, Deirdre N. *The Rhetoric of Economics.* Madison: U of Wisconsin P, 1985. Print.

—. *If You're So Smart: The Narrative of Economic Expertise*. Chicago: U of Chicago P, 1990. Print.

McCloskey, Donald N. "Mere Style in Economics Journals, 1920 to the Present." *Economic Notes* 20.1 (1991): 135-58. Print.

McComiskey, Bruce. *Teaching Composition as a Social Process*. Logan: Utah State UP, 2000. Print.

McDonald, Catherine. *The Question of Transferability: What Students Take Away from Writing Instruction*. Diss. University of Washington, 2006. Print.

McLeod, Susan, and Elaine Maimon. "Clearing the Air: WAC Myths and Realities." *College English* 62 (2000): 573-83. Print.

Medway, Peter. "Fuzzy Genres and Community Identities: The Case of Architecture Students' Sketchbooks." *The Rhetoric and Ideology of Genre: Strategies for Stability and Change*. Ed. Richard Coe, Lorelei Lingard, and Tatiana Teslenko. Creskill, NJ: Hampton, 2002. 123-53. Print.

Miller, Carolyn R. "Genre as Social Action." *Genre and the New Rhetoric*. Ed. Aviva Freedman and Peter Medway. Bristol: Taylor and Francis, 1994. 23-42. Print.

—. "Rhetorical Community: The Cultural Basis of Genre." *Genre and the New Rhetoric*. Ed. Aviva Freedman and Peter Medway. Bristol: Taylor and Francis, 1994. 67-77. Print.

Miller, Carolyn R., and Dawn Shepherd, "Blogging as Social Action: A Genre Analysis of the Weblog." *Into the Blogosphere: Rhetoric, Community and Culture of Weblogs*. Ed. Laura J. Gurak, Smiljana Antonijevic, Laurie Johnson, Clancy Ratliff, and Jessica Reyman. June 2004. Web. 10 April 2007.

Miller, Susan. "How I Teach Writing: How to Teach Writing? To Teach Writing?" *Pedagogy: Critical Approaches to Teaching, Literature, Language, Composition, and Culture* 1.3 (Fall 2001): 479-88. Print.

Mirtz, Ruth M. "The Territorial Demands of Form and Process: The Case for Student Writing as Genre." *Genre and Writing: Issues, Arguments, Alternatives*. Ed. Wendy Bishop and Hans Ostrom. Portsmouth, NH: Boynton Cook, 1997. 190-98. Print.

Mitchell, Sally, and Richard Andrews. "Learning to Operate Successfully in Advanced Level History." *Learning and Teaching Genre*. Ed. Aviva Freedman and Peter Medway. Portsmouth, NH: Boynton/Cook, 1994. 81-104. Print.

Motta-Roth, Désirée. "The Role of Context in Academic Text Production and Writing Pedagogy." *Genre in a Changing World*. Ed. Charles Bazerman, Adair Bonini, and Débora Figueiredo. Fort Collins, CO: The WAC Clearinghouse and Parlor Press, 2009. 321-40. Print.

Mozdzenski, Leonardo. "The Sociohistorical Constitution of the Genre Legal Booklet: A Critical Approach." *Genre in a Changing World*. Ed.

Charles Bazerman, Adair Bonini, and Débora Figueiredo. Fort Collins, CO: The WAC Clearinghouse and Parlor Press, 2009. 99-135. Print.

Myhill, Debra. "Prior Knowledge and the (Re)Production of School Written Genres." *Writing in Context(s): Textual Practices and Learning Processes in Sociocultural Settings.* Ed. Triantafillia Koustouli. New York: Springer, 2005. 117-36. Print.

Natanson, Maurice. "Alfred Schutz on Social Reality and Social Science." *Phenomenology and Social Reality: Essays in Memory of Alfred Schutz.* Ed. Maurice Natanson. The Hague: Martinus Nijhoff, 1970. 101-21. Print.

Neale, Steve. *Genre and Hollywood.* London: Routledge, 2000. Print.

Orlikowski, Wanda J., and JoAnne Yates. "Genre Repertoire: The Structuring of Communicative Practices in Organizations." *Administrative Science Quarterly* 39.4 (1994): 541-74. Print.

Palmquist, Mike. "Writing in Emerging Genres: Student Web Sites in Writing and Writing-Intensive Classes." *Genre across the Curriculum.* Ed. Anne Herrington and Charles Moran. Logan: Utah State UP, 2005. 219-44. Print.

Paltridge, Brian. *Genre and the Language Learning Classroom.* Ann Arbor: U of Michigan P, 2001. Print.

—. *Genre, Frames and Writing in Research Settings.* Amsterdam: John Benjamins, 1997. Print.

—. "Genre, Text Type, and the English for Academic Purposes (EAP) Classroom." *Genre in the Classroom: Multiple Perspectives.* Ed. Ann M. Johns. Mahwah, NJ: Lawrence Erlbaum, 2002. 73-90. Print.

Pappas, Christine C. "Is Narrative 'Primary'? Some Insights from Kindergarteners' Pretend Reading of Stories and Information Books." *Journal of Reading Behavior* 25 (1993): 97-129. Print.

—. "Young Children's Strategies in Learning the 'Book Language' of Information Books." *Discourse Processes* 14 (1991): 203–25. Print.

Paré, Anthony. "Discourse Regulations and the Production of Knowledge." *Writing in the Workplace: New Research Perspectives.* Ed. Rachel Spilka. Carbondale: Southern Illinois UP, 1993. 111-23. Print.

—. "Genre and Identity: Individuals, Institutions, and Ideology." *The Rhetoric and Ideology of Genre: Strategies for Stability and Change.* Ed. Richard Coe, Lorelei Lingard, and Tatiana Teslenko. Creskill, NJ: Hampton, 2002. 57-71. Print.

—. "Writing as a Way into Social Work: Genre Sets, Genre Systems, and Distributed Cognition." *Transitions: Writing in Academic and Workplace Settings.* Ed. Patrick Dias and Anthony Paré. Creskill, NJ: Hampton, 2000. 145-66. Print.

Paré, Anthony, and Graham Smart. "Observing Genres in Action: Toward a Research Methodology." *Genre and the New Rhetoric.* Ed. Aviva Freedman and Peter Medway. Bristol: Taylor and Francis, 1994. 146-54. Print.

Pennycook, Alastair. "Vulgar Pragmatism, Critical Pragmatism, and EAP." *English for Specific Purposes* 16 (1997): 253-69. Print.

Pereira, Tânia Conceição. "The Psychiatric Interview: Practice in/of the Clinic." *Linguistics and the Human Sciences* 3.1 (2007): 25-46. Print.

Perelman, Les. "The Medieval Art of Letter Writing: Rhetoric as Institutional Expression." *Textual Dynamics of the Professions: Historical and Contemporary Studies of Writing in Professional Communities.* Ed. Charles Bazerman and James Paradis. Madison: U of Wisconsin P, 1991. 97-119. Print.

Perkins, D.N., and Gavriel Salomon. "Teaching for Transfer." *Educational Leadership* 46.1 (1988): 22-32. Print.

Perloff, Marjorie, ed. *Postmodern Genres.* Norman, OK: U of Oklahoma P, 1989. Print.

Peters, Brad. "Genre, Antigenre, and Reinventing the Forms of Conceptualization." *Genre and Writing: Issues, Arguments, Alternatives.* Ed. Wendy Bishop and Hans Ostrom. Portsmouth: Boynton/Cook, 1997. 199-214. Print.

Quint, David. *Epic and Empire: Politics and Generic Form from Virgil to Milton.* Princeton: Princeton UP, 1993. Print.

Reiff, Mary Jo. "Mediating Materiality and Discursivity: Critical Ethnography as Meta-Generic Learning." *Ethnography Unbound: From Theory Shock to Critical Praxis.* Ed. Stephen G. Brown and Sidney I. Dobrin. New York: SUNY P, 2004. 35-51. Print.

Romano, Tony. *Blending Genre, Altering Style: Writing Multigenre Papers.* Portsmouth, NH: Boynton/Cook, 2000. Print.

Rosmarin, Adena. *The Power of Genre.* Minneapolis: U of Minnesota P, 1985. Print.

Rothary, Joan. "Making Changes: Developing an Educational Linguistics." *Literacy in Society.* Ed. R. Hasan and G. Williams. London: Longman, 1996. 86-123. Print.

Russell, David. "Rethinking Genre in School and Society: An Activity Theory Analysis." *Written Communication* 14.4 (1997): 504-54. Print.

—. "Writing in Multiple Contexts: Vygotskian CHAT Meets the Phenomenology of Genre." *Traditions of Writing Research.* Ed. Charles Bazerman et al. New York: Routledge, 2010. 353-64. Print.

Russell, David, Mary Lea, Jan Parker, Brian Street, Tiane Donahue. "Exploring Notions of Genre in 'Academic Literacies' and 'Writing Across the Curriculum': Approaches Across Countries and Contexts." *Genre in a Changing World.* Ed. Charles Bazerman, Adair Bonini, and Débora Figueiredo. Fort Collins, CO: The WAC Clearinghouse and Parlor Press, 2009. 395-423. Print.

Salomon, Gavriel, ed. "Editor's Introduction." *Distributed Cognitions: Psychological and Educational Considerations.* Cambridge: Cambridge UP, 1993. xi-xxi. Print.

Schryer, Catherine. "Genre and Power: A Chronotopic Analysis." *The Rhetoric and Ideology of Genre: Strategies for Stability and Change.* Ed. Richard Coe, Lorelei Lingard, and Tatiana Teslenko. Cresskill, NJ: Hampton, 2002. 73-102. Print.

—. "The Lab vs. the Clinic: Sites of Competing Genres." *Genre and the New Rhetoric.* Ed. Aviva Freedman and Peter Medway. London: Taylor and Francis, 1994. 105-24. Print.

Schutz, Alfred. *The Phenomenology of the Social World.* Trans. George Walsh and Frederick Lehnert. Evanston: Northwestern UP, 1967. Print.

Schutz, Alfred, and Thomas Luckmann. *The Structure of the Life-World.* Trans. Richard M. Zaner and H. Tristram Engelhardt, Jr. Evanston: Northwestern UP, 1973. Print.

Segal, Judy Z. "Breast Cancer Narratives as Public Rhetoric: Genre Itself and the Maintenance of Ignorance." *Linguistics and the Human Sciences* 3.1 (2007): 3-23. Print.

Selzer, Jack, ed. *Understanding Scientific Prose.* Madison: U of Wisconsin P, 1993. Print.

Smart, Graham. "Genre as Community Invention: A Central Bank's Response to Its Executives' Expectations as Readers." *Writing in the Workplace: New Research Perspectives.* Ed. Rachel Spilka. Carbondale: Southern Illinois UP, 1993. 124-40. Print.

—. "Reinventing Expertise: Experienced Writers in the Workplace Encounter a New Genre. *Transitions: Writing in Academic and Workplace Settings.* Ed. Patrick Dias and Anthony Paré. Cresskill, NJ: Hampton, 2000. 167-82. Print.

Smart, Graham, and Nicole Brown. "Developing a 'Discursive Gaze': Participatory Action Research with Student Interns Encountering New Genres in the Activity of the Workplace." *Rhetorical Genre Studies and Beyond.* Ed. Natasha Artemeva and Aviva Freedman. Winnipeg: Inkshed, 2006. 240-79. Print.

Smit, David. *The End of Composition Studies.* Carbondale: Southern Illinois UP, 2004. Print.

Smith, Frank. *Understanding Reading.* 5th Ed. Hillsdale: Lawrence Erlbaum, 1994. Print.

Smith, Summer. "The Genre of the End Comment: Conventions in Teacher Responses to Student Writing." *College Composition and Communication* 48.2 (1997): 249-68. Print.

So, Bronia P.C. "From Analysis to Pedagogic Applications: Using Newspaper Genres to Write School Genres." *Journal of English for Academic Purposes* 4 (2005): 67-82. Print.

Sokolowski, Robert. *Introduction to Phenomenology.* Cambridge: Cambridge UP, 2000. Print.

Soliday, Mary. "Mapping Classroom Genres in a Science in Society Course." *Genre across the Curriculum.* Ed. Anne Herrington and Charles Moran. Logan: Utah State UP, 2005. 65-82. Print.

Sommers, Nancy, and Laura Saltz. "The Novice as Expert: Writing the Freshman Year." *College Composition and Communication* 65.1 (2004): 124-49. Print.

Sousa S.C.T., and Soares M.E. "Developing Writing Skills through the Use of Blogs." *L1—Educational Studies in Language and Literature* 9.2 (2009): 71-90. Print.

Spilka, Rachel, ed. *Writing in the Workplace: New Research Perspectives.* Carbondale: Southern Illinois UP, 1993. Print.

Spinillo, Alina G., and Chris Pratt. "Sociocultural Differences in Children's Genre Knowledge." *Writing in Context(s): Textual Practices and Learning Processes in Sociocultural Settings.* Ed. Triantafillia Koustouli. New York: Springer, 2005. 27-48. Print.

Spinuzzi, Clay. *Tracing Genres Through Organizations: A Sociocultural Approach to Information Design.* Cambridge, MA: MIT Press, 2003. Print.

Spinuzzi, Clay, and Mark M. Zachry. "Genre Ecologies: An Open-system Approach to Understanding and Constructing Documentation." *Journal of Computer Documentation* 24.3 (2000):169-81. Print.

Sutton, Brian. "Swales's 'Moves' and the Research Paper Assignment." *Teaching English in the Two-Year College* 27.4 (May 2000): 446-51. Print.

Swales, John M. *Genre Analysis: English in Academic and Research Settings.* Cambridge: Cambridge UP, 1990. Print.

—. "Occluded Genres in the Academy: The Case of the Submission Letter." *Academic Writing: Intercultural and Textual Issues.* Ed. E. Ventola and A. Mauranen. Amsterdam: John Benjamins, 1996. 45-58. Print.

—. *Other Floors, Other Voices: A Textography of a Small University Building.* Mahwah, NJ: Lawrence Erlbaum, 1998. Print.

—. "The Paradox of Value: Six Treatments in Search of the Reader." *Economics and Language.* Ed. Willie Henderson et al. New York: Routledge, 1993: 223-39. Print.

—. *Research Genres: Explorations and Applications.* Cambridge: Cambridge UP, 2004. Print.

Swales, John M., and Christine B. Feak. *Academic Writing for Graduate Students: Essential Tasks and Skills.* Ann Arbor: U of Michigan P, 1994. Print.

Swarts, Jason. "Coherent Fragments: The Problem of Mobility and Genred Information." *Written Communication* 23.2 (2006): 176-201. Print.

Tardy, Christine. *Building Genre Knowledge.* West Lafayette, IN: Parlor Press, 2009. Print.

—. "'It's Like a Story:' Rhetorical Knowledge Development in Advanced Academic Literacy." *Journal of English for Academic Purposes* 4 (2005): 325-38. Print.

Tardy, Christine M., and John M. Swales. "Form, Text Organization, Genre, Coherence, and Cohesion." *Handbook of Research on Writing: History, Society, School, Individual, Text.* Ed. Charles Bazerman. New York: Lawrence Erlbaum, 2008. 565-81. Print.

Threadgold, Terry. "Talking about Genre: Ideologies and Incompatible Discourses." *Cultural Studies* 3.1 (1989): 101-27. Print.

Todorov, Tzvetan. *The Fantastic.* Trans. Richard Howard. Ithaca: Cornell UP, 1975. Print.

—. *Genres in Discourse.* Trans. Catherine Porter. Cambridge: Cambridge UP, 1990. Print.

—. "The Origin of Genres." *Modern Genre Theory.* Ed. David Duff. London: Longman, 2000. 193-209. Print.

Trimbur, John. *The Call to Write.* 2nd ed. New York: Longman, 2002. Print.

—. "Composition and the Circulation of Writing." *College Composition and Communication* 52.2 (2000): 188-219. Print.

Troia, Gary A., and Steve Graham. "The Effectiveness of a Highly Explicit, Teacher-Directed Strategy Instruction Routine." *Journal of Learning Disabilities* 35.4 (2002): 290-305. Print.

Trupe, Alice L. "Academic Literacy in a Wired World: Redefining Genres for College Writing Courses." *Kairos* 7.2. (2002): n. pag. Web. 10 April 2007.

Van Nostrand, A.D. "A Genre Map of R&D Knowledge Production for the US Department of Defense." *Genre and the New Rhetoric.* Ed. Aviva Freedman and Peter Medway. Bristol: Taylor and Francis, 1994. 133-45. Print.

Walberg, H. J. "Productive Teaching and Instruction: Assessing the Knowledge Base." *Phi Delta Kappan* 71 (1990): 470-78. Print.

Walvoord, Barbara, and Lucille McCarthy. *Thinking and Writing in College: A Naturalistic Study of Students in Four Disciplines.* Urbana: NCTE, 1990. Print.

Wardle, Elizabeth. "'Is This What Yours Sounds Like?': The Relationship of Peer Response to Genre Knowledge and Authority." *Multiple Literacies for the 21st Century.* Ed. Brian Huot, Beth Stroble, Charles Bazerman. Cresskill, NJ: Hampton, 2004. 93-114. Print.

—. "Understanding 'Transfer' from FYC: Preliminary Results from a Longitudinal Study." *WPA: Writing Program Administration* 31.1-2 (2007): 65-85. Print.

Weisser, Christian. *Moving Beyond Academic Discourse: Composition Studies and the Public Sphere.* Carbondale, IL: Southern Illinois UP, 2002. Print.

Williams, Joseph, and Gregory Colomb. "The Case for Explicit Teaching: Why What You Don't Know Won't Help You." *Research in the Teaching of English* 27.3 (1993): 252-64. Print.

Winsor, Dorothy. "Genre and Activity Systems: The Role of Documentation in Maintaining and Changing Engineering Activity Systems." *Written Communication* 16.2 (1999): 200-24. Print.

—. "Ordering Work: Blue-collar Literacy and the Political Nature of Genre." *Written Communication* 17.2 (2000): 155-84. Print.

"WPA Outcomes Statement for First-Year Composition." Council of Writing Program Administrators, April 2000. Web. 15 July 2007.

"Writing Now." *Council Chronicle* 18.1 (2008): 15-22. Print.

Yates, JoAnne. *Control through Communication: The Rise of System in American Management.* Baltimore: Johns Hopkins UP, 1989. Print.

Yates, JoAnne, and Wanda Orlikowski. "Genres of Organizational Communication: A Structural Approach." *Academy of Management Review* 17 (1992): 299-326. Print.

—. "Genre Systems: Chronos and Kairos in Communicative Interaction." *The Rhetoric and Ideology of Genre: Strategies for Stability and Change.* Ed. Richard Coe, Lorelei Lingard, and Tatiana Teslenko. Cresskill, NJ: Hampton, 2002. 103-21. Print.

—. "Genre Systems: Structuring Interaction through Communicative Norms." *The Journal of Business Communication* 39.1 (2002): 13-35. Print.

Zucchermaglio, Cristina, and Alessandra Talamo. "The Development of a Virtual Community of Practices Using Electronic Mail and Communicative Genres." *Journal of Business and Technical Communication* 17.3 (2003): 259-84. Print.

Index

About the Authors

Anis Bawarshi is an Associate Professor of English and Director of the Expository Writing Program at the University of Washington, where he teaches courses in composition theory and pedagogy, rhetorical genre theory, discourse analysis, and language policy. He is currently Program Profiles Co-Editor (with Mary Jo Reiff) for the journal *Composition Forum* and serves on the editorial board for Studies in Writing and Rhetoric. His publications include *Genre and the Invention of the Writer: Reconsidering the Place of Invention in Composition* (2003); *Scenes of Writing: Strategies for Composing with Genres* (2004; with Amy Devitt and Mary Jo Reiff); *A Closer Look: A Writer's Reader* (2003; with Sidney I. Dobrin); and articles and book chapters on genre, uptake, invention, and knowledge transfer in composition. His current research focuses on rhetorical memory and uptake in representations of the Israel-Palestine conflict.

Mary Jo Reiff is an Associate Professor of English at the University of Tennessee-Knoxville, where she teaches undergraduate and graduate courses in rhetoric and composition theory, research, and pedagogy. Her research interests include audience theory, rhetorical genre studies, and critical ethnography, and articles related to this research have appeared in *College English*, *JAC*, and *WAC Journal*. She has published a book on audience, *Approaches to Audience: An Overview of the Major Perspectives* (2004), and has coauthored a textbook (with Amy Devitt and Anis Bawarshi) entitled *Scenes of Writing: Strategies for Composing with Genres* (2004). She recently coedited (with Kirsten Benson) a textbook entitled *Rhetoric of Inquiry* (2009). Her current research focuses on the genre of the public petition as a culturally embedded site for rhetorical intervention and social action.

CPSIA information can be obtained at www.ICGtesting.com
Printed in the USA
LVOW08s0422150616

492670LV00001B/115/P